Gerald Jacobs is the Editor of the *Jewish Chronicle Colour Magazine* and writes for newspapers and magazines on the theatre and the arts.

Gerald Jacobs

JUDI DENCH
A Great Deal of Laughter

An Authorized Biography

Futura

A Futura Book

First published in Great Britain in 1985 by
George Weidenfeld & Nicholson Ltd

First Futura edition 1986

ISBN 0 7088 3007 2

Set in IBM Journal by 🅰 Tek-Art, Croydon, Surrey.
Printed in Great Britain by Hazell, Watson & Viney Ltd,
Aylesbury, Bucks.

Futura Publications
A Division of Macdonald & Co (Publishers) Ltd
Maxwell House, 74 Worship Street, London EC2A 2EN

A BPCC plc Company

Contents

Author's Acknowledgements   vii
Foreword by Judi Dench   viii

1 Sunlight and cycle trips   1
2 Central line to Stratford   17
3 'Fear no more the heat o' the sun'   39
4 Playhouses and night clubs   59
5 A romantic winter's tale   74
6 Good companionship   96
7 From comedy to catastrophe   112
8 National matters and private concerns   128
9 Big screen, small screen   143
10 Anatomy of a natural   170

Appendix: stage roles 1957–85   189
Index   192

Illustration Acknowledgements
The photographs in this book are reproduced by kind permission of the following: *Yorkshire Evening Press* Judi with John Neville in Sierra Leona during their West African tour, 1963; *BBC Hulton Picture Library* Judi receiving her Television Actress of the Year Award, with Eric Porter, 1967; *Donald Cooper* Judi with Ian McKellen in Trevor Nunn's production of *Macbeth* at The Other Place, Stratford, 1976; *Zoe Dominic* Judi with Nigel Havers in *The Importance of Being Earnest* at the National Theatre, 1982, and Judi discussing her role as Lady Bracknell with Peter Hall; *London Weekend Television* Judi as Laura in the television series *A Fine Romance*, 1981; *Laurence Burns* Judi as Deborah in Pinter's *A Kind of Alaska*, National Theatre, 1982; *Sophie Baker* Judi as Marcia Pilborough in David Hare's *Wetherby*, 1985.

Author's Acknowledgements

In preparing this book I faced a big problem: how to avoid it seeming to be one long tribute. Everybody I interviewed or consulted about Judi Dench had nothing but the highest regard for her whether professionally or privately. Nevertheless each of my interviewees — some of whose words are quoted directly — enthusiastically provided me with valuable material and I thank them all. And I hope that the story of Judi's life and career as it appears in these pages will speak for itself and show that such uniform praise is both genuine and fully merited. The professional story is of course principally a theatrical one but Judi has also appeared many times on the television and cinema screen and the whole of chapter nine is devoted to this activity, which is of increasing importance to her.

I would like to thank and acknowledge the help of a variety of other people for a variety of other forms of assistance and encouragement. These include Ruth Adams, Judi Cheston, Alex Holdcroft, Judy and Philip Jacobs, Mike and Rosie Jennings, Hannah Nemeth, Hilary Parker, Geoffrey Paul, David Roberts and Jane Blackett, Angela and Michael Stern.

I am very grateful for the patience and hospitality shown by the members of the Williams and Dench households and, above all, for the opportunity afforded me by the splendidly talented lady who is the subject of this book.

GJ Feb 1985

Foreword

When the idea of this book was put to me I at first resisted it and went on resisting it for some considerable time. Biographies, I have always thought, should only be written when the subject is — well, older than fifty!

In the past, I have derived great pleasure from reading about such legendary actresses as Fanny Kemble, Sarah Bernhardt and Edith Evans — where a great deal of water has flowed under their particular bridges — so it makes my twenty-eight years on the stage a mere trickle. But with Gerald's patience, recalling incidents and friends has proved very nostalgic and enjoyable.

I realize how irreverent I may seem in my attitude to my work, but I hope my genuine love of the theatre, and the people in it, is apparent. So, I'm very glad that Gerald has taken the time to sort out my ramblings and put it all down. Reading it, I see how fortunate I have been to be in the right place at the right time — and it's made me laugh — I hope it may do the same for others.

Judi Dench, 1985.

1 Sunlight and cycle trips

York is an essentially English city — steeped in history, crisp in climate, commercial yet genteel — but with depths reaching into more ancient and mysterious traditions. A fitting birthplace for Judi Dench, an essentially English actress with a powerful intuition for the universal aspects of human experience that lie beneath the written text.

The youngest of the three children of Reginald and Olave Dench, he a doctor, she a businessman's daughter and Irish beauty with 'piercingly clear, turquoise eyes and dark red hair', Judith — immediately and always to be known as 'Judi' — was born on 9 December 1934, at the Holgate nursing home. Of her childhood and education in York she has vivid and almost entirely happy recollections.

Her family has established its own traditions. Her eldest brother, Peter, ten years her senior, is a General Practitioner in York just like their father. Her other brother, Jeffery, is six years older than Judi. His own notable acting career has been spent largely with the Royal Shakespeare Company, for whom his younger sister has done some of her most memorable work.

Olave Jones came from Dublin, where her father Harry Jebb Jones made gloves. She, too, had two brothers: Johnson and Otto. She met Reginald Dench at Sunday School when they were both fourteen years old. He was from a Dorset family who had gone over to Ireland when Reginald was a small boy of three or four. He grew up there, completing his education at Trinity College, before bringing his childhood sweetheart, now his bride, to England.

He took a practice in Tyldesley, near Manchester, where both Peter and Jeffery were born. Olave couldn't settle there, however. Surrounded by poverty, she felt helpless and frustrated, but a move to York shortly before Judi was born brought fulfilment and the blossoming of her Irish charm and talent for living.

Nowadays Judi joyfully acknowledges the Irish component of her background — it provided an invaluably firm basis for her portrayal of the eponymous Mrs Boyle in the RSC's 1980 production of O'Casey's *Juno and the Paycock* — but as a child she was barely aware of it, not even realizing that her mother possessed a rich Irish accent. And when she went to boarding school and received her mother's first telephone call, Judi couldn't immediately recognize the voice and asked, 'Who's that?'

'Who's that!' came the thunderous response, outraged and very Irish, 'It's your mother!'

'But you've got a funny voice', protested the astonished daughter.

Before then Judi had been too absorbed in the boisterous atmosphere of her home to make any such distinctions. Her parents entered spiritedly into the flow of York life, from amateur dramatics to archaeology. Their front door was left open most evenings and the house resounded with parties and visitors and the rough and tumble of a contented family.

The house was number 54 Heworth Green, a narrow but solid Victorian terrace dwelling on three floors. Judi's childhood bedroom was part of the attic, a former studio with a glass roof. It became for her a real playroom where she was allowed to draw on the walls. The one other attic room was occupied by a maid, a considerable slice of whose duties involved looking after Judi. There were two: Cissie, and her successor, Bridget.

Dr Dench's surgery and waiting-room were at ground level, as was the kitchen, whose red-tiled floor the young Judi would swab obsessively. There was also a cellar from which her mother dispensed prescriptions and which served as a gallery for the children's panoramic school photographs.

At the end of the back garden was a barn, standing within the area of the original Forest of Galters, famous for its owls and for the pilgrims who once used to make their way through it by the light of the Minster's lantern tower.

Though the pilgrims were no more, the owls were frequent visitors to the barn and the garden. Judi's brother Jeff took a particular interest in them. With a pair of tweezers he would pick out bones from the owls' droppings and stick them on pieces of card with labels naming the parts of the mouse from which they had come.

The garden itself was a flourishing one with peonies, hollyhocks and 'a wonderful-smelling cream rose along the left-hand wall.' There was a rockery and a vine producing grapes respectable enough for the Denches to give as presents in boxes.

Certainly there were plenty of occasions for the giving of presents. Celebrations figured prominently in the very active social and family round of the Dench household. And to this day Judi is punctilious about Christmas and birthdays, cards and gifts, and indeed making sure that all around her enjoy themselves as much and as often as possible.

Reginald Dench was a twinkling sort of man. He had a placid, tolerant nature and found it easy to get on with others. No mean actor himself, he once drew an appreciative notice in the press for his performance as Annas in the York Mystery Plays. He was also an impressive after-dinner speaker, his Irish brogue serving him well. But he was basically a vigorous, outdoor type, fond of cycling and swimming (he captained Trinity College at water polo). In appearance, bald and tanned with blue eyes, he was in the mould of Chaucer's yeoman, who too had a 'not heed . . . with a broun visage'.

He was an obviously popular GP and when he went on his rounds it was common for children to run alongside his car in greeting. He had a habit of knocking on the door of a house or room and then, if it was open, walking straight in. Once, he strode into a kitchen on a local estate, smiled at the young housewife washing dishes, and gestured towards the bedroom, where he assumed his patient awaited him. The startled housewife no doubt assumed something altogether different, for Reg had unknowingly entered the wrong flat.

He was thirty-seven when Judi was born and, as Peter Dench recalls, 'I think my father had given up any chance of having a daughter.' Consequently he doted on her and happily indulged her, granting most of her wishes.

Judi's mother was of a contrasting disposition. Fiery and quick-tempered, it was she who imposed the discipline. What she did share with her husband though was a huge capacity for enjoyment. As a couple, Judi recalls them mostly for their 'incredible sense of humour'.

Together they created something of a theatrical environment. They were both active members of the Settlement Players, a well-known amateur group in York, Reg playing leading parts and Olave becoming wardrobe mistress. And when a professional repertory company came to town in the mid-1930s, its actors and actresses, among them John Gabriel and Phyllis Calvert, soon became regular visitors to 54 Heworth Green.

In 1951 the city was enlivened by an adapted revival, by Canon J.S. Purvis, of the York cycle of Mystery Plays. As with the cycles based on other English towns, these were a series of playlets, medieval in origin, on biblical themes, performed in the open air in a festival atmosphere. The tradition has again taken root and some section of the York cycle of Mystery Plays is still staged there every three years, with a professional director and leading actor at the helm.

Then as now, scores of enthusiastic amateurs were recruited to perform or otherwise help with costumes, lighting and props. In 1951 Tenniel Evans played the angel Michael, and David Giles, later to distinguish himself as a professional director, was Gabriel. Naturally Reg and Olave were involved, Olave's flair for costume proving a particularly useful asset. And on that first occasion one of the many angels was played by their schoolgirl daughter.

The family were also keen theatre-goers. Some of Judi's earliest memories are of trips to Scarborough to see open-air productions of *Faust* and *Hiawatha*; of an outing to *Cuckoo in the Nest* from which she had to be taken home having made herself ill with laughing; and, most indelibly, of being taken to see *Caesar and Cleopatra* performed by the boys of St Peter's, York, one of England's oldest schools, in which Peter Dench played Caesar and his young brother Jeffery was Cleopatra.

At home somebody was always dressing up: the children in pure make-believe, or the adults in their more sophisticated forms of the same thing — attending a masque as Lord and Lady Castlemaine or jointly and painstakingly making a dress for Olave's appearance as Queen Elizabeth I at a coronation ball.

Contributing to the bustle were scores of pets: cats, dogs (a particular favourite of Judi's was Dewar, a black and white spaniel owned by the family during the War), rabbits and a budgerigar that tore off the wallpaper with its beak.

Such were the surroundings in which Judi grew up, sustained by an intensely purposeful family life. Although all their relatives lived some distance away during that period, mostly in Dublin or Northampton, Olave and Reg maintained a lively connection with several close friends in York. Foremost among these were John Moffat, editor-in-chief of Yorkshire Herald Newspapers, and his wife Jean, a former schoolmistress — forever 'uncle' and 'auntie' to the children.

Another friend was Cliff Watson, himself a great party-giver. There were many doctors and their families and another adoptive 'aunt and uncle', Hetty and George Walker.

A highlight of the regular gatherings at Heworth Green was the piano-playing of Olave Dench, focal point of spirited group renditions of Gilbert and Sullivan or Hymns, Ancient and Modern. Sometimes her small daughter would listen from upstairs, having crept out to the landing from her bedroom. Later, Judi's voice would be among those around the piano.

But the entire cluster of memories of number 54 in the 1930s and 1940s is as a cadenza played at the close of an era of domestic vitality no longer attainable in the same form. Television came to the Denches' sitting-room with the Coronation in 1953. By then their youngest child was eighteen-and-a-half and almost ready to set her home-grown flair for entertainment upon a wider stage.

Throughout her childhood, Judi's family spent a lot of leisure time together, whether at home or on outings and holidays. Everybody had a bicycle and there would be frequent cycling trips on Thursday afternoons, which was Reg's half-day at the surgery. One popular destination was Castle Howard, some fifteen miles north-east of York, to which Olave, Reg, the boys and Judi would cycle for a swim and then, reinforcing the delightfully ritual nature of it all, stop on the way back for bacon and eggs, always at the same small cafe, the 'Bide a wee'.

Scarborough was another half-day haunt, reached after a brisk car journey across the moors. But Reg couldn't always escape his work on these outings. One time at Scarborough when they were all swimming and Reg was practising water polo, a woman, unrecognizable in a bathing cap, swam up to him and, head bobbing in the water, asked, 'Doctor, do you think you could let me have some more of those white pills?'

When not astride a bicycle, Judi would sometimes go horse-riding with her mother. They were taught by Wilson Marshall, whose stables were in Rawcliff Lane, where Peter Dench now lives. Marshall was a classically horsey individual who wore a cap and jodhpurs and had very bowed legs. Judi was a nervous rider, something which Mr Marshall sought to overcome by slapping her pony, Jimmy, hard across the buttocks and yelling, 'Get on your bloody way!' to send horse and rider careering down the lane.

Family holidays in Judi's early years were generally taken on the Dorset coast at Weymouth or further west in Cornwall. It is the wartime Cornish days which have remained most strongly present in Judi's memory: 'Every summer we would take a train to Liskeard. The carriages were all blacked out. I remember some Americans giving us unlabelled tins of pineapple.

'At Liskeard a car would meet us and we'd go to a place called Lady Cook's Yard where a man wearing a green baize apron took our luggage and our shoes upon a cart and we'd walk barefoot to town and not wear shoes again for the whole month.

'We stayed with a Miss Goater, who kept chickens, and I slept in a tiny room above the front door — a recess, really, from the landing — with a long window seat overlooking Talland Bay. She called it "the poop".'

'Every morning after breakfast we'd head for one of the three bays: Lake Rock, Talland Bay, or "Stinkers" where there were weever fish which made little holes in your feet. At Lake Rock we made a fire and cooked winkles in a rusty tin filled with sea water which we'd hidden in a special place. One year, a French friend, Daphne, whose family had fled from the Germans, came on holiday with us and she collected snails in a box intending to eat them but when we came back next day the snails had all climbed out.

'We saw a lot of Cornwall. We'd walk to Looe, and sometimes see the actor Robert Newton lurching his way to the Three Pilchards in Polperro. We picked mushrooms and hazelnuts, bought fresh mackerel and lobsters, and picnicked in a nearby, glorious cornfield.

'Often we'd arrive back at the house at about a quarter to two, quite ravenous having spent the morning swimming or walking, to find Miss Goater feeding the chickens, crying out to them, "Girls, girls, girls!" and, seeing us, "What, back for lunch already and I haven't even thought of what we're having".'

That French friend, Daphne, was a few years older than Judi. Her younger sister, Pat, became one of Judi's closest childhood companions. As for Daphne, her friendship was claimed by Peter, who was once more to follow in his father's footsteps by marrying *his* childhood sweetheart. Today, Peter and Daphne — at whose wedding in 1949 Judi and Pat were bridesmaids and Jeff was best man — have two grown-up children of their own living with them in York, though their son, Simon, is a dentist not a doctor.

After the War, with Peter and Jeffery making their own ways into the world, Reg and Olave took Judi on holidays abroad. They went to Majorca before all the hotels sprang up; to Italy; and by caravan all over France.

Small and spare, Judi was a supremely vivacious child. Like Peter, she took after her father, while Jeff, with whom she often fought cat-and-dog, inherited his mother's temperament. More specifically, Judi is characteristic of a line of Dench women who, in her brother Peter's view, recall Reg's mother, Bessie: 'I can remember my paternal grandmother on, I suppose, her death bed. I was four or five years old. She was very Dorset in speech, and in appearance so like my aunts Kally (Kathleen) and Betty. I see an awful lot of my aunts in Judi.'

In adulthood, however, Judi has taken on more of the looks and mannerisms of her mother. This struck Peter very forcibly when he saw Judi in Harold Pinter's *A Kind of Alaska* at the National Theatre in 1983, about two months after Olave's death. Judi played a hospital patient emerging from her bed after years of a mysterious kind of sleeping sickness. Peter found the experience 'overwhelming — it stopped me in my tracks because it *was* my mother, appearance, voice, everything.'

Judi's paternal grandfather, 'Gampy' Dench, was a full-blooded character fond of singing and of swimming, well into old age. He it was who, at Castle Howard, first taught Judi to swim as a young child with sixpenny bribes. And when any prospective girl- or boyfriend was brought home to the Dench house in Ireland the question was always, 'Can she/he sing and can she/he swim?'

Sandymount Park was the name of the house and Judi was first taken there by her parents on a mail-boat just after the War. It was a high time of games and sunshine and trips to the Dublin horse show.

Gampy remarried late in life and had a son, thus giving Judi an uncle younger than herself. Though she never knew her other grandparents, or indeed any of her mother's relations at all, 'Gampy' is firmly etched upon Judi's memory.

The family were on holiday in Wells in Somerset when War was declared in 1939. They returned to York and remained relatively unaffected throughout, although extra demands were made on Reg and Olave. Reg ran a mobile first-aid unit with which he was called out on every alert. Olave took on a full-time job as a caterer at the WVS canteen on York station, dealing with the numerous troop trains. Both thereby found new outlets for their abiding sense of dedicated involvement.

York suffered a night of heavy bombardment during the run of *Caesar and Cleopatra* at St Peter's School and, the performance being abruptly terminated, Dr and Mrs Dench brought the two leading players home, where their sister was supposedly taking refuge in the cellar under the supervision of the maid, Cissie. But when mother, father and sons eventually got in, having picked their way through cordoned-off and blazing streets, they found Judi sitting on the stairs. Cissie, whom Judi considered to be 'frightfully old and wise,' was, at sixteen, too frightened to go down into the cellar.

Judi had a zip-up 'siren suit' and in that cellar of 54 Heworth Green she shared the excitements and anxieties of war — as well as her Radio Malt — with a dozen cats. A lastingly vivid highlight of the War's end was the ceremonious distribution of three bananas to the Dench children by their parents, Judi and Peter devouring theirs immediately and greedily while Jeff's was placed, awaiting his return from school, in a tall cupboard covered with netting, like a single strand of the Golden Fleece.

The outbreak of War coincided with Judi's first term at school. This was at Clifton Preparatory, under its founder and headmistress Phyllis Meaby. (Such is the personal scale and association of this establishment of sixty to seventy pupils that even today it is still known as 'Miss Meaby's', long after that estimable lady's retirement.)

It was a school that encouraged its pupils' dramatic talents and there was a lot of play reading and performance. Judi appeared in each of the nativity plays and in *Alice in Wonderland*, although the sprightly octogenarian Miss Meaby does not recall Judi as noticeably outstanding in this or any other field and describes her with affection as 'not a brilliant pupil'.

Judi's own memories are more specific: 'I remember on the very first day learning "Morning has Broken" with Miss Duncan, and learning to count by pointing to squares and circles on brown sugar-paper pasted round the walls. And that's how I still count, pointing at imaginary squares and circles. I can still see the frieze around the room with A for Apple, B for Ball, C for Cat, D for Dog, E for Egg, F for Fish, and so on.

'My best friend was Elizabeth Blackley, and there was a girl called Sylvia Whitehead who had a mass of curly hair.

We used to go for a walk after lunch (Yorkshire pudding with treacle every Tuesday) in a crocodile formation, often to a place called The Homestead, where we'd play on the swings.

'When we were six and Angela Bedford played Mary in the nativity play, I was told I could be in it as a fairy. I thought, "There's no fairy in the nativity play. I'm just being shoved in." And I incited a chum, David Rymer, who was playing one of the Kings, to dump his frankincense on the baby's head. I felt very spiteful, especially as my doll was playing Jesus!'

It was part of the decorous sensibility of a school like Miss Meaby's that when the children needed to yield to the promptings of nature they would put up a hand and ask to go and 'make a call'. The tiny Judi Dench, young and eager to join in, often asked if she could make a call, and it wasn't until her second term that she followed such a request, duly granted, with another to 'please go to the lavatory'.

'But, Judi, you've only just been', replied Miss Thomas, her teacher.

'No I haven't,' said Judi, 'I just went to make a call.'

She had, for more than a term, been going out into the hall on such occasions literally to 'call' out loud over the banisters.

Judi went to school either by bicycle, accompanied by her brothers, or with Olave in the car — Reg wasn't the only driver in the family and neither was his the only car. Olave's car often failed to start, however, leaving Judi sitting in the back wondering yet again how to excuse herself for being late.

For the most part, though, she got about under her own abundant steam. Her days were filled with parties, picnics and the spontaneous inventions and excursions of childhood. She had plenty of close friends, girls and boys, all of whom were constantly in and out of each other's houses.

The ten-year gap between Peter and Judi precluded any really close childhood attachment and eventually he went up to Cambridge to read medicine and to Malaya for his national service. But in such a family atmosphere there could never be any great distance and all three children joined in the endless round of cycle rides and dressing up. When Peter first came down from Cambridge for the vacation, he and Jeff made Judi a brightly-coloured three-cornered stool with her initials on the top and models of microbes crawling up the legs.

But naturally the closer contact was with Jeff, and Judi found herself involved in the plays Jeff wrote unceasingly. A boy called Leland Edinger, known as 'Dingo', used to spend his holidays with them as his parents were in Hong Kong. The three of them went to parties together, on one famous occasion all wrapped in crepe paper for a 'pink party' in Monkcaster.

Jeff's room contained a long brass curtain-rod through which he and Judi used to shoot dried peas at their father's patients waiting in the garden. The long-suffering patients must often have encountered such childish exuberance in Heworth Green. Once, having helped her mother make a salad, Judi swung it round in a wire basket in the garden before an open window. There was a cry of 'Good God!' and then out came Dr Walsh, an Irish colleague of her father's, to remonstrate in thickly Gaelic tones, 'Judi, will you stop showering the patient's stomach. He's hating that.'

Judi had lots of boyfriends, several of them the sons of doctors, including David Laing, John Mackenzie and the boy next door, David Belchamber. Something of a tomboy, she gained a formidable reputation among some of the more delicate young masculine souls. At one children's party at the home of a local surgeon called Conyers, whose two boys were friends of the Dench children, one young man departed early and dramatically with the loud and public announcement, 'If Judi Dench is here, I'm going.'

At home, life was a compulsive, rewarding business, in or out of doors. Whether trundling a wheelbarrow for her brothers while they 'excavated' the garden (rumoured to be on the bend of a Roman road) or making furniture for the dolls' house, Judi's early years were passed in total affirmation.

In 1947 she started boarding school. Even then she stayed near home, for she went to The Mount, the Quaker school for girls in York.

She chose it she says because of the uniform, but however fortuitous her enrolment it certainly offered a most effective environment for her development. The Quaker philosophy appealed to her as yet unconsidered faith in the individual. It afforded her an inner calm with which to underpin her natural dynamism. Eventually, too, the seeds were sewn for an acting career.

Judi was very popular with her fellow pupils at The Mount and attracted many friends and followers, the closest of whom was a girl called Susie Marshall, who is now married to a doctor in Edinburgh and still in touch with Judi. In those days she used to rescue Judi's domestic science disasters.

Life was far from plain sailing with the teachers. Judi was constantly in trouble on account of her high spirits, especially in the first year or two when her pranks included the spraying of an entire dormitory with a fire extinguisher, there being not the faintest flicker of a flame. And she always knew when a reprimand or worse was on the way whenever a teacher addressed her as 'Judith'. But as years went by she acquired a deep sense of responsibility, which she unhesitatingly attributes to Quakerism.

On the other hand, her schooling did not provide her with an easy attitude to young men. The Mount had a brother school, Bootham, for boys, with whom a number of joint ventures were arranged. As a result of such contact Judi met a boy called Christopher Malcolmson whom she allowed to escort her back to school one day along York's city walls. En route an 'incident' occurred which Judi hardly thought of again until, in 1968 when she was appearing in *Cabaret* at the Palace Theatre in London, a card was left for her at the stage door from Mr and Mrs Christopher Malcolmson inviting Judi for a drink after the show.

She was delighted to renew such an old acquaintance and duly met the Malcolmsons that evening. As they were having a drink Christopher said, 'I've got something to show you', and produced from his wallet an extremely dog-eared letter which read, 'Dear Christopher Malcolmson. I can never walk back with you along the walls again as you touched my coat. Yours sincerely, Judi Dench.' All that had in fact happened on that walk those many years earlier was that a gust of wind had blown back Judi's coat and the young Christopher had simply and gallantly replaced it for her.

One year, the Rowntree company in York invited six schools, among them Bootham and The Mount, to a 'Strawberry Party' at which there was to be dancing, a prospect so daunting to Susie Marshall that she couldn't bring herself to go. But Judi went along and promised to give her friend a full report of the proceedings.

The potentially romantic highlight of the evening was when a group of boys and girls went up on to the roof to view the sunset. On the way down Judi and a boy named David Robson were the last and he seized his opportunity and kissed her.

Back at school Susie was agog. 'I'll start counting in steam rollers,' she said, as children sometimes do to measure the distance of a thunder storm, 'and you tell me when to stop to show how long the kiss lasted.' Oh, the disappointment and disdain at Judi's revelation that her great amour was but one steam roller's worth!

On wet afternoons at The Mount when games were cancelled, the girls were sent off in small groups on one of a number of carefully routed 'wet walks' around the town. Each was designated by a colour: the 'red wet walk', 'blue wet walk' and so on. Judi, with one or more friends, would invariably take advantage of these situations to visit her parents — with their happy compliance.

She and her chosen accomplice would set off along the prescribed 'red', 'blue' or 'brown' road and, once safely out of authority's sight, rush into a telephone box and phone Olave. She would always welcome them — 'come on then, as quickly as you can' — and the girls would run to spend a blissful hour or so at Heworth Green. Reg would pop out of the surgery and join them for a cup of tea and, strictly forbidden, cakes. Afterwards Olave would hose them down in the garden and give them an authentic 'wet walk' look and drive them back to within a discreet distance of the school gates.

Though not exceptionally gifted academically, Judi had

a range of talents capable of blooming in the fertile soil of home and school. She was artistic; she could paint, draw, design and make clothes. Here there were family precedents. Apart from her mother's costume work for the Settlement Players and the Mystery Plays, her father was a keen water colourist and his brother, William Dench, was a Royal Academician.

Jeffery also showed an aptitude for drawing, but his first love was acting and when he went to the Central School of Speech and Drama in London it seemed part of an inevitable process. Some of his enthusiasm could not fail to rub off on his younger sister, who would listen rapt as he told her about the dancing and the fencing lessons and showed her all the different ways to bow and curtsy.

She herself had first performed in public at the age of five when she played a snail (Reg made the shell) in a children's show at the Rowntree Theatre. Then there'd been Miss Meaby's and the occasional dancing class, and always in the background her father's accomplishments upon the amateur stage. After her début as an angel in the Mystery Plays in 1951 she played the young man guarding the tomb in 1954 and three years later she was back to play the Virgin Mary. But by then the die was cast. She turned out once for the Settlement Players, as Tuesret, Pharoah's daughter, in Christopher Fry's *The Firstborn*. It was, however, at The Mount that all the elements first began to come together.

Drama was one of the activities in which The Mount combined with Bootham so that the annual school play had a mixed cast of girls and boys. Both schools possessed an enthusiastic drama teacher, John Kay at Bootham and Kay Macdonald, a former professional actress, at The Mount. Both recognized Judi's natural ability and both managed to communicate to her something of their excitement about theatre.

Kay Macdonald spoke racily about life in the London theatre and John Kay sought to mould the talent at his disposal. Judi responded warmly to them both. She appeared in *Tobias and the Angel* and played Titania in *A Midsummer Night's Dream* and the Queen in *Richard II* where she had to alternate each night as a lady-in-waiting with a girl called Rachel Hartley.

Her parents watched her spellbound and after one performance treated her to dinner at the Queen's Hotel in Leeds where they told her, 'Jeff thinks you should try for Central.' It was a suggestion that took her fancy but which at that stage could not quite sway her from her rapidly growing determination to go to art school.

Judi had such an idyllic childhood, such a secure foundation, that she has to some extent retained the qualities of a young girl. It comes as no surprise, for example, to discover that she has kept her first toys: a rabbit and two bears.

Certainly she is endowed with the lustre of youth. Her buoyant optimism, her tendency to giggle and her girlish mien all stem from the early days at Heworth Green. As does her passionate family love and loyalty, exercised now as wife and mother. But she also still seeks some kind of parental approval for her actions, a cushioning, even, from some of reality's rougher edges.

Her constant need for support and reassurance may also derive from the fact that her first major decision backfired. By the time she left The Mount in 1953 she was convinced she wanted to pursue a career in painting or design. She applied and got into the School of Art in York. But she was unhappy there and left before the end of her first year.

The art school was, like most such institutions at that time, somewhat Bohemian in style and outlook, in radical contrast to the graceful formality of The Mount. It was undoubtedly a very difficult transition. For a time Judi toyed with the possibility of going to the Slade in London but really she was disenchanted with the very notion of training to become an artist.

At the same time the world of the theatre, especially under Jeff's influence, was fixing itself more firmly within the orbit of her imagination, even though she had not yet seriously considered *acting* as a career.

A kind of compromise emerged in the form of an ambition to become a stage designer. She briefly assisted Voytek at the Theatre Royal in York and became more and more intent on the idea. And then one day she went to Stratford with her parents to see Michael Redgrave in *King Lear*.

The set, by Robert Colquhoun, so impressed her that suddenly she could no longer face the challenge of theatrical design. She considered herself lacking the creative resources for anything so economical and effective as Colquhoun had achieved.

It was the first really anxious phase of Judi's life. While still at art school she had the only serious row with her mother that she can remember: 'She said I was the most intolerant person she had ever met, and at that point I think she was right.' But generally her parents guided and helped her through it. Her father gave her every chance to foster her artistic interests and took her on a surprise trip to Florence. The impact of seeing the actual Botticellis that she'd come to know through theory and through books was overpowering.

Reg suggested that she spend some time in Switzerland or France and learn about another language and a culture. But Judi was impatient to progress and so applied to Central. She was ill at the time and took part of her entrance examination at home, where she drew a Greek theatre.

It was ironic that her artistic skill helped her gain a place at drama school and when she went to London she was still dogged by the feeling that she was settling for her second choice in life. It was a feeling that would not last beyond the first term at Central.

2   *Central line to Stratford*

The Central School of Speech and Drama, so named for its
solid, middle-of-the-road approach to dramatic technique
rather than its geographical location, was founded in 1906
by the actress Elsie Fogerty. It was first set up in rooms at
the Royal Albert Hall, where it remained for half a century,
moving to its present Swiss Cottage home just as Judi
Dench was leaving.

Miss Fogerty's pressing concern was with speech and
diction. Having established Central she became an inspirational coach to many actors and actresses, among them
Laurence Olivier and Peggy Ashcroft. The profession
today is well stocked with Central graduates. Julie Christie,
James Bolam, and more recently Kate Nelligan and Rupert
Everett are all beneficiaries of Elsie Fogerty's dream.

Judi Dench arrived there in September 1954. The principal was Gwynneth Thurburn. Judi's contemporaries
included Anna Dawson, Julian Belfrage, who later became
her agent, and Vanessa Redgrave. In the year ahead of her,
and regarded with awe, were Ian Hendry and Rowena
Cooper. The first term was devoted exclusively to breathing,
mime and relaxation. Judi was still a slightly reluctant
student, dreaming more of brushes and easels than of
greasepaint and footlights.

At the end of that term the first-year students were
asked to perform individual mimes on which they were to
be adjudicated. Judi couldn't decide upon a theme until
almost the last minute. Eventually the subject she chose
was 'Walking in a familiar garden'. The adjudicator, Walter
'Dickie' Hudd, thought it a quite remarkable performance
and said so. This was the trigger Judi needed. From that
point her choice of career was never more in doubt.

Dickie Hudd wasn't always so unstinting in his praise,

however. He once gave Judi a terrible dressing-down for 'corpsing' — laughing during a speech on stage. This happened in a performance of J.B.Priestley's *Time and the Conways*, staged for the internal consumption of Central students only, not the public.

Judi's character is at one point discovered hiding behind a curtain by a young man who then kisses her. The young man on this occasion was fellow student Richard Page-Jackson. As he pulled back the curtain, intent upon the kiss, the two lengths came off the rail and part of the ceiling came down on Judi. At this moment her line was, 'I suppose you do this to all your girlfriends' but she was laughing so much she couldn't utter a syllable.

A few years later Judi found herself on a professional stage with Dickie Hudd and was amused to recall his anger at her. Playing her father, he corpsed so badly one night that he had to walk off, his lines unspoken.

For the whole of her three-year stay at Central, Judi shared a room with her colleague Jennifer Daniel at Queen Alexandra's House, a hostel under the benevolent and imposing direction of Charis Fry, daughter of the distinguished sportsman and journalist C.B. Fry. Situated alongside the Albert Hall, Queen Alexandra's catered for students at the Royal College of Music as well as those from Central, and its friendly, institutional character eased Judi's path from boarding school to the big city.

Not that the city daunted her in any way. She readily grasped its social and cultural opportunities, albeit on a limited budget, and danced, went to concerts and saw numerous plays. She devoured the London Theatre, going to as many productions as time and her pocket would allow. The old family friends, the Moffats — 'auntie Jean and uncle John' — had moved to London and took Judi to several shows.

Her appetite for the peculiar magic of her newly-chosen profession grew with the feeding. She practised and studied enthusiastically and attended professional performances avidly. During her Central years she saw Richard Burton in *Henry V*; Lilli Palmer in *Bell, Book and Candle*; Barbara Jefford and Keith Michell in *Much Ado About Nothing*; her fellow old girl from The Mount, Mary Ure, in *Time*

Remembered; Paul Scofield in *The Power and the Glory*;
Sam Wanamaker in *The Lovers*; Peggy Ashcroft, Michael
Redgrave and Ralph Richardson. She went to revues,
musicals, and thrillers, classics and new plays, tragedies and
comedies, and laughed uninhibitedly at Paul Rogers as
Falstaff in *The Merry Wives of Windsor*, at Robert Morley
in *Hippo Dancing*, and Peggy Mount in *Sailor Beware.*

Many of these plays and players left a strong impression.
Judi would watch in mingled admiration and aspiration.
She became a devoted fan of several performers, among
them John Clements and Kay Hammond, fondly remembered as 'Dresden characters' in *The Little Glass Clock*;
Dorothy Tutin, whom she saw four times in *I Am a Camera*;
and Barbara Jefford, whose performance as Julia in *The
Two Gentlemen of Verona* at the Old Vic in 1957 was
seminal as far as Judi was concerned.

At Central, Judi thrived on her regular contact with Reg
and Olave and their obvious interest in what she was doing.
They were also tolerant of her youthful obsession with
every aspect of acting. At the time of her first visit home
she had just begun to learn make-up and there was more
than a touch of the flamboyant about the young lady who
stepped out on to the arrival platform at York station, clad
in a 'very unsuitable hat' and burdening a porter with a
bulky trunkful of clothes.

Judi recalls with amusement greeting her mother by
telling her she had found 'the most incredible way of doing
eye make-up'. Olave's reply — 'So I perceive' — was a fine
example of that parental art of combining warmth and
ambiguity in the same statement, addressed as it was to
someone of whom Ariel might have said, 'Those are coals
that were her eyes.'

Charis Fry used to organize dances at Queen Alexandra's
which were attended by young officer trainees from the
Royal Naval College at Greenwich. It was at one such dance
that Jennifer Daniel and Judi met a pair of appropriately
dashing sub-lieutenants. For several weeks thereafter the
girls would visit Greenwich regularly. A typical Sunday
found them attending chapel at the college in the morning,
followed by lunch in the famous 'painted hall' prior to an
afternoon outing by car or motorbike. Judi's beau was

Sub-Lieutenant John May, with whom she once went on a motor rally where their car overturned in a ditch, a predicament from which they both emerged free from injury.

Judi had no problems finding boyfriends. Before long, however, her social activities became intertwined with student life at Central, and Sub-Lieutenant May gave way to young men at the drama school like Bill Johnston and later Jeremy Kemp. They went to dances held at the Royal Court's Theatre Upstairs, the girls in black dresses, the men debonair and hopeful.

Another favourite haunt was the Mogambo coffee bar in Knightsbridge: 'They used to do lovely hot chocolate. Also a little copper dish of bacon and eggs which cost four-and-something. We never had enough money and used to club together to see if we could muster one dish between us to have with our hot chocolate and still be able to pay the bus fare from Kensington Gore'.

Although there were institutional meals at the hostel, Judi and Jennifer sometimes held 'dinner parties' in their room, ill-equipped though it was for the purpose. Jean and John Moffat were frequent guests on such occasions. The meal was always the same: herb omelette with salad, cooked one at a time on the single gas ring. To enliven the menu Jeremy Kemp taught Judi to make *Igel*, a German sweet dish in which plain biscuits and chocolate were sliced into a tin and frozen. The girls had no fridge and so they used to leave their tin of *Igel* outside on the window-sill to cool. One evening, the Moffats' patience over their 'individual' omelettes went unrewarded by the keenly-awaited sweetness of the *Igel*. Judi, in her eagerness to push open the window, sent the dessert clattering into Jay Mews, a good many feet below.

Central's situation within the Royal Albert Hall afforded its students various opportunities to hear music, both in rehearsal and performance. This was fully appreciated by Judi, who was thereby enabled to hear, among other things, Gigli rehearsing for his last concert.

Ever keen to exploit London's cultural largesse, she certainly didn't confine her musical appreciation to rehearsals at the Albert Hall. Memorably, she once witnessed the rich, satisfying *Tosca* of Renata Tebaldi at Covent Garden. And, crammed into the gallery slips, Judi and her companions Vanessa Redgrave and Roderick Horn leaned over perilously to toss hyacinths on to the stage. The evening concluded on a bathetic note, however, when Judi, Vanessa and Roderick went round to the stage door to see Tebaldi come out and enter a taxi which failed to start. The three drama students each lent a shoulder and got the cab going with a push. And then, in a bizarre reversal of what had taken place earlier in the opera house, Tebaldi threw carnations to them from the taxi window.

In those days there was little to detect of Vanessa Redgrave's future political leanings, though she was one of the more serious Central students. She and Judi were good, if not particularly close friends, who couldn't help but be aware of each other's outstanding talent. Judi recalls Vanessa as 'the only student who could do Restoration epilogues'.

Despite their common start, shared years of high achievement and a brief period of overlap at Stratford in the early 1960s, Vanessa and Judi weren't to work together until 1984, in the David Hare film, *Wetherby*.

One person much in demand in that impecunious student world was Julian Belfrage, who had a car. This was an especially welcome luxury when lectures were held, as some regularly were, a short distance from the Hall, at 52 Hyde Park Gate. Julian used to charge Judi twopence for each lift.

After leaving Central he spent only a short time as an actor before deciding to set up as a theatrical agent. Clearly a perceptive man, he engaged the young Judi Dench as his first client in 1958, and represents her still — along with the likes of Alan Howard, David Warner, Penelope Wilton and others on a long, impressive list. Today, Julian Belfrage's first client teases him about twopenny lifts in far-off days meriting deduction from his fees.

Elsie Fogerty's great personal interest in the vocal side of acting had led the Central School to be notably strong in that department. In Judi's day, 'Fogie's' legatees in this respect were Clifford Turner, Oliver Reynolds and Cicely Berry.

Clifford Turner was very jokey, possessed of a light, staccato laugh, but very thorough. Judi remembers him keeping her standing for half an hour pronouncing over and over the word 'armchair'. He first taught her how valuable *words* are to an actor, their individual sounds and strengths aside from their existence as mere links in the chain of story-telling.

Oliver Reynolds used to sit silently for minutes at a time before passing comment on students' work. One day, after one agonizingly long pause, he told Judi that her voice was too quiet, speculating that 'perhaps because you're a small person you simply can't speak very loudly.' He and Cicely Berry worked hard with Judi on voice projection and not only did she overcome her problems in that quarter but she very definitely ensured that hers was a voice to be recognized and reckoned with. Years later, at the Palace Theatre, she was to pin up a notice in the foyer reading, 'Miss Judi Dench does not have a cold, her voice is always like that.'

Judi's indebtedness to Cicely Berry stretches over many years, both women having served the Royal Shakespeare Company with distinction. At Central, Miss Berry was a precise and technical tutor, explaining physiology and demonstrating the importance of relaxation and breathing techniques. This, maintains Judi, is where the difference lies between the professional and the amateur:

'The amateur thinks it's a case of getting up, saying the lines and interpreting them. That's the icing, but it's the fruit-cake that matters. It's all about conserving breath and energy. You learn about earning a pause — so that the reins are firmly in your hands and the whole thing doesn't run away with you.

'At Stratford before a performance, we all lie out on our backs with our eyes closed and do Cicely's breathing techniques, starting by breathing on a vowel and building up. She then comes round and when she lifts up one of your arms, totally limp, suddenly you know about relaxation.

'When I did *Cymbeline* in 1979, I had an appallingly bad throat on the first night so I went to Cis. She worked the magic : laying you out on your back on the floor, legs crooked up, working your neck, "talking" you along your spine and gradually bringing your knees down to rest.'

Judi's other teachers at Central included the actor Esmé Percy, who directed her in a student production of *Good King Charles' Golden Days*, and the actress Beatrix Lehmann, who coached Judi for her final-year 'audition speeches'. This was a triumphant time, for at the outgoing Central students' matinée of scenes from various plays, held at Wyndhams theatre in June 1957, the Elsie Fogerty prize and gold medal 'for best all round performance' was awarded by the judges — Renée Asherson, Peter Ashmore and James Donald — 'to Miss Judi Dench'.

Auditions, however, were more meaningful than accolades at that point. Each final-year pupil chose two pieces to read in which he or she would be carefully coached. Beatrix Lehmann took Judi through Miranda's 'Alas, now, pray you work not so hard' speech from *The Tempest* and one of Julia's from *The Two Gentlemen of Verona*, in which Judi promptly and receptively went to see Barbara Jefford at the old Vic.

These would then be delivered to a seemingly empty auditorium, but out in the darkness would be one or two representatives of some leading professional organizations. Judi went on, wearing a plain black leotard, to give her speeches accompanied by a student called Tony Benson who read the part of Ferdinand for her *Tempest* extract. When she had finished, the silence was broken by a quiet 'Thank you, Judi' from Dickie Hudd.

Afterwards she was called to Dickie who told her simply, 'They want to see you at the Vic on Saturday.' She had also caught the interest of Tennent Productions. Judi was thrilled, especially as her boyfriend, Bill Johnston, was already working at the Old Vic.

Bill went with Judi to her audition and then waited for her outside a church on the Waterloo Road. Inside the theatre where there was a large crowd of hopefuls waiting to audition, tension was high. Judi was eventually collected from the throng by John Dexter, then a stage manager at the Old Vic, later to direct at the National and elsewhere.

The Old Vic's artistic director, Michael Benthall, asked Judi to perform her two pieces and also to sing something from *The Beggar's Opera*. Then he told her to learn Ophelia's

'Oh what a noble mind is here o'erthrown' speech from *Hamlet* and to come back the next day, Sunday.

She duly returned the following morning and auditioned once more. After that there was need for further auditions and she never did go to Tennent's.

When she had finished, she was summoned to Michael Benthall's office. It was a bewildering, slightly unreal encounter, him peppering her with questions and instructions like, 'How tall are you?' 'Can you sing?' 'Let your hair down.' 'Walk across the room.' So far as she was then aware, this was all for the sake of a walk-on part. Then he stopped for a moment or two and said, 'I'm going to take this gamble. If after two weeks it doesn't work, you can understudy.'

The gamble Michael Benthall was about to take was to cast an unknown young woman opposite one of the country's leading actors, on its foremost stage, in its most famous play. She was to be Ophelia to John Neville's Hamlet.

Judi could hardly have chosen a more exciting moment in English stage history to begin a professional acting career. John Osborne's *Look Back in Anger* had opened at the Royal Court on 8 May 1956, just a few months after Samuel Beckett's *Waiting for Godot* had so confounded London's arbiters of taste (Judi had been to see both). And now a tidal wave of British playwrights, including John Arden, Harold Pinter and Arnold Wesker, was about to break and transform the theatrical landscape.

Even so, the 'angry young men', the Theatre of the Absurd, and 'kitchen-sink' realism were yet to make their lasting impact. And Judi had after all entered the mainstream where she was to stay. But it was a mainstream soon to be radically altered by the flowing in of such currents as took their force from those exceptional times.

Judi approached her role in *Hamlet* confidently, conscious more of the privilege of her position than its pressures. Barbara Leigh-Hunt, who had recently joined the Old Vic company, recalls Judi's arrival at the theatre for the opening of rehearsals for the season: 'She walked on to the stage, this petite blonde girl with her hair done up in a pleat at the back, and she looked navy blue. I think she had on a blue skirt with a blue and white check shirt, but her face looked blue as well. It transpired that she had an allergy. It was discovered that it was to the soap powder in which her landlady was washing her bed linen.' (By this time Judi had moved out of Queen Alexandra's House and was living in digs in Queens Gate.)

Whether or not Judi's symptoms were aggravated by nerves it is hard to say, but she was quickly made to feel welcome by the company. Coral Browne, who played Gertrude in *Hamlet*, joked that the object of Judi's allergy was Michael Benthall. And when later in the season Judi went down with flu, Coral and her husband Philip Pearman looked after her at their flat in Chester Terrace.

Just prior to her Old Vic début, Judi returned to York at the invitation of Martin Browne, who was directing the 1957 Mystery Plays and wanted Judi to appear as the Virgin Mary. She played the part in a state of bursting excitement – she had been forbidden to say anything about Ophelia, although she did tell her parents.

Judi has no recollection of first-night nerves for *Hamlet*. But then she barely remembers that first night at all. There had been a certain amount of publicity and press comment about her getting the part but, fresh from drama school, she was able to preserve a degree of anonymity. And if she needed any prompting for this, it came in the shape of her first telegram — addressed to 'Tudor Bench, Old Vic Theatre'.

In the event, the production was not an immediate success. It previewed quietly at the Royal Court Theatre in Liverpool and came to London on 18 September 1957. *The Times* called it 'lifeless' and dismissed Neville as a 'clockwork *Hamlet*'. The critic Richard Findlater, writing in the *Sunday Chronicle* took Michael Benthall to task for displaying such a raw, unsuitable Ophelia as Judi Dench's within the national show-case. She had, he wrote, 'tripped over her advance publicity and fallen on her pretty face . . . A few years hard labour in proper obscurity will do wonders.'

In November 1957 Judi opened in the much more modest role of Juliet in *Measure for Measure* with John Neville as Angelo and Anthony Nicholls as the Duke. Isabella was played by Judi's heroine, Barbara Jefford.

This time Judi was scarcely noticed by the press and her troubles lay on the other side of the footlights.

It was an unhappy production under the American director Margaret (Peggy) Webster, who arrived on crutches with one leg in plaster and proceeded to transmit some of her discomfort to the cast. She was particularly severe on Judi.

The designs were of an abstract, modern nature and the actors disliked them intensely. Peggy Webster insisted upon them, however, until she saw the finished costumes at the dress parade. They were manifestly inappropriate and the director verbally lambasted her designer in front of the entire company, who, as one, united in his defence against such treatment. As Barbara Leigh-Hunt recalls, 'loyalty is a strange thing. He had made people look absolute idiots in some of those costumes.'

Judi was to have her chances later to shine in this dense, enigmatic play about the weakness and pretensions of human nature, *Measure for Measure* being one of a nap hand of plays to which she has returned to play a more prominent part (the others are *A Midsummer Night's Dream, Twelfth Night, The Importance of Being Earnest* and *The Cherry Orchard*). On the other hand she has never gone back to *Hamlet* — it is too late now for Ophelia and she is an unlikely Gertrude.

A Midsummer Night's Dream and *Twelfth Night* were both presented in that first 1957—8 Old Vic season. The comedian Frankie Howerd was brought in to play Bottom in the *Dream*, to some acclaim. *The Times* described his Bottom as 'the play's most poetic character and its most delightful.' He was also popular with the rest of the cast despite, or perhaps because of, his habit of making up a lot of his dialogue as he went along. Judi played the first fairy, and six younger fairies were imported from the Royal Ballet School, all sylph-like girls of fifteen or sixteen. Rehearsals sometimes went on until 3 a.m. to get the movements right.

This was probably the first public revelation of Judi's now well-known propensity to fall over. Michael Benthall's memorable observation of her less than graceful ballet was made before the whole assembly: 'Miss Dench, will you try not to knock the other fairies over. You're coming in with your hands like a pair of finnan-haddies.'

Twelfth Night, in which Judi was Maria, had a strong cast, incorporating Paul Daneman, Derek Godfrey, John Humphrey, Barbara Jefford and John Neville. Once again, *The Times*' critic disapproved of Michael Benthall's efforts and rebuked Judi for playing Maria 'as a soubrette with a northern accent instead of a lady-in-waiting.' That summer the production went up to Edinburgh where Judi was thrilled to read Harold Hobson's review likening her to 'a chamois'.

By this time she was settling down well in London and had forged a strong alliance with 'Bar' Leigh-Hunt, which has lasted ever since. She also carried over from York and Central her popularity with the opposite sex and was continually falling in and out of love. Not that she was the most sophisticated of young ladies. Trying to impress her escort on one particular date she made use of a lip pencil which had been given away in a magazine — 'just touch the corners of your mouth and look amazing' — and, wearing a new dress, ran to their meeting place alongside Waterloo Bridge. She did not, alas, impress in the way she'd hoped. His immediate reaction was, 'Judi! Why have you got that comedy mouth on?'

Bar Leigh-Hunt was living in a flat at the top of a house in Eaton Terrace, a fashionable and expensive part of Belgravia, which she had obtained through a contact in her home town of Bath. At £9 a week the rent was affordable on the basis of sharing with two others. Originally her flatmates were Adrianne Hill and Juliet Cook, two colleagues from the Vic. After a while Adrianne dropped out and Judi offered to replace her. She was accepted on the spot and the three girls spent a joyous year together.

Judi and Bar shared one bedroom and Juliet, who was a little more independent, had the other. One day they discovered that by standing on a dresser they could just about see into the flat occupied by Michael Benthall and Robert Helpman in Eaton Square. Michael roared with laughter when they told him and thereafter offered them an occasional lift to the theatre. Mostly, though, they would take the tube from Sloane Square or a number 46 bus, leaving home at 9.20 a.m. and not returning until past 11 p.m., when exhausted but cheerful, they would clamber up the long flight of stairs. Judi frequently fantasized that a 'hamper from Fortnums' would be awaiting them at the top. In reality they had to start cooking. Cleaning and shopping were left for Saturday mornings.

It was a sociable flat, from which could be heard the sounds of a fairly steady stream of visitors along with the strains of Sarah Vaughan and Frank Sinatra records. Reg and Olave came down once or twice and took the girls out to tea. On Sundays Bar and Juliet would sometimes go home to their parents. Since York was too far for Judi to go back at all regularly she often accompanied Bar to Bath, christening Mrs Leigh-Hunt the 'OM' (Other Mother).

Professionally, it was a vitally formative period for Judi. She had worked hard at Central and now applied herself with equal thoroughness at the Vic. She would stand in the wings and watch her more experienced colleagues, looking to learn from them. She felt proud to be working with Barbara Jefford, whose performance in *The Two Gentlemen of Verona* had so excited her as a student.

Michael Benthall and John Neville were also very important influences. Judi still remains grateful to Michael Benthall for teaching her the effectiveness of speaking lines *legato*, giving each word its due weight. Neville always made rehearsals enjoyable, sometimes downright zany. He had his tonsils out during the rehearsal stage of the *Dream* and came back unannounced into the dress parade, appearing among the fairies in a lurex fig-leaf, long green socks and a big hat out of *Measure for Measure*. He once remonstrated with Judi for crying while she had the flu: 'Never do that. They haven't paid to see Ophelia crying with a headache. Get on and do it properly or let your understudy do it.' Judi took his advice to heart as a maxim of professionalism.

Michael Benthall endorsed this view of the fundamental value of discipline, telling Judi, 'Always, whatever you've got, do it *definitely*. Be definitely good or definitely bad, but for God's sake don't go on and be nothing.

In fact, Judi was far from being the only member of the company to go down with flu in that year. In 1957 London was struck by the so-called 'Asian flu' epidemic. The Old

Vic was not immune. At the close of *Hamlet*, with the epidemic at its height, Fortinbras' call for 'four captains' to 'Bear Hamlet like a soldier', was answered by two ladies-in-waiting, Claudius and a stage-hand.

Henry VI was notably depleted and for a good deal of the run Judi was one of the few people fit enough to go on. At one point the three inhabitants of the Eaton Terrace flat — Judi, Barbara and Juliet — formed the entire contingent of Cade rebels. Cade's rebellion seemed somewhat less than plausible when his rousing call: 'Now go some and pull down the Savoy; others to th'Inns of Court; down with them all' was addressed to a trio of young girls all trying not to giggle. The audience, however, could not hold back its laughter at the sight of Juliet Cook heading off in the notional direction of the Savoy bearing a nineteen-foot pole which happened to have a toffee stuck on the end.

It was a singularly blighted production. As Jack Cade, Derek Francis was called upon to leap athletically about the stage and one night he slipped, injured his leg and had to be taken to hospital. During another performance a series of loud explosions was heard — an attempt at beer-making in a room off-stage by the stage manager, John Wayne (Naunton Wayne's son), had miscarried.

Judi undoubtedly seized firmly the golden opportunity offered to her by Benthall, and most of the time felt elated to be in such distinguished company. But perhaps the most valuable lessons were those she learnt in adversity, like working through the Asian flu epidemic, or having to face criticism and rejection.

The critical notices for *Hamlet* had got her down — Findlater's comments disheartened her considerably — although a more reflective and scholarly view by M. St. Clare Byrne in the *Shakespeare Quarterly* some twelve months later held that 'Judi Dench received less than her due of priase for Ophelia, if her first-night performance was as good as the one I saw . . . her outburst at the end of the nunnery scene was, like Dorothy Tutin's, strongly and clearly carried for the sake of what it has to say . . . her madness had an effective darting vigour . . . I found her playing touching and honest.'

Nevertheless, the general opinion was that Michael Benthall's gamble hadn't come off and at the end of the season, with the company preparing to tour Paris and America for six months, Judi was called in for another awkward interview in the director's office.

Michael was looking out of the window, not at Judi, when he said, 'I don't know how to say this but when the company goes to the States I'm going to give the part of Ophelia to Barbara Jefford.' Judi's compensation was the Princess of France in *Henry V* with Laurence Harvey, and the retention of Maria in *Twelfth Night*. But it was a heavy blow. Judi went to her room in tears, and then off to have her distinctive blonde hair cut short. It was never to be long again.

There were just two productions in Paris: *Hamlet* and *Henry VIII*, for the latter of which the company were joined by John Gielgud and Edith Evans playing Wolsey and Katharine to Harry Andrews' Henry. The performances took place during a heat-wave and the actors sweltered on the stage of the Sarah Bernhardt Theatre. It was a great thrill for Judi and other members of the company to be taken out on the first night to dinner in a smart restaurant where all the other diners stood and applauded their entrance. However, their spirits were soon dampened when, after they had seated themselves at an open-air table and ordered their food, the skies opened and the rain poured down upon bare heads and arms.

Amid the excitement of Bastille Day, Judi was joined in Paris by Reg and Olave, on their way down to Biarritz for a holiday, and they came to see *Hamlet*. The tour also took in Brussels and Antwerp, where a lavish party was thrown for the company by a wealthy local industrialist. This took place on a fine, dry evening, at the height of which Paul Daneman, Paul Rogers and Daniel Thorndike ran gaily out through the open doors of the house, down to the bottom of a flight of steps beside a magnificent stone parapet and into the garden. Unfortunately, what they believed to be a lawn at the foot of the steps was in fact an enormous lake covered in duckweed.

But the main objective of the tour was America, and in particular New York and Broadway. Judi was the only member of the company not in *Hamlet* and it was a lonely experience for her to watch from the wings especially at the very end of the tour when the production was filmed on a New York stage.

If she didn't quite take America by storm, it certainly conquered her. She was a wide-eyed and enthusiastic tourist, whether visiting Sardi's or the Empire State. The company crossed the States on a three-day train journey from New York, and passed through places like Salt Lake City, Green River and Laramie in a permanent condition of collective euphoria. This big new experience was lapped up in gleeful moments like that when Harold Innocent bounded from his window seat to exclaim to all and sundry along the carriage that he had just seen a bear.

In New York, Judi was introduced to the celebrated jazz musician, Gerry Mulligan. A few days later he rang her at her hotel, inviting her to a late-night jam session. To Judi it was all a new dimension: 'It was music I'd never heard. I didn't really know anything about jazz before then. I went to lots of concerts — a highlight was hearing Muggsy Spanier. I was taken to Birdland to hear Count Basie with Joe Williams. We arrived to find a hole in a plate-glass door through which somebody had been knocked in a fight. I remember thinking, "this is real life; life in the raw." '

Christmas day was spent rehearsing on Broadway for *Henry V*. At the time, the American actor Edward Mulhare was playing Henry Higgins in *My Fair Lady* and he invited some of the Old Vic members for drinks at his home. Her first Christmas away and in a whirl, Judi put through a call to her parents, not even thinking about the time lag, and when her father answered she said, 'Hello. Who's with you?' He replied, 'Mummy, of course. Who did you think was with me? It's five o'clock in the morning!'

In Philadelphia the cast had problems negotiating the circuitous route between the dressing-rooms and the stage. The opening production was *Twelfth Night*. Judi, as Maria, had the line, 'Madam, there is at the gate a young gentleman much desires to speak with you' which referred to the disguised Viola, played by Barbara Jefford, and was addressed to Jane Downs as Olivia. From there the scene proceeds a while before the entry of Viola on the cue:

'We'll once more hear Orsino's embassy.' In Philadelphia it went on somewhat longer, with Jane and Judi exchanging improvised lines like, 'I do hope this young man will come soon' until Barbara Jefford at last appeared, a little flushed, having lost her way.

In the next act the same thing happened to Judi, whose entry line: 'What a caterwauling do you keep here!' was delivered, scarlet-faced, to two poor actors who had just sung the catch, 'Hold thy peace', an unconscionable number of times while she was finding her way on to the stage.

The actors' resistance finally and totally dissolved a scene or two later when Judi again had trouble and virtually sprinted on to say, 'Get ye all three into the box-tree. Malvolio's coming down this walk,' at which point John Neville, as Sir Andrew Aguecheek, intervened with the devastating stage whisper: 'Wanna bet?'

But the mood was effervescent, not disruptive, and the show received tremendous reviews. In Dallas, the Old Vic troupe found themselves part of 'British fortnight' and sponsored by the large Nieman-Marcus store, who asked to borrow some costumes for an exhibition. The actors couldn't believe their eyes when they duly attended the unveiling of the exhibition, beautifully mounted and illuminated in the windows of the Neiman-Marcus building. Whoever was responsible for displaying the costumes on the models had lost the list of descriptions so that some weird and wonderful combinations were on view. Edith Evans' top, for example, would be with Paul Rogers' jacket and John Neville's breeches, and labelled 'Hotspur'. Once again laughter demolished the actors' formal front.

The tour was an undoubted success, not least because the individual players had jelled as a company. Michael Benthall emphasized this aspect in a newspaper interview on his return: 'I feel very strongly about this. Nobody realizes the enormous care that goes into it.'

What he had attempted to do with his carefully chosen set of performers was to remove the starchy, Thespian image of the English Shakespearian actor which then prevailed, aiming to substitute a 'colloquial' form of verse-speaking for the 'intoning' style of previous generations. Indeed he liked to use the term 'verse-*acting*' as opposed to verse-speaking.

Judi learnt a lot on tour, partly from having to stand outside of *Hamlet* and watch Barbara Jefford earn the plaudits. The first night in San Francisco, where the company was completely unknown and Barbara gave a triumphant performance, was notably salutary.

Back in London, Judi and Bar Leigh-Hunt rented a rather gloomy bedsitting room together in Notting Hill and faced the approaching season in a more sombre frame of mind than that of a year before.

However, there was to be an unexpected fillip. The company were invited to Yugoslavia, which was just opening up again to tourism after the War. Moreover, Barbara Jefford was already committed to appear elsewhere in *The Cenci* and Michael Benthall restored Ophelia to Judi for the tour. This time she gave a more considered and mature performance, the production itself was more polished and the Yugoslav audiences were warmly enthusiastic. One night in Belgrade there were seventeen curtain calls.

Judi didn't return to the Notting Hill bedsit and, for that next Old Vic season, moved into digs in Elm Park Gardens, Chelsea. It was about this time that she did her first television work. Her earliest screen appearance was in a play called *Family on Trial* starring Andrew Cruickshank, followed by the title role in a dramatization of Arnold Bennett's *Hilda Lessways* and an episode of *Z-Cars* in a part which served as a model for the character she was to portray so effectively a few years later in John Hopkins' *Talking to a Stranger*.

Back at the Vic she played Cynthia in *The Double Dealer* in a production by Michael Benthall which did very well at the 1959 Edinburgh Festival. This was Judi's second successive trip to Edinburgh with the company, and she was beginning to feel at home there. She thrived on the cultural hurly-burly of the festival, mingling with other performers and going to see other plays and concerts or getting tickets to watch Ansermet or Klemperer rehearsing. But more than that, she was able to give vent to a personal sense of 'Scottishness'.

She has developed an almost mystical attachment to Scotland and nowadays goes there regularly on camping holidays with the family. More than once she has uncannily described in accurate detail an area in the Scottish country-side — a camp site, perhaps, or a village — before arriving there and without ever having been there before.

In *The Double Dealer*, Judi was required to sing on stage for the first time but Michael Benthall promptly cut her song, saying, 'Oh no, Miss Dench, we can't have that.' Once more Benthall was the perfect catalyst for an intriguing mixture of performers, including Donald Houston, John Woodvine, Joss Ackland, Miles Malleson and Maggie Smith.

Judi also appeared in *The Merry Wives of Windsor* and as Phebe in *As You Like It*, a 'pretty, petulant teenage pony-tailed Phebe' *The Times* called her. The director was Wendy Toye and the cast included Barbara Jefford, as Rosalind, Maggie Smith (Celia), Donald Houston (Jaques), John Justin (Orlando) and Alec McCowen (Touchstone).

In *The Importance of Being Earnest* which opened in October, 1959, Judi, as Cecily, built up an effective team-work with Barbara Jefford, who played Gwendolen. Alec McCowen was Algy and John Justin, Worthing. The key role of Lady Bracknell was taken by the distinguished actress Fay Compton, then in her mid-sixties.

Like other Lady Bracknells before and after her (including Judi Dench), Miss Compton had to contend with the redoubtable shadow of Edith Evans. She it is with whom the role is forever associated in the public mind, and against whose legend Lady Bracknells will surely be measured until the end of time.

So anxious about this was Fay Compton on the first night at the Vic in 1959 that, addressing Judi's Cecily Cardew, she uttered the marvellously tangled phrase, 'Thirty-four is a very attractive *name, Mister* Cardew.' Alec McCowen and Judi, in contagious nervousness, immediately began to giggle. Miss Compton was *not* amused and the elder actress lectured the younger long and hard backstage.

That same season Douglas Seale directed Paul Rogers in *King Lear* and in the early stages of rehearsal mystified some of those with smaller parts, including Judi, by the poses he asked them to strike. Standing behind a chair representing the throne for the opening scene, in which

Lear divides his kingdom, were Judi, with her arms spread wide; Adrianne Hill, with her arms stretched out in front of her; and Barbara Leigh-Hunt, with her hands held high above her head. Only when it came to the technical rehearsal was it revealed that Adrianne was to hold a stunted tree; Barbara a six-foot sword, which caused her arms to lock; and Judi a vast, smoking chalice, which obscured her face but made her cough every few seconds. All considerable feats of endurance.

Three years after bringing Frankie Howerd into *A Midsummer Night's Dream*, the Old Vic management secured another 'non-acting' star for a leading role in a dramatic classic. In the autumn of 1960, Tommy Steele was signed to play Tony Lumpkin in Goldsmith's *She Stoops to Conquer*. Douglas Seale directed and Judi Dench played Kate Hardcastle.

This time the guest star attracted crowds of young female fans to the Vic. Judi likened her role to being 'bottom of the bill at the Palladium' since a large portion of the audience was chattering in between Tommy's appearances, impatient for his return. Even so, Tommy was, like Frankie Howerd, popular behind the scenes. Initially, though, he had to overcome his fears at appearing with a group of skilful Shakespearian actors, while they in turn had to get over the considerable reservations about appearing with a famous pop star.

Later that year, the company returned to *A Midsummer Night's Dream*. This time the director was Michael Langham, and Judi Dench and Barbara Leigh-Hunt stepped up from the ranks of the fairies to play Hermia and Helena, the female members of the lovers' quartet.

Michael Langham drove the whole company exceedingly hard, but reserved his sharpest words for Judi and Bar, reducing them to tears on several occasions. He was very ill at the time although neither of the girls was aware of the fact.

He had already undergone a serious operation while the company were in the United States and the English actors had been exhorted to give a pint of blood to help pay for his treatment. Barbara Leigh-Hunt was one of those who responded to this plea — unknown to Langham himself.

And when she later had to suffer the slings and arrows of his directorial methods in the *Dream*, she was heard to say, 'I'm going up to him and demand my pint of blood back now!'

But it was not all blood, sweat and tears. For one thing, Hermia and Helena wore wonderfully slinky silk costumes, which were very daring at that time. They were low-cut at the front and had slits at the sides. During the fight between them, Hermia was supposed to pull off a piece of Helena's costume — it had been carefully made to come off — but on the first night Judi pulled the wrong piece and exposed Barbara's bottom for the rest of the scene. At the end of the day they were both singled out by the critics for the highest praise.

In the repertory with *A Midsummer Night's Dream* and *She Stoops to Conquer* was *Romeo and Juliet*. This, Tommy Steele and Michael Langham notwithstanding, was the production which made the biggest impact. It was also the most controversial. The man responsible for all this was its director, Franco Zeffirelli. Renowned for his grand-scale, colourful operatic productions (he had originally been a set designer in his native Italy), the very engagement of Zeffirelli to direct caused a stir. He is said to have regarded the invitation as a joke at first, in view of the 'laughably small' fee offered, but he came, he saw, and — if audience figures are a guide — he definitely conquered. The play ran for a record 122 performances at the Old Vic. Romeo was played by John Stride, Juliet was Judi Dench.

Both the principals were chosen for their youthful qualities. From the outset Zeffirelli concentrated on the passion of the love story at the expense of the poetry. To a large extent he rehearsed and directed John and Judi separately, therefore seeking a more natural and precarious union, as if they were two real young lovers.

In place of the traditional lyrical and bookish treatment of the play here was a tale very much of flesh and blood, and it outraged a few people. Nothing was sacrosanct. Even the balcony scene had Romeo climbing up a tree so as to *touch* his Juliet, who in turn leaned forward in earnest desire to greet him.

It was all too much for many of the critics. *The Times* praised the sets: 'To visit the squares and walled gardens of Mr Franco Zeffirelli's Verona is to breath the air of an enchanted Italian late summer', but concluded that the whole enterprise foundered on the lack of poetry. Robert Speaight, writing in the *Shakespeare Quarterly*, summarized the general objection succinctly: 'Romeo and Juliet move in a convention inescapably poetic; poetry is the rhythm to which they breathe.'

On the other hand John Russell Brown admired Zeffirelli's refusal to condescend to the two young lovers, resulting in a natural sense of excitement in their love. Brown's view was that 'Zeffirelli has been unusual among our contemporaries in unifying Shakespeare's words and an inventive, youthful and apparently spontaneous action.' Kenneth Tynan thought the production one of the Old Vic's best for years.

It certainly proved popular with the public. Joe Mitchenson, the theatre historian, who with his partner Raymond Mander was soon to become a very close friend of Judi's, first realized her power as an actress when he saw her Juliet: 'Seeing Judi at the Vic I felt a thrill I hadn't experienced since I'd seen Peggy Ashcroft in the part opposite John Gielgud many years before.' Mander and Mitchenson went back to see the production on its last night, by which time they and Judi were firm friends — she gave them a kitten called Juliet to replace a beloved pet cat that had died. Despite their influential position in the theatrical world — Mander and Mitchenson were indispensable to any important first night or presentation — they could only get seats in a box at the side of the stage normally given over to lighting equipment, so successful did the play prove.

Zeffirelli had made an enormous impression on the Old Vic and he was asked back four years later to direct *Hamlet* and *Much Ado About Nothing*. But it wasn't just at the box office. Judi found him remarkably inspiring and one of the few directors able to show what he wants by example: 'You'd be rehearsing on the stage and then out of the corner of your eye you'd see Franco doing it himself — and so much better you'd have to stop and gape.' He showed her how to convey passion from the heart rather than the head, and to give Juliet the manner and feelings of a young girl, not a woman.

After its London success Zeffirelli's *Romeo and Juliet* was taken on tour to Italy. The play formed part of the Venice Festival, at which Judi was awarded the *Paladino D'Argentino*, given by the Committee of the Palermo International Prize to the 'best actress of the year'. She had a beautiful dressing-room at the Fenice Theatre, overlooking the waterways, and took delight in her surroundings, even cherishing the experience of starting an hour and a half late one evening because of a gondola traffic jam.

The first night there was eventful for the antics of two Venetian stage hands charged with the task of holding up the piece of scenery representing the tomb. Judi needed all her powers of concentration as they chatted and flirted with her while she lay upon the tomb in performance. And in the last scene they started to move it away before the curtain came down.

But Venice saw her last appearance as Juliet. The company was to embark upon another American tour but Judi had decided not to go. Zeffirelli prevailed upon her to give a handful of performances in Venice, but that was to be the end of her involvement with the Old Vic. She felt it was time to seek new directions.

Just before she left for Venice she was approached by the fledgling Royal Shakespeare Company and introduced to one of its associate directors, Michel St Denis, who had seen and admired her as Juliet. An offer was made and accepted, and Judi left the Old Vic tour after Venice. She did, however, accompany the party to Turin, where, somewhat distracted and vulnerable, she was taken out to dinner by some friends from England, the actor Frank Duncan and his wife.

She returned to the theatre just in time to see, from the wings, the tumultuous reception given at the close to her replacement, Joanna Dunham. It was like San Francisco all over again but with one important difference: this time it had been her decision.

3 'Fear no more the heat o' the sun'

The Royal Shakespeare Company was created in 1960 out of the company then housed at the Shakespeare Memorial Theatre — thereafter to be known as the Royal Shakespeare Theatre — in Stratford-upon-Avon. Its first artistic director was Peter Hall. Michel St Denis became a general artistic adviser to the company and directed a number of productions at its London base, the Aldwych Theatre.

St Denis had made a name for himself in France, his homeland, and in England, where he founded the London Theatre Studio just before the Second World War. He was in his sixties and something of a daunting figure when Judi first met him. He told her, 'If I had been looking for Eliza Doolittle I'd look no further', and seemed doubtful about how and where to slot her into the company. But he did cast her in *The Cherry Orchard* as Anya.

This was Judi's first change of company; a big step and it felt like it. After leaving her *Romeo and Juliet* colleagues in Turin, she escaped to the South of France, joining her brother Peter and his wife Daphne on holiday in Nice. Here, she totally relaxed, soaking up the sun and enjoying being with the family.

She needed to let go. She was reacting to the exhilaration of Juliet and at the same time feeling anxious about what lay ahead at the RSC. Consequently she was a bit dreamy and absent minded. One day she accidentally removed the top of her swimming costume on the beach (later remarking that since nobody turned a hair she didn't know whether to be embarrassed or insulted) and when she baby-sat for Peter and Daphne one evening they returned to find her and their daughter Louise asleep on the floor, the latter having fallen out of her cot without Judi noticing.

Back in London Judi moved into a basement flat at 1

Regent's Park Terrace, home of a family called Carey and close to London Zoo. It had previously been occupied by the actor Paul Hardwick, who was in the cast of *The Cherry Orchard*. Judi originally intended it to be a short let but stayed for seven years, during which time she became very friendly with the Careys, acting as godmother to their daughter Liz's little girl Jenneth. Bar Leigh-Hunt came to stay frequently until her marriage to the actor Richard Pasco.

That first rehearsal period for *The Cherry Orchard* was a tense one for Judi. Not only was she a newcomer in a fairly well-knit group, but some of her fellow actors were of a considerable stature. The cast list for *The Cherry Orchard* bore ample testimony to the RSC's wealth of talent. It included Peggy Ashcroft as Madame Ranevsky, John Gielgud as Gaev and Dorothy Tutin as Varya, as well as Patience Collier, George Murcell, Patsy Byrne, Patrick Wymark, Roy Dotrice, Paul Hardwick, David Buck and Ian Holm as Trofimov.

Judi never felt so unsure of herself professionally. Although Michael Langham had given her an immensely difficult time in the *Dream*, he had always said he was pushing her towards something he knew she was capable of, whereas Michel St Denis told her, 'you've got to prove to me that you're worthy of it.'

When he gave notes to the actors at the end of each rehearsal he would throw up his hands in despair when it came to Judi. She was very unhappy but Peggy Ashcroft and John Gielgud were both supportive. Dame Peggy's advice was, 'If you're the whipping boy, don't let him see you cry.'

The Moscow Arts Theatre had visited London with a production of *The Cherry Orchard* only months before the RSC version. Indeed they had played it at the Aldwych and St Denis needed to emulate their success. He also had a strong memory of another Russian staging many years previously, in which there had been an outstanding Anya. Judi was being made to try to live up to these models. He rehearsed her one whole afternoon on the line: 'The birds are singing in the garden', which Anya delivers both laughing and crying, unsure which emotion she feels. By the end of the day Judi was in a similar hysterical quandary herself.

When it came to the first night and she turned to go back on after Act One, during which she had been extremely nervous, John Gielgud said to her, 'If you had been doing that for me I'd be delighted.' As ever, authoritative encouragement was exactly what she needed and she settled into the role precisely from that moment. She had been worried that Michel St Denis might have taken the part away from her but once the play opened, his manner altered and he became genial and complimentary. Furthermore, she gained satisfying recognition from fellow professionals for her performance as Anya when British Actors' Equity presented her with the 1962 Clarence Derwent Award for the best supporting actress.

During the run of The Cherry Orchard, Peter Hall asked Judi to participate in the Stratford end of the RSC's operations. She was to play Isabella in Measure for Measure and Titania in the Dream. John Blatchley was the director of Measure and Hall himself would take charge of A Midsummer Night's Dream. Judi was back on familiar Shakespearian ground, continuing the process of moving up from the minor parts to the major ones.

After that uncomfortable start in The Cherry Orchard, Judi soon came to find work agreeable at both RSC venues and 1962 was an intensely happy year. She landed the part of Major Barbara in a television production of Shaw's play and was having to attend rehearsals for that in London while based in Stratford. It was hectic but it was part of the fun of growing in confidence as an actress.

In Stratford she rented a tiny workman's cottage in Scholars Lane and struck up a close friendship with Tom Fleming, who was at that time a leading member of the company. She used to cycle out to Tom's place at Hampton Lucy for breakfast. He would put the porridge on and she'd buy the cream on the way. Then he'd put her bicycle in the back of his car and they would drive to the theatre.

On Shakespeare's birthday that year, Tom and Judi were both invited to the celebratory lunch in Stratford. The town beadle asked each guest his or her name on arrival and having been told, 'Tom Fleming', he announced 'Mr Albert Finney!' And, even more mysteriously, to Judi and Tom together: 'A horse, a horse, my kingdom for a horse!'

Measure for Measure opened in April. It was characterized by John Bury's grey, sombre set, incorporating a massive wall and echoing the depressed, prison-like nature of the Vienna in which the play is set. Angelo, the man 'whose blood is very snow-broth', was played by Marius Goring, and the Duke by Tom Fleming. Ian Richardson, Clive Swift and Ian Holm were Lucio, Pompey and Claudio respectively. Judi, as Isabella, did not wear the habit of a novitiate nun as is customary but remained in plain dress throughout. John Blatchley's production was generally held to offer a bold, clear reading of the text.

Judi's performance showed signs of that nervous strength which was to inform so much of her later and greater work. It also attracted, from Philip Hope-Wallace in the *Guardian*, the kind of lofty review to which she has been prone from time to time. Managing to combine an almost nursery-rhyme reference to her lack of inches with unfavourable comparisons to previous Isabellas, he wrote that 'where Miss Jefford gave us grandeur and simplicity and where Dame Flora Robson once memorably gave us a terrible puritan hysteria, little Miss Dench was content with sincerity and an orderly, if not very affecting, use of language.'

Judi has always bridled at reviews of her performances which refer to her physical appearance. This is partly because she is undeniably sensitive about her height (she is 5 feet 1½ inches) and sometimes wishes she were tall and slender, and partly because the assumptions that often accompany or underlie such comment are irrelevant to any appreciation of acting of the highest standard. This is a view shared by the director of her next play at Stratford: 'Anyone looking at her as a young girl would have said "What a pretty girl, but rather short, and she'll be confined to *ingénue* parts." But she's become a great leading actress. It doesn't matter if you're tall, short, fat, thin, if you have genius. She's got genius.'

Judi impressed Peter Hall right from the beginning of their work together in *A Midsummer Night's Dream*. By now her inner power as an actress was firmly apparent. Hall sees it as something earthy and sensual: 'She can be very sexy on stage. And her feet are very firmly on the ground — it's very important to Judi what shoes she wears, what the floor of the stage is made of, how she stands. When we did *A Midsummer Night's Dream* the whole part of Titania was released when I suggested she played it bare-footed. She could be nimble and earthy — bang her heels and run off. I think she's the definitive Titania, certainly of my lifetime.'

A Midsummer Night's Dream is indeed not just an ideal vehicle for Judi's acting talents; it creates the perfect setting for her personality. It is surely one of the most enchanting works in our literature, full of mystery and mischief, hilarity and celebration, and innocent but solid good cheer — all qualities with which she herself is filled to the brim.

In that 1962 Stratford production it was the ensemble playing that caught the eye. A sense of *company* communicated itself to the audience in the interplay between Ian Richardson, as Oberon, Ian Holm, as Puck, and Judi, whose Titania was compared by the critic J.C. Trewin to 'spun crystal'. Others in the cast all made their contributions, too, including Tony Steedman as Theseus, Paul Hardwick as Bottom, Diana Rigg and Patricia Brake as Helena and Hermia and Tony Church, Ian Hewitson, Clifford Rose, Clive Swift and Bill Travers as the mechanicals.

A special performance for children was given at the Central Hall, Westminster with the Royal Philharmonic Orchestra playing the Mendelssohn score. Ian Holm was unavailable for this. His replacement — who was to take over when the play transferred to the Aldwych — was a young member of the company whom Judi had not long got to know, but with whom she was ultimately destined to experience the closest interplay of all: Michael Williams.

It was, and is, the achievement of a harmonious *blend* that Judi finds most satisfying in the work of actors within top companies like the RSC. When she arrived at Stratford in 1961 Peter Hall and his lieutenants were rigorously instilling in the RSC's troops what Judi calls 'the Stratford seal of democracy'.

No company can be without its leaders, but in certain groups those leaders are expected to lead from the front and muck in with the menials, listening sympathetically to everybody's views. And everybody is encouraged to express a view. Such a company, *par excellence*, is the Royal Shakespeare Company. Under Peter Hall and, perhaps even more obviously, his successor Trevor Nunn, the RSC has striven for and established a reputation for ensemble playing that is unsurpassed in the contemporary British Theatre.

This is something in which Judi Dench, whether as a junior or a senior member, has felt completely at home: 'I like knowing a company so well that you are not embarrassed about making a fool of yourself. I would dare to do almost anything. You push yourself beyond a kind of limit. And the democracy means that nobody need mind offering a view and it is taken into account. At the Vic I remember you wouldn't dare say anything, and everyone was "Miss Browne", "Mr Nicholls" and so on. At the RSC the production evolves out of a co-operative endeavour. The finished result is something that all hands have been involved with.' All parts of the winds of change, perhaps, ushered in by the theatrical revolution of the 1950s.

Although it all sounds so constructive, democracy is not the simplest idea to implant in the fragile egos of theatre people. It is not widely appreciated, for example, that the period at the RSC in the early 1970s when Trevor Nunn instituted the much lauded policy of giving small parts in some productions to leading actors, was an immensely trying time for him. He had to spend 'hundreds of hours' on the telephone convincing people who expected star billing that it was healthy for them to play a supporting role to a junior colleague. And then there were the follow up thank you calls that such stars expected. But it did work for a while and Nunn recalls Judi's collaboration as vital:

'It was a remarkable time in the life of the company — when you think that Alan Howard played an eight-line part, and Ian Richardson played Marcellus in *Hamlet*, for instance. Judi Dench played a walk-on in *Much Ado*. There are no small parts for girls in that play. There are four parts and they were required for girls in the company who needed them to make their season. Therefore to make the doctrine work Judi played a walk-on. Not only did she do it, she did it completely anonymously, no *I hope you're all noticing me*. She did her professional job, the whole season through. More than anybody, she was responsible for the experiment lasting as long as it did.'

The final play of Judi's first term with the RSC in 1962 was presented at the Aldwych. *A Penny for a Song* had launched its author, John Whiting, in 1951, with a production by Peter Brook at the Haymarket Theatre. Whiting subsequently achieved prominence with his vivid and spectacular psychological drama, *The Devils*, based on an historical book by Aldous Huxley, produced by the Royal Shakespeare Company in 1961.

But *A Penny for a Song*, which Whiting rewrote for the RSC's 1962 staging, was in marked contrast. An extraordinarily tender comedy, its subject is the eccentric and varied response of a group of people in Dorset in 1804 to the supposed threat of a Napoleonic invasion. The title is taken from a poem by Yeats about the relationship between age and idealism, a central theme of the play. Judi played Dorcas Bellboys, daughter of Sir Timothy Bellboys, the quaintest and gentlest of warmongers (played by Marius Goring). She is the one character who is not obviously and deliberately one-dimensional. She is affable, pretty, innocent, but with an observant, down-to-earth quality, and is charged with expressing the play's concluding message, a sober warning about the childish absurdity of treating war lightly.

Apart from that, Dorcas is not much in the foreground and the part can really only be viewed as a stepping stone in Judi's career.

John Whiting worked closely with the director, Colin Graham, and the actors. Judi found the playwright to be intelligent, understanding and gentle and he made a great impression on her. He was a writer of the highest promise. A year later, at the age of forty-five, he died of cancer.

Judi quickly formed an affection for the Aldwych Theatre and it has since remained fixed in second place in her personal league table, permanently headed by the Old Vic. She is a great believer in the idea that buildings retain the spiritual attributes of their inhabitants, and that the Aldwych is a happy, lively place through the continuing influence of its past masters of farce like Tom Walls, Ralph Lynn and Robertson Hare. It also felt good coming into

London from Stratford to work on a smaller stage, the reverse of the normal transfer situation.

By the season's close, Judi had gained a firm footing on the theatrical ladder. Early promise had been given substance by craftsmanship, energy and enthusiasm by vitality and versatility. She had definitely arrived as an actress. The days of her longing for success as a painter or designer were long gone. Her ambitions now were theatrical. It wasn't so much that she hankered after specific roles but that there were certain people she strongly desired to work with.

High on the list was the director Tyrone Guthrie, whose legend she had imbibed at the Old Vic and whose career she had followed ever since. At about the time *A Penny for a Song* was ending its run, plans were being finalized for the opening of a new theatre in Minneapolis named after Tyrone Guthrie and at which the great man himself would be directing.

Meanwhile Judi had received an offer to appear in a 'whodunit' comedy called *A Shot in the Dark*, an American version of a play by Marcel Achard, in a part Julie Harris was then successfully playing on Broadway. Judi wasn't keen but her employment at the RSC was coming to an end and her agent advised acceptance. Accordingly she was sent a contract which she read and signed on her way into the theatre to do a matinée. There was a letter for her at the stage door. She picked it up, went to her dressing-room and got ready before opening it. It read 'Dear Judi Dench. Will you come to my first season at Minneapolis to play Ophelia, Marianne in *The Miser* and Irina in *The Three Sisters*. T. Guthrie.'

Judi at once wrote to Guthrie to explain about *A Shot in the Dark*. He replied to say he couldn't break her contract for her — 'a contract is a contract is a contract' and that 'there'll be other times.' Sadly, there weren't. He died a few years later leaving that particular ambition of Judi's unrealized.

To rub salt into the wound, *A Shot in the Dark* was a dismal failure and folded within a short period of its opening in May 1963. But prior to that Judi did manage to get some foreign experience, though in a place and a manner she could not have foreseen.

Her mentor, colleague and close friend from the Old Vic days, John Neville, had gone to Nottingham Playhouse in 1961, becoming its artistic director two years later. As Judi was coming to the end of her first period with the RSC, Neville approached her with an exotic offer. The British Council had invited the Nottingham Playhouse to take a company to West Africa. John Neville and Frank Dunlop were to direct, between them, three plays: *Macbeth, Twelfth Night* and Shaw's *Arms and the Man*. John Neville wanted Judi for Viola, and Frank Dunlop wanted her to play Lady Macbeth.

The tour was to take in three countries: Nigeria, Ghana and Sierra Leone, and they were to be the first British theatre company to visit the region. John Neville was to act as well as direct and other company members included Polly Adams, James Cairncross, Paul Daneman and Jill Gascoigne. Judi jumped at it.

The British winter of 1962–3 was the most severe this century. There were gales, deep cold frosts, and the worst fog in London since the Great Smog of 1952. Glasgow, with three inches of snow, had its first post-War white Christmas. Snowdrifts elsewhere reached fifteen to twenty feet. Whole communities were isolated. The New Year began with the coldest January since 1814. It was the coldest single month this century. The sea froze in several places and there were ice-floes at Tower Bridge.

The Nottingham Playhouse Company flew out of Heathrow on one of the few flying days in January. The aircraft took them from one extreme of climate to another. Just before she left, Judi had her hair permed. She boarded the aircraft with it soft and wavy, she disembarked in Africa with it completely frizzy.

The heat was a constant companion, insistent and omnipresent. The actors suffered from it and delighted in it by turns. They sent home mocking tape-recordings, giggling while they pretended to commiserate over iced-up cars or burst pipes.

The company performed at a wide variety of venues, but only one purpose-built theatre. That was in Lagos, where the stage manager was a Mr Obeyme, renamed 'Mr

Disobeyme' by the cast when he began to miss cues and forget props. Also in Lagos the company were treated to a reception at the home of the British High Commissioner.

The tour was geared to a hectic schedule. Playing at universities and colleges and the barest of open-air arenas, staying at government rest-houses in Ibadan, Accra, and Freetown, and arriving at some of the more obscure destinations, such as cocoa plantations, only to find they weren't expected, the company lived and worked at a high pace. pace. They travelled a great deal by aircraft, a small DC4, with the scenery — made by the drama department of the University of Ibadan — strapped inside, next to the passengers. Or they were driven by jeep for miles along red dusty roads, and when they reached the end of their journey they would be covered in dust themselves.

They inevitably played to packed houses — 'even if they didn't want to see the plays they came to look at this band of red-faced strangers.' The audiences usually contained a sprinkling of British expatriates but the great majority were Africans, among them scores of children studying the plays at school as 'set texts' for examinations.

It was a new and taxing experience for the actors. The spectators were enthralled and excitable. They would chatter, scream and laugh incessantly throughout the performances, but always in response to, or by way of commentary upon the action. *Macbeth* invariably provoked a noisy accompaniment and the performers struggled to make themselves heard. The proceedings would be interrupted constantly by cries of 'Oh look!' or 'Say that bit again!' amid loud laughter and applause.

Rhyming verse had a sensational effect, and, in the sleep-walking scene, the line, 'The Thane of Fife had a wife' was a showstopper. Judi had to steel herself for it every time, coming as it does at a high emotional point yet here being greeted as the greatest-ever comedy line.

In the same scene, Lady Macbeth performs the action of washing her hands, probably the *locus classicus* for guilt expressed through drama. Here, too, the audience reaction was electric: 'She's washing her hands and there's no basin! What's the matter with her now?'

But, although John Neville and Judi came to refer to

themselves, not entirely ironically, as 'the Morecambe and Wise of West Africa', the company soon realized that the audience involvement was both genuine and total. At the end of each performance the reception was overwhelming, and when in the closing act of *Twelfth Night* Sebastian was reconciled with Viola, the audience would go wild, and stand and cheer and throw programmes, flowers, shoes and all manner of things on to the stage in utter breathtaking appreciation.

Quite aside from the challenge posed by the audiences there was a full quota of on-stage mishaps to cause panic or laughter. A number of the performers went down with illness throughout the tour and when Polly Adams was laid low with a tooth infection and Judi and the others were already covering extra parts, a lady from the British Council volunteered to play the third witch in *Macbeth*, claiming a sound working knowledge of the text. Only the fact that the witches wore masks (a fact which in itself tickled many Africans, indicating as it did the white man's superstition towards witchcraft) prevented pandemonium around the cauldron when, after the 'Double, double, toil and trouble' invocation, the British Council lady's offering to the brew was 'Scale of dragon, tooth of wolf, Witches' mummy, two pork chops'!

One time, Judi entered for the already notorious sleep-walking scene and the lamp she was carrying crumbled away in her hands. In Accra, she collapsed with malaria in the middle of a scene. The audience thought it was wonderful and clapped. Fortunately, this occurred just before a break of a few days and Judi recovered suffic-iently not to miss a single performance. At a swimming-pool in Kaduna, northern Nigeria, she organized an 'aquatic show' which Paul Daneman filmed and James Cairncross recorded.

On a stopover in Cape coast, they were given singularly dubious accommodation. Judi's bedroom had an enormous, uncurtained window out on to the corridor, along which she was able to observe much coming and going throughout the night.

In Port Harcourt, where the company was billeted in an unfinished hotel, Judi was at first given a room which still had men's clothes in the closet and a large pair of shoes under the bed. She insisted on changing to another room and was given what she describes as 'a cupboard — no bath, no hot water, and a shower with no drain so if you did decide to have a shower you had a flooded room for the rest of your stay. When I got up the next morning I happened to touch the shower tap with my shoulder and the whole thing fell into the room.'

Some of the acting locations demanded a similar resilience. Sometimes lizards would race the actors across the stage and run up and down the set. In Ibadan a violent storm cut off the electricity and stopped the show. One performance took place before a high, curved stone wall which also served as a cinema screen. Happening to glance up, Judi saw several vultures perched there, prompting her to advise those of her *Macbeth* colleagues called upon to die on stage not to lie too still!

Probably a more genuinely unnerving experience was appearing before President Nkrumah of Ghana, whose armed guards, resplendently attired in red and gold, kept the closest possible watch on the Nottingham players, even following them to the lavatory.

It was a tough, rigorous couple of months. When the last performance of the tour ended in Freetown, Sierra Leone, John Neville, who had been playing Macbeth, ripped off his armour, threw it to the ground and, thankful to be delivered from night after night of furnace-like endeavour, ceremoniously urinated over it. But even then he was not rid of it — when the actors had cleared away, a small boy spotted the abandoned armour and dutifully carried it back to the company's hotel.

If ever there was an engagement to confirm Judi's belief in professional discipline, this was it. Each member of the troupe had to fetch and carry equipment, become familiar with various bus timetables, put on make-up under the blazing sun only to have it run during performance, rehearse and play in varying conditions within a tight schedule in front of a noisy and distracting audience, and all in relentless, torrid heat. One or two had to return to England through illness, among them Frank Dunlop with gastric malaria.

The arduousness of it all was underlined by two fatalities. Pat Farrell, an administrator, collapsed and died upon his return to Britain, as did the actor Patrick Duffy, who was suffering from a kidney disease.

Nevertheless, for the most part the company looked back upon the tour with great satisfaction. It was certainly a success in that it generated tremendous interest in drama throughout the region, and local and visiting theatre groups came thick and fast in the wake of the Nottingham Playhouse Company.

Judi was glad to have been able to tackle two such important Shakespearian roles and regarded her work in Africa as a good grounding for the future. It was undoubtedly a little raw in one or two places. In the light of the audiences' attitude to Lady Macbeth, for instance, she tended to play Viola in a fairly untrammelled comic fashion, while in *Macbeth* itself her approach was possibly a little too dogged.

But it is more than a faint possibility that the African experience amounted to a necessary apprenticeship in the career of an actress who was later to demonstrate, by adding an extra dimension to both Viola and Lady Macbeth, that she was a supreme exponent of her craft.

Events between the springs of 1962 and 1963 propelled Judi into maturity. Professionally she came through the prodigious trials of the RSC and Africa, and also suffered the the disappointment of the missed opportunity with Guthrie. Privately, she received a stab of more than mere disappointment.

In 1954, while in London judging a St John's Ambulance Brigade first-aid competition, Reginald Dench had suffered a heart attack. He managed to travel home by train but was admitted to hospital a day later. He seemed to regain his health fairly quickly and over the next few years lived a normal, active life. Then in 1963, while Judi was in Africa, she felt intimations of mortality in the heat and a terrible sense of foreboding. She telephoned home to hear indeed that her father had experienced a second, more serious coronary. Suddenly, the parental rock on which she was so accustomed to lean was cracked.

On her return she went to see him in hospital in York,

the healer ministered to by healers, one of whom, a staff nurse named Susie Taylor was a great prop. Sympathetic and supportive even beyond the call of duty, she and Judi became and have remained the firmest of friends. They lost touch for a period during which Susie was divorced. Remarried — to businessman Gerald Bodmer — and living on the outskirts of London, she is now in constant, almost daily contact with Judi, and both families get together at regular intervals.

Reg was eventually discharged from hospital, his strength vitally sapped. Judi, meanwhile, entered rehearsals for the ill-fated *A Shot in the Dark*.

Early prospects for the production weren't at all bleak. The Broadway show had done extremely well and there was talk of a film (which eventually surfaced as a Peter Sellers vehicle).

Judi met the American adapter, Harry Kurnitz, at the Ritz for tea. In a miniature scene absolutely in the spirit of the piece under discussion, Harry and Judi disturbed the cool, English equilibrium of their surroundings when he said, 'Yes, I think you'll be wonderful in the part' and gave her a congratulatory push. Judi, taken aback by the un-Ritz-like gesture, was caught off balance and slipped, breaking the leg of a small sofa.

Rehearsals seemed to go well, under the direction of Jerome Whyte and subsequently Harold Clurman from America, and the cast, which included Polly Adams, George Baker and Peter Sallis, began to dovetail smoothly into the comedy routines. They opened in Liverpool to rave notices. Then Brighton and a similar reception. Then London, and an echoing thud.

The Times sank its teeth into Harry Kurnitz's scripts — 'long-winded and insensitive to cliché ... Broadway at its sniggering, priggish, blunt-witted worst.' Judi's old friend, Philip Hope-Wallace in the *Guardian*, after complaining about the production's 'tedium and vulgarity' and 'unrelieved flippancy', grandly opined that 'Judi Dench, squawking and grimacing pluckily, has the audience on her side, but the character refuses to establish itself in the circumstances.'

On that first night at the Lyric, Shaftesbury Avenue, Judi was deeply upset by a clumsy, if apparently well-meaning gesture by the management, who sent her the dress Julie Harris had worn in the New York production feeling it to be more appropriate than the one originally designed for Judi. Joe Mitchenson went to see Judi in her dressing-room before the show and she sobbed on his shoulder about this.

Uncharacteristically, she needed a pre-curtain drink to help her feel right for going on. But what was in character was that, amid the critical shambles of a doomed, unsuccessful production, she derived plenty of fun. Her memories of *A Shot in the Dark* are almost all humorous:

'It was agony. Nobody came, nobody laughed. Once, Polly failed to come on. It was in a scene where I was being interrogated by George Baker and Peter Sallis. She was supposed to burst into the proceedings, play the scene and depart. Well, not only did she not appear, she wasn't even standing by. We just froze. We couldn't ad lib and we couldn't think what to do — I remember taking my shoe off and looking at it for bit. We heard the stage management rushing upstairs. Peter said, "I'm going to see what Monsieur Du Pont has to say about this," and he walked off and we heard him shout, "Polly!" up the stairs. Then we heard him go to the prompt corner and look through the book so we could pick up the scene.

'He came back and said, "Monsieur Du Pont suggests what you say is this . . . " and he gave me my line. George asked, "What do I say?" and Peter replied, "If you think I'm going off to look up your line, you've got another think coming." We laughed and the audience didn't.

'Polly had been in the loo, knitting. And even at the curtain call she still didn't realize she had missed the scene. There'd been a matinée that day and she thought she'd done it.

'And then came the fateful day when the cast were called together between shows for the announcement that we were closing. As we all made our way to the stage Polly caught up with me and, wondering at the reason for the assembly, whispered, "Do you think it's because the Pope has died?" A smashing girl, Polly.'

In 1964, Judi joined the Oxford Playhouse Company, run by Frank Hauser, to play leading parts in five plays, *Three Sisters*, *The Twelfth Hour*, *The Alchemist*, *Romeo and*

Jeannette, and *The Firescreen*. She had encountered Frank
Hauser just once before. Introduced to her in a pub he had
embarrassed Judi by whimsically enquiring whether she
had previously been with the Bluebell Girls dance troupe.
Then she heard that he had walked out of the Zeffirelli
Romeo and Juliet. So Hauser's was a name which did not
exactly have a sweet sound in Judi's ear. But all that was
to change and before long a strong bond of affection had
grown up between them.

Certainly the Oxford offer was an attractive one enabling
Judi to put behind her the disappointments of *A Shot in
the Dark* though she was surprised to receive it, given the
dismissive opinion she assumed Frank Hauser to have of her.

When they began to work together, whatever prejudices
they held towards each other quickly evaporated in the
hard-working, often hilarious rehearsals. Hauser had in fact
assembled a rich collection of personalities who between
them produced some sparkling work. In the cast of *Three
Sisters* were John Standing, Elizabeth Sellers, Patsy Healy,
Roger Livesey, James Cairncross and Joseph O'Connor,
and other company members that season included John
Hurt, John Moffatt, Frank Shelley, Simon Ward and John
Turner. Judi thought Turner the most frightening man she'd
ever met after seeing him, huge as he was, sitting on a
corner of the stage during rehearsal eating raw meat with
an egg beaten into it.

Three Sisters opened towards the end of April 1964.
Frank Hauser orchestrated the Chekhovian intricacies with
notable precision and it was well received. Judi, as Irina,
displayed her natural instinct for poignant comedy, and
the whole production flowed smoothly.

She had her hair streaked for the part at Ellison and
Cavell's hairdressers in Oxford where unfortunately an in-
experienced girl who had never streaked hair before left
Judi's exposed by half an inch or so from the roots. The
hairdressers agreed to put right the resultant disaster at
their own expense and dyed Judi's entire hair ash blonde.
Reg and Olave were due down that day and Judi was more
nervous of confronting them as an ash blonde than of
appearing on stage in the evening. In the event, Reg's first
words on seeing her were, 'Oh, that looks very good!'

Also in the audience was Dirk Bogarde, who came back-stage afterwards to see Elizabeth Sellars, an old friend. Judi was introduced and was completely tongue-tied. Years later, when she was doing another season at Oxford, he again came round and said, 'I don't think you'll remember but we met some time ago.'

The Twelfth Hour, by the Russian writer Alexei Arbuzov, and set in his homeland in the wake of the Soviet Revolu-tion, brought John Hurt to the fore in a praised performance as Judi's idealistic husband. Judi, as a spoiled, calculating, young woman, also responded well to the atmosphere created by Arbuzov and the Oxford season proceeded along its successful path. One of the more teasing problems facing Frank Hauser in this play lay in the logistics of arranging for the tiny Judi Dench to embrace the giant John Turner passionately during a scene at a party. This was finally overcome by having John conveniently collapse on to a tree stump as they danced.

Also in the cast were James Laurenson, as a zealous young revolutionary; John Moffatt, contributing greatly to the mood in a white suit; and Ursula Jeans, who joined late for this one role, her husband Roger Livesey having been with the company from the start of the season. Ursula nonplussed Frank Hauser somewhat with her nonchalance in rehearsal and a lasting image in the minds of everyone associated with *The Twelfth Hour* is of Ursula, still reading from her book a matter of days before opening, peering out at the dark auditorium and saying, 'Frank, I know it will only take me an evening to learn this part — it's just that I haven't chosen the evening yet.'

The quintet of plays at Oxford extended, with tours, well in 1965. In the midst of all this Judi appeared in the television trilogy *Parade's End*. More shatteringly, her father died on 1 December 1964.

Judi was in London, having just returned home from filming *Four in the Morning* for Anthony Simmons, when her brother Peter rang and broke the news. It was almost six o'clock in the evening and Judi decided to travel up to York the next morning. She put down the telephone and was hit at once by despair and isolation. Most of her close friends, including Bar Leigh-Hunt, were away. She called

Frank Hauser at his London flat, who came straight over as soon as he heard her voice — she didn't even say what had happened.

When he arrived he sat silently doing *The Times* crossword while Judi packed sadly for her journey. It was some time before either spoke and then virtually the only words Frank said were, 'I presume it's a member of the family.' He judged, kindly and accurately, the sort of quiet, steady support Judi needed at that moment.

The next day Judi joined the family in York. Her mother was devastated and Judi felt a strong responsibility to ensure that life would continue to hold a purpose for her. It was an emotional landmark and, although Olave never fully recovered from Reg's death, mother and daugher were brought closer together than ever.

A week after Reg's funeral, it was Peter Dench's son Simon's birthday. Reg had bought him a recording of *The Mikado* as a present and was actually listening to it when he died. Peter and Daphne had planned a party and Judi and Olave insisted it shouldn't be cancelled. It turned out to be a most warm-hearted and animated occasion, largely due to Judi's spellbinding presence. She was the driving force. Children queued to sit on her knee.

It was time, however, to return south for rehearsals at Oxford. At this point Frank Hauser stepped in to prevent what would have been an enormous wrench for Judi. He telephoned York and suggested that she brought Olave back with her — 'I'll give her jobs to do.' So Judi and her mother came down together and Olave found some distraction from her grief in attending the odd rehearsal, making tea for the company and generally being around Judi and her work.

Dol Common in *The Alchemist* provided Judi with her next part. Although the production perhaps made less of an impact than others in the repertory, Jonson's eternally effective satire was as pungent as always and there was a diversion in the form of a short tour to Cumbria. This was to perform in the exquisite private theatre designed by Oliver Messel in former stables attached to the house owned by Miki Sekers in Rose Hill, Whitehaven.

Touring reinforced the company's existence as a generally self-contained unit. In Oxford there was little or no contact with the students or the university — although Judi and others gave a few special lectures in local schools — and the actors would spend a lot of off-duty time together, in pubs, lodgings, or over dinner in The Welsh Pony. Judi was staying at the Turf Tavern, one of Oxford's famous old pubs and a magnet for American visitors.

Other touring dates included Cambridge, where there was more involvement with the students, and Middlesbrough, where Judi had a room next door to Joan Rhodes, who did a 'strong-woman' music-hall and television act and whose exertions could be heard through the wall as she practised bending iron bars.

The remaining two plays in that Oxford season were Anouilh's *Romeo and Jeannette*, and *The Firescreen*, a comedy by Alfred de Musset. In the former, a robust, romantic piece, Judi played the wild heroine of the title who compellingly drags her lover (played by Nicholas Pennell) from a respectable, bourgeois life into a passionate joint suicide. John Turner made a fiery contribution as Lucian, Jeannette's brother, and David Swift played their weaker father. Tony Tanner directed.

The Firescreen, with Frank Shelley, John Turner and Simon Ward, was directed by Minos Volanakis. Judi played the part of Jacqueline, a woman who, in order to conceal an affair she is having, sets up another man as a decoy, or 'firescreen', between her husband and her lover, only to fall in love with the man brought in as the firescreen.

The first scene opened with Judi lying on a bed. Just before one matinée she ate a very large lunch and, taking up her position a little early, fell asleep. When the stage manager saw her on the bed he brought the curtain up and the play began. Judi awoke with a jolt to see Frank Shelley — playing André, her husband — standing before her. Not realizing for a second or two what was happening she stared at him in sleepy confusion and said aloud, 'Frank?'

Such minor aberrations apart, all went well and the production transferred to the Nuffield Theatre, Southampton where Minos Volanakis drew a favourable notice from *The Times* for his direction and the set, which he designed himself. Judi, too, was commended as 'a woman absorbed and absorbing'.

Ahead lay a period of adjustment, especially for Olave. She became much more involved in the life and work of her daughter. And for Judi, a time of consolidation in the theatre and some first steps into film. Her early professional years had seen her in two major national companies, two leading repertory organizations, three vastly contrasted foreign tours, on television and Shaftesbury Avenue. To each of these categories — often on the very same stages — she would in due course return with renewed vigour and greater distinction.

4 Playhouses and night clubs

After Oxford and Frank Hauser it was back to Nottingham again and John Neville, this time strictly on home base. No cocoa plantations, malaria or running greasepaint. In some ways, though, it was quite as lively. There were many hysterical moments — it could hardly be otherwise with John Neville. Paradoxically, in the theatre this is often a mark of hard, serious work. The closer and more intensively a group of actors works together, the greater their familiarity and the greater their need for the occasional release of pressure, usually in crazy, unbounded laughter.

Judi's second Nottingham Playhouse season in 1965 gave her the chance to tackle Isabella once more in *Measure for Measure*, her third appearance in the play. At the Old Vic she had played the minor part of Juliet and at Stratford in 1962 her 'plain-clothes' Isabella was set in the sober, dark-grey context of John Blatchley's production.

At Nottingham, Isabella was back in nun's attire but this was the only concession to tradition. In Neville's modern-dress production the moated grange became a night club with Ewan Williams, wearing a green shade, playing 'Take O take those lips away' on the piano, and Mariana seated at the bar in an advanced alcoholic state. At the dress rehearsal Judi, in demure white habit and cropped hair, halted at the door of this particular scene, much to John Neville's annoyance.

'Why aren't you entering?' he yelled.

'I'm not sure how to enter correctly,' was the reply.

Then, in the heat of the moment oblivious of the splendid incongruity of his instruction, he barked out, 'You enter in the way any fucking nun would enter a night club after hours!'

When *Measure for Measure* opened, Edward Woodward was in it as Lucio but after a while he dropped out and Jimmy Thompson replaced him. There was one speech

that Jimmy could never remember properly. This was at
the close of Act I when Lucio urges Isabella to beg Angelo
to save her brother's life.

> Go to Lord Angelo,
> And let him learn to know, when maidens sue,
> Men give like gods; but when they weep and kneel,
> All their petitions are as freely theirs
> As they themselves would owe them.

At Nottingham this was addressed to Isabella by a dist-
inctly contemporary, white-raincoated Lucio, through an
S-shaped grille designed by Patrick Robertson to adapt to
prison or nunnery. On Jimmy's first night in the role,
when he came to the above passage he said, 'Go to Lord
Angelo, And let him learn to know . . . that when maidens
kneel down they can have anything they want!' With that, he
put his hand inside his raincoat, pulled out a cigarette case
and, turning to face Judi, said, 'Would you like a cigarette?'

John Neville's modern appurtenances made for an enter-
taining evening, though the general verdict was that he had
tampered too much with Shakespeare. Judi, on the other
hand, was singled out for praise by the press. *The Times*
described her Isabella as 'a triumphant portrayal'.

With *Private Lives* in October 1965, Neville gave Judi
her first, never-forgotten taste of Coward. Playing opposite
Edward Woodward, she revelled in the sheer, audacious
style and the unashamed theatricality, still potent in a
world in which playwrights were increasingly turning to
'relevant' social issues.

Going out on stage as Amanda was, said Judi, 'like having
a wonderful love affair each evening. I felt terrific. When
we came up to the dress rehearsal I put on this marvellous
wig — dark red and Marcel-waved — and when I passed Teddy
Woodward on the set he didn't recognize me. Wearing that,
and all those lovely clothes, you couldn't help feeling good.'

'Teddy' Woodward and Judi, both incorrigibly fond of
pranks, seemed together to generate a stream of miniature
acts of chaos, mostly unintentional. One night as Judi threw
her arms up in greeting, her bracelet flew off into the audience.
Another time the top of a coffee pot came off and Teddy

put it in his pocket. In yet another performance the drinks trolley, which was meant to go over when he pushed her against it, failed to do so and Judi fell into it. She remained stuck there while Teddy walked away without lifting her out.

Edward Woodward's character, Victor — a part of course originally conceived by Coward for himself — is called upon to play the piano. Woodward couldn't and so Ewan Williams played for him on a piano placed directly behind a piece of scenery through which the concealed Williams could see the stage piano. The two men built up a routine which worked well until the night Teddy Woodward spent too much time downstage and his piano started 'playing' without him.

One play in that Nottingham repertory in which Judi was not appearing was *Richard II*. This did not prevent her from playing a practical joke on the cast. The day they were dress rehearsing she went out early and obtained a suit of armour, boots, a cloak, a wig, false eyebrows and a beard. And that evening, when Alan Howard as Richard entered the jousting scene in the first act on a flourish of trumpets, he was followed by a strange little man.

The whole proceedings ground to a halt around this mysterious intruder. John Neville thought it was an old man whom he'd earlier turned down at audition. At last, Judi revealed herself to an uproarious remonstrance.

Practical joking was rampant throughout the company, in the image perhaps of its director, whose sense of humour was well known. In *St Joan*, in which Judi played the lead, the part of the Inquisitor was taken by Harold Innocent. Just before the production opened, some members of the cast approached John Neville to ask for a run-through, in costume, of the entire trial scene. One person not in that deputation, however, was Harold Innocent, whose character is the central one in the scene with a 900-word speech. Nevertheless, Neville agreed to it and once Innocent had launched into his marathon the real reason for the actors' request, perpetrated by Job Stewart, became apparent. It was an elaborate practical joke.

Stewart, who was playing D'Estivet, produced a flask from his cassock, along with several cups and some biscuits. As Harold Innocent continued his speech Job Stewart quietly poured out cups of tea, passing them with the biscuits along the row of monks. And then Ronald Magill, in the person of the Bishop of Beauvais alongside Innocent's Inquisitor, suddenly took out a length of purple knitting on which he promply began to work. All this while Harold Innocent continued boldly about the Holy Inquisition and Church and Empire. He was understandably rather angry. John Neville, meanwhile, lay down on the floor helpless with laughter.

Joan was an ideal part for Judi. Elfin-like yet charged with inner strength, she was equal to Shaw's 'sane and shrewd country girl of extraordinary strength of mind and hardihood of body.' She had already been offered the part several times but had turned it down on account of other engagements or lack of confidence in particular productions. But at Nottingham the Maid of Orleans provided an intriguing counterpoint to Isabella's cooler brand of girlish, religious idealism in *Measure for Measure*.

The production of *St Joan* under John Neville's direction with sets and costumes by Patrick Robertson and Rosemary Virgo, was a success; but Judi again came to regard that first attempt at a role so well suited to her talents as preparatory grounding for a more effective later performance. To date, apart from a radio version directed by John Theocharis, this has not materialized. In 1983 there was a chance to play Joan at the National Theatre in a production by Ronald Eyre. But there were other commitments and she felt unhappy about following Eileen Atkins' portrayal for Toby Robertson at the Old Vic in 1977, so it went instead to Frances de la Tour.

Some critics thought de la Tour manifestly too old to be convincing, despite her undoubted ability as an actress. Would the same have been said of Judi? And would it be true? Perhaps, after all, the time has passed for a memorably redefined Joan in the manner of her Viola or Lady Macbeth. If so, the English stage has missed the opportunity of presenting a richly rounded version of Shaw's heroine, one that might convey her basic, flawed humanity as never before. Judi's maturer view is to 'dislike the character more. I think she was a fanatic, dogmatically intolerant of other people's views. I concentrated too much on the spiritual aspect then. I'd do it in a more earthy way now.'

Judi appeared in two other plays in the Nottingham Playhouse 1965–6 season. They were *The Astrakhan Coat* by Pauline Macauley, whose husband Donald McWhinnie was the director, and Wycherley's *The Country Wife*, directed by Ronald Magill.

The Astrakhan Coat was a thriller with comic overtones. Judi played the part of Barbara, one of a gang of three (the others were Job Stewart and James Villiers) who plot a clever murder. Compounded of slick writing and energetic direction it was the season's pot-boiler.

Ronald Magill brought out the full Restoration flavour of *The Country Wife*. Judi played Margery Pinchwife with Harold Innocent as her husband and Michael Craig as the lecherous Horner. Written in 1675, Wycherley's most popular play concerns the antics of a licentious man-about-town who pretends the loss of sexual potency in order better to gain access to his ladies. The principal object of his desires is the wife of the puritanical and pathologically jealous Pinchwife, who tries to keep his naive new bride, Margery — the country wife of the title — under lock and key away from the attentions of the pseudo 'eunuch', Horner. Though the play has a moralizing tone, it is, to say the least, equivocal, with invitations to laugh both with and at the spectacle of quickening human frailty.

Judi delighted — as in *Private Lives* — in the frisky theatricality of the plot; in Wycherley's incandescent, sardonic language; and, as always, in the costumes — the dressing up.

It was at Nottingham that Judi first started giving poetry readings and recitals, an activity she had kept up ever since. It began with poetry and jazz in the Playhouse after shows and on Sunday nights. The actors would declaim lines by e.e.cummings and other suitable writers while the Johnny Southgate Band improvised an accompaniment.

But as the season drew to a close it was Shakespeare's words — from *Measure for Measure* — rather than cummings' which were appropriate to the occasion as Judi answered a call back to that other influential playhouse at Oxford:

Break off thy song, and haste thee quick away.

*

Her next professional engagement in Nottingham was not until 1983, on tour with the National Theatre. She found places and faces greatly changed. Looking in vain for the old County Hotel she eventually found its welcome mat and swing doors swallowed up by the new Theatre Royal extension. John Neville had resigned controversially in 1968 and subsequently gone to Canada. One way and another, he and the Nottingham Playhouse had given quite a boost to the theatrical career of Judi Dench, a career in which 1966 was an important year. Not only did she move from Nottingham to Oxford, she also met a new young director from the Royal Shakespeare Company called Trevor Nunn.

Outside the theatre, too, Judi's professional future looked brilliant in that autumn of 1966 when she and Leonard Rossiter were rehearsing Pirandello's *The Rules of the Game* in the perhaps unlikely setting of the town which Matthew Arnold had pointedly addressed one hundred years previously as 'Beautiful city! so venerable, so lovely, so unravaged by the fierce intellectual life of our century.'

Judi, in contrast, was making her mark now very much in twentieth-century terms and winning awards for screen as well as stage work. She had already completed three feature films — all within the previous few months — and, during that Oxford rehearsal period, was appearing on television in an unusual quartet of plays dramatizing the same situation from different standpoints. It was written by the successful *Z-Cars* scriptwriter, John Hopkins, and was called, *Talking to a Stranger*.

The stranger Judi got talking to one November day in the pub next to the Oxford Playhouse was not concerned with television, however, even though he had been the recipient of an ABC TV training scholarship not too many years before. Neither did he remain a stranger very long.

Trevor Nunn had been with the RSC for a year when he was assigned *The Taming of the Shrew* to direct. It did not fill him with excitement. There were many other Shakespeare plays he was passionately keen to tackle and he felt he had nothing to say about the *Shrew*. Nevertheless, *The Taming of the Shrew* it was, the task alleviated by the planning committee's suggestion that he might try to persuade Judi Dench to rejoin the company and play Kate. At that stage Trevor had only seen Judi act on television but that was enough to send him to Oxford full of enthusiasm.

Within minutes of the meeting in the pub, that enthusiasm was kindled: 'It was one of those meetings that are a form of love at first sight. She was the most delightful person I had ever stumbled across. We got on so famously that she was *entirely* convinced that what she most wanted to do was to play Kate in a production of the *Shrew* at Stratford directed by myself.'

By that time *The Rules of the Game* had opened. There was only one other play in the season and Judi added a rider to her acceptance of Trevor Nunn's offer to the effect that should this second play — 'a very strange new Russian three-hander' — have any extended commercial life then she was committed to remain with it. But, she assured him, there was no chance of that; it just wasn't commercial.

The piece in question was *The Promise* by Alexei Arbuzov, author of *The Twelfth Hour* in which Judi had appeared two years earlier at Oxford. *The Promise* also featured Ian McKellen and Ian MacShane. Within two months it had transferred to the Fortune Theatre in London, where it stayed until September 1967. Judi never did get to play Kate.

In *The Rules of the Game*, a rarely performed play in this country, Judi played a wife who deliberately sets out to make her husband jealous. Not for the first time, Judi was given a lift by wearing exquisite, sophisticated clothes. Leonard Rossiter gave a finely controlled performance as the husband, who turns the tables in the end by contriving the death of his wife's lover (John Rollason). But Pirandello was somewhat eclipsed on the occasion by the success of Arbuzov's play. Set in Leningrad, it spans the period from 1942 to 1960. The three characters are Lika, a wartime teenager bent on a medical career, and the two men who love her: Leonidik, a very minor poet, and Marat, even more of a dreamer than the other two.

The action takes place entirely in one room in which the three occupants have been very much thrown together and which, like them, undergoes a gradual transformation. Each member of the young trio is scarred by the war — orphaned, wounded or disillusioned — and each has to cope with the difficulty of coming to terms with insistent needs while retaining as much dignity as possible.

Judi played Lika, Ian McKellen was Leonidik, and Ian MacShane was Marat. Throughout the ensuing months this trio evolved a deft, tight cohesion and the foundations were laid for even more accomplished teamwork between Ian McKellen and Judi in the future.

On the first night the three members of the cast went out to dinner with Frank Hauser. A group of theatre critics, having filed their copy, were at another table. In an unusual deviation from the etiquette of these matters, the critics asked the director and actors to join them, so positive was the overall feeling about the production. The mood was congratulatory and celebratory, several bottles of wine were discharged and Frank Hauser was at his merriest.

The Promise is a long play, running well over three hours, and imposes heavy demands upon its three performers. There were two intervals, during which the characters had to age, so these were taken up with full make-up sessions. And at the Fortune, where it opened in January 1967, there are lots of stairs up to the dressing-rooms. It was exhausting but rewarding work.

A good many well-wishers climbed the stairs up to those dressing-rooms between January and September, among them Michael Williams, then in *The Representative* at the Old Vic. He and Judi shared tea in a cafe, sympathized with each other about their currently lacklustre love lives, and bid each other farewell. Ironically Michael was engaged to appear in Trevor Nunn's production of *The Taming of the Shrew* at Stratford.

Judi often gets ravenously hungry before a performance and once during *The Promise* this almost led to a situation comparable to her falling asleep on the set of *The Firescreen*. In *The Promise* Judi again had to be on stage before the curtain rose, this time concealed in a sack. Shortly before the performance in question, she sent the assistant stage manager out for a veal and ham pie and he took longer than anticipated. When he arrived back, Judi hastily took the pie from him, raced on stage and ate it inside the sack. Fortunately, she finished it before she had to emerge.

As Lika, Judi had to convey a very wide range of emotions, thoroughly testing her technical acting skills. For this reason, it sometimes felt like one long audition. Certainly her portrayal was watched closely throughout those months by a number of producers and directors. One of these was Harold 'Hal' Prince, the American director and co-producer of *Cabaret*, a musical enjoying outstanding success on Broadway. This had an impressive genealogy, embracing Christopher Isherwood's literary and biographical musings on Berlin in the 1930s and, their offspring, John Van Druten's play *I am a Camera*, in which Judi, while still a drama student, had been so moved by Dorothy Tutin. Among the thousands who had been to see the new show was Judi's old chum, Barbara Leigh-Hunt, then touring the United States with the Bristol Old Vic company:

'I saw *Cabaret* on a night off and felt pole-axed. I couldn't get up from my seat during the interval. I didn't want to break the spell. As it happened Peter Bridge, producer of *The Promise* at the Fortune, was in New York and I ran into him. He was on his way back to England and I sent a copy of the cast recording of *Cabaret* over with him as a present for Judi.

'When I got back a few weeks later I went to Regent's Park Terrace to see Judi. She wasn't at home but there was a note for me to ring her at the theatre. I rang and we asked after each other's health, she enquired about my flight home, and then she said, "Guess what I'm doing next."

' "I don't know", I said, "Getting married?"

"No, no no! *Professionally.*"

"Making a film?"

"No."

"Well I don't know, you could be doing anything."

'Heavy silence and then, "*What* record did you sent me from America?"

"*Cabaret*. Well?"

"Well? I'm playing Sally Bowles."

"*You* are?"

"Yes!"

"But you can't sing!"

"I know I can't, and I haven't been able to play that damned record ever since I knew I was going to do it." '

Judi's vulnerable but demonstrative Lika had struck a chord with Hal Prince. Here was a woman, he believed, formed of the same fibre as Sally Bowles, the central figure in *Cabaret*. He got in touch with Julian Belfrage and when Judi was told of Hal Prince's interest she went out and got drunk. And when it came to singing at the audition, she couldn't bring herself to go on stage and she delivered her musical numbers from the wings.

Judi's was clearly not a singing voice but Hal and his fellow producer Richard Pilbrow thought it had the right emotional qualities for Sally, and she was given the part for the British premiére of one of the most successful of modern American musicals. Judi was dispatched to the singing tutor, Gwen Catley, who told her, 'I can't teach you to sing, Judi, but I'll teach you how to put a song over. It doesn't matter about hitting the notes, just act it.'

Despite Hal Prince's perception of the similarities between Lika and Sally Bowles, there was no doubt that in *Cabaret* Judi was taking on something vastly different, in purely theatrical terms, from anything she had done before. All this was part of the thrill. She resents being neatly categorized or stereotyped as an actress, and always fights to avoid becoming locked in a particular image. The roles that most attract her are those far removed from the present or the immediately previous job; those where she is called upon to try something new.

In this respect she once described the offer to play Sally Bowles as 'just like the most wonderful present, and everything else beside it appeared dross.' She also responded favourably to the fact that Hal Prince was prepared to take a gamble on her, just as she would years later when the gamblers would be Trevor Nunn and then Peter Hall backing their judgment with the ladies Macbeth and Bracknell respectively.

Cabaret was to be staged at the Palace, a large London theatre with a long musical tradition. Just before she began rehearsals Judi went, with James Cairncross, to see a show there for the first time. It was *The Desert Song* and the experience was a useful one. It gave her what she calls 'the measure of the theatre', enabling her to see how a performance can best be projected in a particular auditorium, and of course to soak up the atmosphere of the place. Seeing

Barbara Jefford at the Old Vic in *The Two Gentlemen of Verona* had been similarly helpful in 1957 and it is now a common practice of Judi's to attend a performance at the theatre in which she is next to appear.

As to the musical aspect, this agitated her increasingly as the February opening drew nearer. On the day before her band call — the rehearsal when the singer performs for the first time with the full orchestra — she had lunch at Julian Belfrage's home. It was unseasonably mild and they ate in the garden. The actor David Hutcheson was there and he helped to soothe Judi's fears by assuring her that the band call would be 'one of the most exciting days of your life.'

At the theatre the next day she was still extremely frightened but the moment the orchestra began to play and give shape to the songs she had so far rehearsed only with a piano, she was lifted beyond her imaginings — 'it's like an enormous pillow being blown up with you on top of it' — and she never quite came down.

That is not to say she felt completely on top of things. A fortnight prior to the start of full rehearsals at the theatre, she went to a health farm where she spent a lot of time in a card-playing foursome and met somebody who sent her four dozen baby bottles of champagne. Each night before the show she drank one to give her courage.

Given the massive proliferation of recorded popular music and the dazzlingly polished qualities of the American musical, with the attendant gloss of Hollywood — the rise of which in a turbulent world must surely constitute one of the grandest, most glamorous seductions in all history — audiences, or at any rate those up to and including the 1960s, have come to expect a slick, smooth, harmonious and mellifluous range of sensations from such shows. A ticket denotes not merely admission to the theatre but a transportation, an escape from the harsh and the mundane.

It is easily forgotten (sometimes perhaps as a result of commercial packaging by Americans themselves) that this art form has emerged through *theatrical* conventions, that George Gershwin, Rodgers and Hart, Cole Porter and Irving Berlin, not to mention John Kander and Fred Ebb, composer and lyricist respectively of *Cabaret*, were all, to a greater or lesser extent, making their contributions to stagecraft. Admittedly the mirror thereby held up to nature may sometimes have been rose-hued and viewed through the wrong end of a long telescope; nonetheless all those singing and dancing numbers form part of a greater whole, which in the best of instances tells a story about life as valid, if not as richly-textured, as those of Shakespeare, Moliére and Tennessee Williams. While this may be demonstrably evident in the collaborations of Bertolt Brecht and Kurt Weill, in the recent history of the Broadway musical, too, a composer like Stephen Sondheim has rooted his characters more obviously in 'real life' or generally striven to avoid seams showing between the story and the song and dance.

In *Cabaret*, with its evocation of a decadent city crumbling in the grip of Nazism, librettist Joe Masteroff was certainly attempting to present a coherent, overall statement. And, as Hal Prince explained to his non-singing star in 1968, the songs are part of a continuum. They should emerge naturally from their context. Gwen Catley also emphasized that singing on stage is not a throat-clearing, band-striking-up business which announces, 'I'm stopping speaking and starting singing.' It should flow, be an outpouring that ideally makes the audience believe that a song is the only way of conveying that particular piece of the story.

Thus, having a good singing voice is not the primary consideration. In the absence of those rare mortals who can sing, dance *and* act surpassingly, an actor with expressive vocal powers is bound to be truer to the spirit of the book than somebody with a beautiful voice who can't act. Theatre-goers were probably less prepared to acknowledge this in 1968 than they are today and Judi undoubtedly disappointed some of them.

Some of the critics were disappointed at a more fundamental level. Philip Hope-Wallace relegated 'a gorgeously lit, smartly staged and energetic production' to 'empty entertainment' casting a sympathetic line to Judi for her 'infectious glee', expressed, he felt, through an insubstantially conceived character. Irving Wardle mentioned *Cabaret's* literary prototypes in his review in *The Times* and commented that 'Judi Dench has certainly lost weight and enlarged her technical range, but her Sally is essentially an affectionate home girl with none of the glittering inconstancy of the unattainable original. You wonder how she ever got to Berlin; and her performance sometimes suggests the thwarted fantasies of a Pinner secretary.'

The verdict of her friends Joe Mitchenson and Raymond Mander was considerably less detached. They took Olave to the first night and she sat between them. All three linked hands anxiously as Judi began her first song. By a nice touch of irony this happened to be 'Don't Tell Mama' which Judi delivered in appropriately suburban English tones with the faintest, quavering suggestion of night clubs, whisky and cigarette smoke. Everybody applauded except Olave, Raymond and Joe. Instead, they remained with their hands locked together, an electric impulse of nervous excitement passing through them.

By the time she sang the title song at the close, the quavering had grown less faint, the Englishness less suburban. Gwen Catley's lessons in 'putting over' the songs were bearing fruit. In her performance of that final number, walking a musical tightrope held secure by Gareth Davies, the musical director, who sang along with Judi from his position in the orchestra pit, Judi summed up her Sally Bowles: simple but powerful, vulnerable but defiant.

Another American musical in town in 1968 was *Sweet Charity* based on an Italian film called *Nights of Cabiria* and starring the American dancer and actress Juliet Prowse. A rather unfortunate link emerged between Juliet and Judi when both fell prey to the constant attentions of the same overzealous admirer, a young man who laid siege to their respective stage doors at the Palace and the Prince of Wales. Eventually he got to speak to the two leading ladies, independently telling them that he had only a short time to live, and thereafter exploiting their kindnesses. Judi was profoundly shocked when, weeks later, he was discovered to be fraudulent.

A happier off-stage occurrence for Judi during the run of *Cabaret* was the purchase of an eighteenth-century cottage in Hampstead. She had lived in Regent's Park Terrace for seven years and friends persuaded her that she should be thinking about buying a home. Marty Feldman, the comedian, and Theo Cowans, the theatrical publicist, took her along to the cottage and she was completely and immediately enchanted by it. As soon as she walked inside, and before inspecting the rooms, she told the owner she would take it at the asking price.

Two of Judi's traits had here combined: impetuosity and her feeling for places, whether buildings, towns or countryside. She felt comfortable in those surroundings; that little room in that little cottage, set in a brief, bright terrace, itself hidden from metropolitan clamour along a pretty path of flowers and trellis. It was an Alice-in-Wonderland-like sensation of stepping from the middle of Hampstead into the heart of the countryside. With Theo and Marty on hand to underpin her decision and her mother subsequently giving the requisite ratification, the deed was done. Judi now had a home of her own.

It was a warren of small, low-ceilinged rooms of irregular shape, grouped around a narrow, winding staircase, and has in time become a family home where Judi still lives with her husband and daughter. In those early days during 1968 when she first moved in she recruited gangs of willing friends to help strip walls and woodwork, expose the fireplace, put up shelves and generally redecorate. She quickly introduced her own taste in the furnishings, and steadily amassed collections of mementoes, ornaments and pictures. She has a passion for hearts, for example, and throughout the house can be found heart-shaped cards, pillows, boxes and numerous other items, arranged in a carefully scattered fashion.

Gradually, with the establishment of her independence and then family life, the cottage has provided a warmth and solidarity akin to that of Heworth Green, despite a great difference in size and structure. And, while Judi and her husband, Michael, have since bought bigger, second homes, the tiny cottage in Hampstead has so far remained their base.

As Judi was entering into the purchase of her cottage, *Cabaret* was beginning to make money and she was attracting plenty of personal popularity. Another favourite with audiences was the Russian-born actress Lila Kedrova who, like Judi, was new to musicals. Her previous London appearance had been as Ranevsky in *The Cherry Orchard*, for which she had won the 1967 Evening Standard Best Actress Award and in which Hal Prince and Richard Pilbrow no doubt detected signs of Fraulein Schneider, her character in *Cabaret*. Judi did not find her the easiest person to befriend, however. Barry Dennen was brought over from America to play the important part of the Master of Ceremonies while Clifford Bradshaw, the character emanating from the young Christopher Isherwood, went to Kevin Colson. In Herr Schulz, Judi was reunited with a fellow casualty from *A Shot in the Dark*, Peter Sallis.

Although the London production was popular, it fell well short of the success achieved in America but anyway the notion of *Cabaret* as a stage musical was soon superseded in the public imagination by the film starring Liza Minnelli. Judi has avoided seeing the film. She did once watch a few moments of it on television but rapidly decided that 'this wasn't the story of a failure but of a huge success', and switched off her set.

With changes of fashion and the decline from the prosperity of the sixties to the austerity of the eighties, Judi's Sally Bowles has gained something of a retrospective cult status and people now recall it a shade or two more enthusiastically than they actually received it at the time. The London cast recording has become a collector's item.

In reality, Judi's impact was modest but emphatic. When she left the cast to take up a new Shakespearian challenge, Elizabeth Seal was brought in to take her place and a farewell party was arranged. Judi had forged a strong bond with the company and always said of the chorus that 'they taught me to dance.' In the early weeks they had been protective towards her and now they planned an affectionate send-off at the Arts Theatre Club. But the moment Judi withdrew, the bookings dwindled and by the time the party took place notices had been posted announcing the show's imminent closure. Elizabeth Seal had rehearsed in vain; her Sally was never seen.

Today, most people still think of *Cabaret* as a spectacular movie with a bravura performance by Minnelli. Even for those who admired Judi in the role, points of comparison with the American are easily conceded — who was the real singer, the better dancer, the star? No contest. But then, who was the true Sally Bowles?

5 A romantic winter's tale

In 1968 Trevor Nunn became the Royal Shakespeare Company's artistic director and he set about planning the following year's Stratford season. He devised a grouping of some of Shakespeare's late plays and romances — *Pericles, The Winter's Tale, Henry VIII* and *Twelfth Night.* Nunn considered Judi Dench vital to his conception of *The Winter's Tale* as did John Barton in his vision of *Twelfth Night.*

During the run of *Cabaret*, Judi frequented a small Italian restaurant behind the Palace Theatre, and that was where she went, one night after a performance, to hear what Trevor Nunn had to say. She was very much on home ground; the waiters were assiduously attentive and protective towards her, at the same time regarding her dining partner with suspicion. They needn't have worried. Once again the lure of Stratford was magnetic. Once again she accepted Trevor Nunn's offer unhesitatingly.

This was the case even though the part he suggested she play in *The Winter's Tale* was Hermione, the mother, and not Perdita, the daughter. At thirty-three this was chastening — 'What, mothers' parts already?' she'd laughed when he stated his proposal. But this didn't for a moment prevent her from agreeing, especially since John Barton wanted her to play Viola in *Twelfth Night.* By this time too, her brother Jeffery was an established RSC player, having joined the company in 1963. Between 1968 and 1969 he was in *The Merry Wives of Windsor, The Relapse* and *Henry VIII.*

Three weeks later Trevor Nunn contacted her again. 'I've been reading the play a lot', he said, 'and though I cannot claim that it was Shakespeare's idea — and there is a scene where mother and daughter both speak — I just now have a vision of the play where, were you to play both Hermione and Perdita, the ironies between the central, pastoral section of the play and the very cruel, tragic first part would become much more pronounced, much more painful and the play would become much more coherent.'

It had been done before but not for a long, long time — the American actress Mary Anderson had played both parts at the Lyceum in 1887, when she was twenty-eight. Judi leapt at the idea with not a hint of caution.

Nunn very painstakingly and deliberately plotted the divisions between the 'central, pastoral' and the 'cruel, tragic', between Bohemia and Sicily, Perdita and Hermione. In 'Sicily', together with his designer Christopher Morley, he created a cool, light atmosphere, with white suits and pale grey and green silk dresses. In stark contrast, 'Bohemia' was all orange and yellow, wild hair and beads.

He rehearsed Judi solely as Hermione at first and then switched over to Perdita, totally dropping Hermione. Accordingly Judi kept the mother and daugher in two separate mental compartments. It was as if she were rehearsing for two different plays. Then the two were brought together and it all slotted very neatly. And when the production was under way Judi found herself in a strange, schizophrenic state whereby when she got ready for Hermione she would sit in her dressing room waiting for visitors or stand quietly in the wings, but when she became Perdita in the interval, she would rush around and visit everybody and go in the wings and dance, a completely different person.

Rehearsals for *The Winter's Tale* were a creative feast, much enjoyed by those involved. Taking equal care with the administrative side of his new job, Trevor Nunn found he had a long preliminary period with the principal members of his cast. This had much to do with Terry Hands, who was to direct *Pericles*, as Trevor Nunn recalls:

'Terry had elected to have a small cast — twenty-six people playing Shakespeare was in those days revolutionary. All of Terry's twenty-six were in *The Winter's Tale*. Terry had come up with a startling production concept that required all twenty-six to be on stage for the entire play. In my first season I had to be seen to be extremely generous and allowed Terry to have them when he wanted. There was almost nothing that I could rehearse for the first four weeks of my rehearsal period *except* that I had Judi Dench, Barrie Ingham, Richard Pasco, Nick Selby and, for a lot of the time, Brenda Bruce. All remarkable, accomplished actors. Nobody could have predicted that they had it in them to become that close. I learnt more from that group of actors at that time than at any previous time in my artistic career.

'We had a great deal of fun and there was a great deal of laughter — I come back to that repeatedly in talking about Judi. You do run to rehearsal because you know it's going to be fun. I do associate that kind of rehearsal with Judi more than with anybody else. Really startling ideas come out of fun. People starting to feel anarchic and a bit mad — you can accomplish anything, why not? If it goes wrong it's still fun.

'I think I can say without reserve that the early rehearsal period of *The Winter's Tale* in Stratford in 1969 was the happiest, most enchanted, most idyllic rehearsal period I've ever been through.'

Barrie Ingham played Leontes and Richard Pasco, Polixenes. During that first rehearsal period Trevor Nunn stimulated all sorts of activity, continually experimenting and building. Working just with Barrie, Richard and Judi on the theme of unwarranted jealousy, he posited a situation in which Barrie and Judi were to imagine themselves to be a wealthy couple with a villa in the South of France to which they had invited Dickie Pasco, the husband's — Barrie's — best friend. From that premise, Trevor invented a series of incidents and actions designed to fabricate jealousy.

He would place his trio of actors face down alongside each other on the 'beach', with Judi in the middle. Thus, if Judi faced Barrie, Dickie would be excluded and vice versa. So intense did the actors become in this Riviera ménage that at one point Barrie waded out into the 'ocean' and performed an elaborate swim around the conference hall, the Royal Shakespeare Theatre's main rehearsal space, where they were working. Wild laughter was released like steam from a pressure cooker.

Some of the fun of rehearsal spilled over into perform-ance. It was bound to as such an intimate project was unveiled before the public. Judi began to organize games and competitions among the company, both off and on stage. Creativity bordered on frenzy.

The luxury of the long rehearsal period, the closeness of the players and the inventiveness of the director were all thrown into the melting pot in May 1969, when *The Winter's Tale* opened in Stratford. It was a production that perfectly matched the *zeitgeist.* The impact of R.D.Laing's treatise on schizophrenia, *The Divided Self*, originally published in 1960 by the Tavistock Institute of Human Relations, had long ceased to be merely psychiatric or academic. By the late sixties, with a massive American and British paperback circulation, Laing's work had, in a faint echo of Freud, reclaimed the agonies of the mind from the confines of medical diagnosis. Schizophrenia was elevated to a cultural concern and *The Divided Self* became prescribed reading on university campuses. Art and literature were subjected to vigorous, if sometimes superficial reinterpretation. Students of Shakespeare were encouraged to look anew at the plays in the light of Laing's insights.

Trevor Nunn's intelligent reappraisal of the evidently schizoid world of Sicily and Bohemia in *The Winter's Tale* focused some of these concerns. It also consummated weeks of thorough, professional preparation. It was a triumph. And ultimately it was Shakespeare, rather than Laing, who had been vindicated; the playwright rather than the psychiatrist.

Hilary Spurling, writing in *The Spectator*, called Judi's Hermione 'as rare and precious as the text suggests.' Gareth Lloyd-Evans, in the *Guardian*, wrote that the character achieved 'a presence which touches greatness.' Ronald Bryden, in *The Observer*, said Judi had 'never been better or looked better.'

The doubling of Hermione and Perdita, perhaps not sufficiently saluted for the feat it was, proved most effective. And if it was Hermione who drew the acclaim, she is after all the character with the depth and the dignity. Where critics sought to make a forceful contrast with Perdita — Irving Wardle in *The Times* dismissed her as 'barely more than skittish' in comparison with her 'superbly dignified' mother — they were in fact underlining Judi's achievement. She had aimed to lend a 'slightly earthy, slightly Yorkshire' quality to Perdita, and while she did this she still maintained the girl's *apartness* from Mopsa, Dorcas and the rest. It was her finest Shakespearian performance yet.

Outside of Shakespeare — though not far — the RSC's 1969–70 season included Thomas Middleton's tragedy, *Women Beware Women*, directed by Terry Hands. A neglected work, written about five years after Shakespeare's death, it contains some fine writing terminating in the whirlpool of blood conventional in Jacobean drama. The plot centres on the seduction of Bianca, the young bride of the earnest, social-climbing Leantio, by an older man, the Duke of Florence. It is a moral tale through which vivid characters emerge, speaking vivid language. T.S. Eliot considered that, in Bianca, Middleton had created 'a real woman; as real, indeed, as any woman of Elizabethan tragedy.'

It was potentially a rich part for Judi but, possibly in reaction to the intensity of *The Winter's Tale*, she never quite became as engaged in her work with Terry Hands as she had with Trevor Nunn. She has always found Hands a little frightening; his method of hurling his actors in at the deep end, making them examine themselves, creating for Judi an insecurity altogether absent in Nunn's continuous attachment to the actors as they construct their roles.

In the cast of *Women Beware Women* with Judi were Richard Pasco as Leantio, Ann Dyson as his mother, Brewster Mason as the Duke, and Elizabeth Spriggs, who gave a scintillating performance as Livia, a courtly procuress. Characteristically, Terry Hands created an exciting spectacle and Judi loved the handsome period costumes. Her tendency to fall over manifested itself on one or two occasions but generally she made an upright and visually satisfying contribution to the grand operatic style of it all.

Having played Viola in the testing conditions of the Nottingham Playhouse tour of West Africa, Judi came to John Barton's 1969 production with confidence. She was eager to build upon those rudimentary beginnings, to learn both from experience and from Barton's scholarly approach.

This was the first time Judi had worked with John Barton and she found him inspiring. He imparted the play's bittersweet tone to her, revealed layers of meaning and possibility and related the performance to the text with a rigour she had never before encountered. 'The Merlin of Shakespeare', she calls him, affirming that 'once you've worked with John you know exactly where the full stops are, and the half-lines, and where the pauses are intended. And you can't get away with anything. If you're slack, he knows.'

John Barton's intellect and Judi Dench's instinct combined to produce, in that Stratford season of 1969, a memorable *Twelfth Night* and, in Trevor Nunn's words, 'the definitive Viola'. Here, he was echoing the language of his predecessor as the RSC's artistic director, Peter Hall, in his description of Judi's performance as Titania (which earlier that year had been reproduced on film).

What Barton's production brought out most beautifully was the deep, autumnal humanity of the play, heralding the late romances. In this a key factor was the music, arranged most hauntingly by Michael Tubbs from old English airs. Another connected one was the Feste of Emrys James, investing the songs with a weight and humour that gave them enormous breadth. Another was the sureness of Donald Sinden's comic portrayal of Malvolio, adding body. Another was Judi's Viola. Penetrating far beyond the frothy comedy she had purveyed in Africa, she caught the resonances of sadness and isolation with which *Twelfth Night* is laden.

Several people have described Judi as someone hovering on the verge of tears and laughter; she could go either way. In *Twelfth Night* she brought something of that personal quality to the playing of Viola. And with the suggestion that Viola could either laugh or cry went the capacity to make the spectator laugh and cry too. Decidedly boyish in her Cesario guise, she gave the most powerful indications of a woman's heart within, and one that ached with sympathy and sadness. While she charmed and mocked and played well the knowing side of her role, this was a Viola sensitively aware of her own and others' plight.

In proof of his glowing assessment, Trevor Nunn cites a moment in Act II, Scene IV when, having watched the Duke indulge himself listening to Feste's song, Viola's verdict on the music is that 'It gives a very echo to the seat/Where love is throned' and Duke Orsino replies, 'Thou dost speak masterly.'

'It was absolutely choking', recalls Trevor Nunn, 'because Judi *had* spoken masterly. She had understood what Feste was doing as Orsino hadn't. Her Viola did feel herself to be a kind of monster caught in a trap of her own invention, dressed as a boy and confronted with a woman's love, a mirror of her own feelings.

'I've never seen an equivalent performance . . . Judi seemed to me to be at the very heart of the play.'

Roger Rees, who played the minor part of Curio in *Twelfth Night* maintains that it was Judi Dench's spirit that kept the company going through the three years on and off that the production lasted. He has since become a close friend. In those days he was in awe of her. In the early part of the play, accosting Viola in man's attire, he thumped her on the chest — 'a joke about Viola's sex that you put in somewhere. The audience always laughed. I'm not sure that in the great scope of playing Viola she ever thought about it, but it meant a lot to me because here I was, getting a laugh with Judi Dench.'

There was plenty of 'unofficial' laughter too, much of it at Judi's instigation. She devised a variety of games to be played during the long last act of *Twelfth Night*, which comprises just one scene, throughout which the stage gradually fills up with people. One of her inventions was for everyone on stage to scratch his or her nose each time the letter 'f' was mentioned. Two others were 'Badger in the Boot' and 'Rabbit in the Ruff'. For these, each character — and they were all in Elizabethan costume — had to behave as if possessed of a wriggling animal in ruff or boot. One day there was a 'regatta' when everybody had to come on doing a rowing action.

These diversions are invariably concealed from the audience but keep the actors on their mettle. Roger Rees is all in favour of such madness as pervaded the stage in *Twelfth Night*: 'It gave such a great deal of strength. The finest times I've known as a human being have been laughing, jet-propelled tears, on stage, with Judi Dench.

'Once when playing Viola she had a big red spot on her nose. So, one by one, we each came on in that final scene with red spots on our noses. And when Donald Sinden, as Malvolio, the last to enter, a spot prominently placed on his nose, was led in by Fabian to the Duke's enquiry, "Is this the madman?" Judi was in pain from laughing.

'She organized the first "art competition" so that people are not only playing Leontes or Aguecheek but are also worrying about their entries in the art competition which have to be hanging on the wall of the green room by the second act. She always used to have three categories: something like a landscape, something about the play, and the third would always be "a brown study".'

In a performance much later on in the production's three-year life a moth flew distractingly into Judi's light and landed on her mouth. She ate it.

And certainly not all of the fun emanating from Judi was contrived. She was, and is, a mistress of the *faux pas*. At one point during the 1969 season a reception was held in Stratford for members of the company to meet the mayor, who happened to be blind. In the course of this gathering the mayor, chatting to a group which included Judi, said, 'I believe the theatre has been redecorated.' In jumped Judi — 'Oh! Has it been redecorated? Oh, absolutely beautiful; wonderful flame-coloured seats, just wait till you see them.' An embarrassed silence followed, broken by Judi's stifled giggles as others tried to cover up — which she found as funny as her original *faux pas*.

A week later she was walking through Stratford with Trevor Nunn, *en route* to a restaurant, when they saw the mayor and his wife walking along the other side of the road. The wife waved and told her husband whom she'd seen. Trevor said, 'I think we should go over' and whispered to Judi to take care not to commit another gaffe about the mayor's blindness. When they had crossed the road Judi walked staight up to the mayor, shook him warmly by the hand and said, 'Mister Mayor, how lovely to hear you again!'

In late 1969, between the end of the Stratford season and the beginning of the Aldwych transfers in 1970, Judi was invited back to West Africa. Not this time with the Nottingham Playhouse but with an actor who had been a fellow member of that company six years earlier, James Cairncross. The two of them were to embark on a six-week lecture tour to schools under the auspices of the British

Council, covering a similar geographical area to that of the 1963 tour. Their material consisted of three plays in the general examination syllabus: *Macbeth*, *Twelfth Night* and *Henry V*, and they were expected to give a lot of reading direct from the text with question-and-answer sessions at the end.

It was gratifying to see the marked growth in interest even in the six years since the pioneering Nottingham tour, though in some ways it was harder this time without the back-up of the company. And some of the up-country locations were tough going when, after a fatiguing aeroplane trip, James and Judi were faced by rows upon rows of children who simply stared, without asking a single question. They also lectured before General Gowon, the Nigerian leader, in slightly constrained circumstances recalling the 1963 performance for Nkrumah. But generally things went smoothly with none of the strange, frenetic adventures of the original tour.

She sent Olave a shoal of letters, her tone loving, concerned, reassuring, and conveying a host of impressions. In Jos, in Nigeria, she and James visited a convent school where the nuns were Irish, except for a few young Nigerian girls, all of them dressed in white — 'when we stood in the wings waiting to begin, they all stood up and everyong sang the Nigerian National Anthem while a nun played the piano. Then we walked on and everyone was dressed in a bright-blue school uniform. They looked *wonderful*.

'Afterwards we had a vote of thanks by the head girl — very perfect English and beautifully said — and then another girl came up and gave me a huge bunch of roses, all colours and such a size.

'The Mother Superior had grown them in her garden and always won all the prizes with them. Then we went off to coffee with her and saw the chapel, and sat in a cool, pretty room and ate home-made cakes.'

Judi was to spend a substantial portion of that English winter period of 1969—70 in the southern hemisphere. Shortly after her return from Africa she was packing her bags again, this time for an RSC tour of Japan and Australia. Once again she was a pioneer — the Royal Shakespeare Company's visit to Japan in January 1970 was the first by any British theatrical company. The productions they took with them were *The Winter's Tale* and *The Merry Wives of Windsor*, plus a compilation piece entitled *To Be or Not to Be*. The venues were Tokyo, Fukuoka, Osaka and Nagoya.

For actors used to coughing spectators, tourists shuffling uncomfortably in their seats in Stratford, the occasional soul asleep in the front row and — on the credit side — bursts of laughter and other reactive sounds, the Japanese audiences were a revelation in their quiet and stillness. At first, the British performers thought the play was going extremely badly but at the end the audience erupted and that's how it was throughout the rest of the tour.

The centrepiece of the Stratford set for *The Winter's Tale* was a huge white perspex box, which was taken on the tour. It was assembled from a rather complicated arrangement of square sections and when the Japanese stage-hands came to piece it together — refusing all assistance — they not unexpectedly experienced considerable difficulty. However, they persevered and eventually erected it on stage only for the actors to discover scores of black footmarks criss-crossing the ceiling.

Judi was excited by Japan and felt very content among the Japanese people, recognizing in their serene self-containment something of the Quakers' desired objective of inner peacefulness. She found out as much as she could about the Japanese and their culture and wrote home about them to Olave in the most enthusiastic terms: 'They are such beautiful people . . . and have such a profound standard to live by . . . they make us all look so clumsy and large and ill-mannered.' And many identified with her, too, believing her playing of Hermione to be rooted in Zen Buddhism.

She visited Expo 70, Mount Fuji, the ancient Nanzenji Temple in Kyoto, saw some traditional *Noh* and *Kabuki* theatre, and stayed in a traditional Japanese inn where the guests had to surrender their clothes and wear kimonos. Everywhere, she was showered with hospitality and gifts. It was a happy, inspiring start to the tour and Judi was thrilled when two years later she was able to return with John Barton's *Twelfth Night* production. But for the moment Australia lay ahead, and, after an unruffled three weeks in Japan, upheaval.

The Australian tour began on 8 February and lasted until 18 April. The schedule contained three cities: Melbourne, Adelaide and Sydney, and two plays: *The Winter's Tale* and *Twelfth Night*. Critically and commercially it was an unmitigated success. Emotionally, the pendulum swung through its full arc.

Orsino, in *Twelfth Night*, was played by Charles Thomas, a talented, broody, passionate, Welsh actor and seasoned RSC campaigner who had joined the company in 1964 to play Aumerle in Richard II, with David Warner — whom he understudied — and had gone on to play Berowne in *Love's Labours Lost* and Lorenzo in *The Merchant of Venice.* He and Judi were very close, though his proneness to depression always ensured some distance. Once, in Stratford, during rehearsals for *Women Beware Women*, he came in with blood on his gym shoes. He said he had cut his hand. It was an image that Judi would carry with her across Australia. But Charlie Thomas never got further than Melbourne. That was where he killed himself.

It was not the happiest of times anyway. Judi disliked the brashness of Melbourne and was distressed by the large amounts of litter on the beaches. Trevor and Jeffery were both able to provide some comfort after Charlie's death, however. Jeff was by now playing Sir Andrew Aguecheek in *Twelfth Night* — as a bagpipe-blowing Scotsman — and Judi was positively feted through Australia. Audiences and the press adored her. One columnist described her as 'one of the most sensitive, intelligent, brilliant and beautiful actresses in the English-speaking world, and a wonderful woman to match it.'

By this time Judi had become romantically involved with Michael Williams, and he paid her a surprise visit in Australia. Trevor Nunn flew back to London and met Michael at the airport. He told him about Charlie Thomas and that Judi's — and the company's — mood was not exactly buoyant at that moment but that the tour was to continue.

It was Raymond Mander and Joe Mitchenson who had first brought Michael and Judi together. This was in 1961, when Judi was playing Juliet at the Old Vic and Michael was in a play called *Celebration* by Keith Waterhouse and Willis Hall at the Duchess Theatre. Joe and Raymond had known Michael since he was a student at the Royal Academy of Dramatic Art, through his involvement with a Catholic theatre club. They had been introduced to Judi at the Players Theatre Club soon after the opening of *Romeo and Juliet* and had taken her under their collective wing. When she wasn't appearing at the theatre she would accompany them to first nights and gaze excitedly at the celebrities in the audience, most of them known to Joe and Ray. Through them she met Emlyn Williams, John Gielgud and many others — including Michael Williams.

Joe, Ray and Judi had all met in the Opera Tavern prior to a first night at Drury Lane. Michael happened to be in the pub. By that time Judi had received the offer from Michel St Denis to join the RSC, where Michael was already a member. He called Joe over and asked to be introduced to Judi, which he promptly was as 'a future colleague'. They chatted for a while in a friendly way until Judi stood up, looked at her watch and said to Joe and Ray, 'Isn't it time we were going?'

Over the next few years, when they weren't actually working together at the RSC, Michael and Judi bumped into each other in the way actors do, but they never got closer than that cup of tea in the cafe when she was in *The Promise* and he was in *The Representative*, exchanging a few desultory words about relationships that had recently ended for them both. But their paths crossed often enough at the RSC to provide hints that they were at least kindred spirits. And then in 1969 Michael damaged a cartilage playing football for an RSC eleven. While he was recuperating he decided to see *Twelfth Night*.

The night before, he invited Judi to dinner at the Black Swan, known to all Stratford theatre people as the 'Dirty Duck'. The conversation surged; more than mere friendliness was apparent. Judi, a non-smoker, nervously smoked seven or eight cigarettes and burnt a hole in the lino. There was an intoxication about the evening that had little to do with alcohol. Michael gave Judi a note when they parted. Referring to her Viola, he wrote, 'If you're good I will weep you, an 'twere a man born in April.' This was based on a quotation from *Troilus and Cressida* in which he had recently been appearing. Michael, though in fact thirty-five the previous June and not April, had discovered, like many before and since, that Shakespeare is a wondrous match-maker.

Shortly after that night in the Dirty Duck, Michael was in a film, *Eagle in a Cage*, being shot in Yugoslavia. He knew that Judi had a week off and invited her to spend it with him. She accepted and flew out to join him on location. They had come a long way from that curtailed encounter at the Opera Tavern.

And now Judi and *Twelfth Night* had moved on to Australia. Judi found out about Michael's visit, although it was intended as a surprise, and she was eager to see him. Even so, there were one or two genuine surprises still to come.

In the sunshine and heightened atmosphere of Australia the relationship deepened and Michael found it impossible to tear himself away. He made four or five attempts to leave, going so far as to book himself on to an aeroplane. He then turned back from the airport and, fixing it with Trevor, came on stage that night in *The Winter's Tale* as one of the rustics in Perdita's dance scene. He had blacked out several of his teeth, and his general costume, make-up and demeanour were grotesque. This time Judi, as Perdita, had no inkling that Michael was in the theatre. So far as she was aware he had returned to London.

It took extreme professional control to cope with the sudden and unexpected entrance of this crazed-looking hippie among the dancers and at first she froze with shock. One of the other people in the scene later remarked, 'I've never before seen anyone dry during a *dance*.'

Ultimately Michael stayed for the remainder of the tour and, one sunbaked day in Adelaide, he proposed. Judi's reaction was cautious. Here was a man she had known for years, a good friend and now more than that. But to marry? They were both establishing firm careers for themselves; could she adapt sufficiently from the life that this entailed? Indeed, could she reconcile her idea of married and family life, based on the sound and steady model provided by Olave and Reg, with a union between a couple of actors? And, more immediately, were their present feelings influenced by the holiday mood of the tour and the Australian sunshine? And so she said to Michael, 'Ask me again on a wet day in London.'

That they were a couple who felt and looked happy together was obvious to all. Trevor Nunn certainly noticed this, so much so that when the company's aeroplane landed at London Airport he called Mike and Judi aside and suggested to them that Mike would make an ideal Charles Courtly to Judi's Grace Harkaway in the RSC's forthcoming production, *London Assurance* by Dion Boucicault. They agreed, and soon found themselves at the centre of a highly successful production.

The success of *London Assurance* was a triumph of professionalism. The RSC does not have to take too many literary risks; with Shakespeare it is on the safest possible ground. But it is a company which never loses sight of the fact that the plays were written for the stage, not the page. Peter Hall, Trevor Nunn, Terry Hands and their cohorts have always tried to maintain a living theatre. The directors look at how best the texts can be *performed* to an audience. Ronald Eyre's espousal of *London Assurance* was a glittering example of this approach.

Boucicault's play, first staged in 1841 at Covent Garden, when the author was not yet twenty-one, reads most unpromisingly. Shaw wrote that 'if *London Assurance* were revived (and I beg that nothing of the kind be attempted) there would be no more question of dating about it than about the plays of Garrick or Tobin or Mrs Centlivre.' Poe described it as a 'despicable mass of inanity'. Eyre, however, was alive to the possibilities of it working on stage with a well-trained cast. And out of Boucicault's fairly fatuous pot-pourri of mistaken motives and identities Ronald Eyre created a breezy, amusing piece of theatre.

Judi's character, Grace, is a country girl compounded of innocence and wisdom, who is betrothed to an elderly, narcissistic sophisticate, Sir Harcourt Courtly, but who falls in love with the man's son, Charles. Contrasts, parallels and morals are drawn constantly, bolstered in this instance by stage manoeuvres finely executed by Eyre's cast, in which Donald Sinden was a splendidly indulgent Sir Harcourt, and Judi a bespectacled, prim-looking Grace, whose appearance belied a bouncing sense of fun ever likely to break out.

The story is sustained and complicated by the foibles of such characters as the hearty Maximilian Harkaway, Grace's uncle (in fact played by Judi's brother Jeff), the vivacious Lady Gay Spanker (Elizabeth Spriggs) and the sponging Dazzle (Barrie Ingham).

Ronald Eyre saw the play as a story of four vastly different love affairs including 'the love affair of Sir Harcourt Courtly and his mirror.' His treatment, which involved substantial textual adaptation, was thoroughly popular with audiences and the production was destined to be revived.

Twelfth Night and *The Winter's Tale*, much seasoned since their Stratford openings and tightened and polished still further in Australia and Japan, duly took their place in the 1970 Aldwych repertoire. Three new productions in which Judi had a leading role — *Major Barbara*, *The Merchant of Venice* and *The Duchess of Malfi* — were to be added in the course of the next year. Also in 1970, she was awarded the OBE in the Birthday Honours — 'It's a wonderful thing to have. You can wear a tiny badge, though I never use it. It was lovely going to the palace to receive it. As I went up to get it they played "Half a Sixpence"!' It was a heady, eventful time, and in the midst of it she got married.

The emotional climate between Michael and Judi had not been entirely satisfactory following their return from Australia, and in the absence of clear, reciprocal commitment, Michael severed the relationship. But of course they were both working at the RSC and could hardly avoid each other.

Michael was involved in an experiment under the guidance of Terry Hands and the young director Buzz Goodbody intended to create a production on the theme of the 1926 General Strike, but this failed to achieve positive results and after about four weeks it was abandoned. At the end of the final, abortive rehearsal for this enterprise, Michael and the rest of the would-be cast trooped off, for mutual commiseration, to the Opera Tavern, coincidentally the scene of his and Judi's first meeting. After a short time Judi entered, trailing a little dog belonging to the writer

David Benedictus, who had been working on the script of the General Strike piece. Whether or not she knew Michael would be there and whether she knew how winningly vulnerable she would look to him with that borrowed dog are matters best left to speculation. By the end of the evening they were reconciled. By the end of the month wedding plans were being made.

Michael's background is rather different from Judi's. Born into a staunchly Catholic, working-class family in Salford, he was brought up and worked for a while in Liverpool before winning a scholarship to RADA and eventually making his way into the Royal Shakespeare Company. Like Judi, he has a strong sense of family and of religious values, and here there was a problem.

They both wanted to marry in the little Catholic church around the corner from the Hampstead cottage and so Michael went along and spoke to the priest there, detailing his and Judi's contrasting denominational backgrounds and beliefs. It was explained that, although they were able to marry there, the service would be in a truncated form, excluding nuptial mass. Judi remembers finding this extremely difficult to accept:

'I asked Michael to get a copy of the "script" of the proposed marriage service and saw that it was weighted against me. Michael would be able to take communion but I wouldn't. I had been confirmed before becoming a Quaker and felt that I could and should take communion. The local priest also said that any children of the marriage had to be brought up in the Catholic faith. I just couldn't promise that. I felt if that had been said about me I couldn't have become a Quaker.

'So Michael rang up a very good friend, Joseph McCulloch, the rector of St Mary-le-Bow, and told him about this apparent impasse. Joseph invited us to dinner to talk about it. He also invited Edward Carpenter, Dean of Westminster and Tom Corbishley, a Jesuit who had formerly been Master of Campion Hall.

'There ensued the most complex theological discussion that Mike and I couldn't touch the fringe of. It was like a foreign language. Eventually Tom Corbishley said, "Why don't you come to the Jesuit Church in Farm Street the day before the wedding. Have your service with a mass with communion." So we went to Farm Street and he gave us a nuptial mass in a little room. Michael prepared the bread and wine for both of us, and then Tom gave a sermon.

'From that moment he became an absolutely cemented, close friend and gave us a great deal of help and advice until he died about eight years ago.'

After that private ceremony, the more public wedding went ahead as planned the following day in Hampstead. But in between there was a performance of *Twelfth Night* to be given. When Judi arrived at the Aldwych Theatre she found that the company had put up signs proclaiming 'This way to the wedding' along the corridor leading to her dressing room. Mike, who was having a quiet family party that night, called to see Judi in the interval, when all the cast brought them drinks and a present. At the curtain call they threw confetti, which the audience may well have considered appropriate for a play which ends on a note of nuptial promise.

The next morning, Friday 5 February 1971, at five minutes to eleven, the narrow road leading from Judi's cottage to the church was packed with people and cars. Judi was putting the final touches to her make-up and receiving a long, congratulatory telephone call from John Hopkins. Her brother Peter, who was to give her away, waited patiently. She wore a tuck-pleated silk dress, and a long, off-white, fine wool coat with a hood edged in white fur. Ready at last, and with a thousand thoughts and memories between them, Judi and Peter walked together the few score paces to where the congregation waited. As they turned the corner somebody took a photograph. Behind them a man was sweeping the road, and so he too had his place in the album. Judi arrived at the crammed-full church, paused at the entrance, saw Michael and said to herself, 'I am most frightfully glad I'm doing this.'

A Dominican monk conducted the service; Joseph McCulloch, a Church of England rector, gave the address; James Cairncross, a Catholic actor, read a passage on love by the seventeenth-century religious writer, Thomas Traherne. Music was played by the Royal Shakespeare Company Wind Band; the singing of the hymn 'Praise, my soul, the

King of Heaven' leapt deafeningly to the rafters; Barbara Leigh-Hunt wept 'for sheer joy'; Peggy Ashcroft was given Judi's large bouquet of lilies-of-the-valley; and, as Michael and Judi walked down the aisle, Donald Sinden was heard to say, 'there go the Start-rite children.'

The reception was held in the members' room at London Zoo, in Regent's Park, a choice in keeping with the bride and groom's love of animals. In a typically theatrical mixture of beauty and foolery, the bridal car was festooned with daffodils and toilet paper. Peter and Daphne missed the party as they had to take Jean Moffat, who had stomach pains, to University College Hospital and look after an uncle, who'd fainted.

Mike and Judi flew to Dublin, where they had dinner with her aunt and cousin who had been unable to attend the wedding. They were then driven to Galway, by a man called John Brennan, who sang 'This is your lovely day' at the top of his voice while driving at such hair-raising speed that the bride and groom clutched each other for safety. The rest of the weekend was spent at a more amiable pace, cycling through the countryside. On Monday Judi was back in the theatre.

She had once mentioned how sometimes she longed for old-fashioned theatrical manners when managements issued formal calls for 'Mrs Bracegirdle', 'Mr Kemble' and so on. Consequently she was delighted when over the tannoy that evening came the call for 'Mr Sinden' and . . . 'Mrs Williams'.

Few of the guests at Michael and Judi's wedding could have been happier than Olave. She had come to know, like and respect Michael and recognized in him a solid, prospective husband for Judi, in contrast to one or two previous boyfriends whom Olave, at least, thought of as being of uncertain temperament.

Admittedly, Michael did have the advantage of a fortuitously good start. He was first introduced to Olave in The Dirty Duck in Stratford, where he bumped into Judi and her mother one evening in 1969. He happened to have called in on his way to a formal reception for which he was dressed in a dinner-jacket. Olave was very impressed with this combination of smart appearance and polite manners. Others were not so sure of the match and thought Michael and Judi so different as to be completely incompatible. But, as Olave possibly perceived, they complement rather than duplicate each other, dovetail rather than run parallel. Mike is the realist, the careful thinker; Judi is the idealist and impulsive doer. She is allegro to his penseroso. They themselves often express it astrologically — Michael is Cancerian, prone to scuttling away into the darkness, while Judi is Sagittarian, leaping into the light. They have an inbuilt system of checks and balances to stop either of them going too far down any particular road. Though Michael can be over-serious and Judi frivolous, they unite in laughter and generosity. It is a bond which has strengthened over the years, notably through the birth of a daughter, and which has latterly been professionally productive.

Major Barbara had opened in October at the Aldwych and comfortably established itself. In Brewster Mason, Judi was facing the same Undershaft she had encountered in the television production eight years' earlier, and both profited from the experience. In Clifford Williams' production, sympathy inclined towards the arms-dealing capitalist Undershaft, the father who pedals sweet reason, leaving Judi's salvationist daughter, offering faith, a defeated figure at the end.

Elizabeth Spriggs chalked up another personal success as Lady Britomart and the production helped to keep the RSC's pennant aloft. There was a largely favourable critical reception, Harold Hobson acclaiming, in *The Sunday Times*, Brewster Mason's performance as 'tremendous' and Judi Dench's as 'touching', in their exchange of issues 'presented with dazzling dramatic force and wit.'

Soon after their wedding, Judi and Michael went up to Stratford for the new season and in March opened together in *The Merchant of Venice*. Judi played Portia to Emrys James' Shylock and Michael was Bassanio. Terry Hands was the director and once again Judi was unable to respond to him enough to give herself completely to the role. She seemed to hold back a little. And in the case of *The Merchant of Venice*, unlike *Women Beware Women*, she felt a strong distaste for the play. She originally turned down the offer to play Portia but yielded to persuasion.

In all her work, consciously or subconsciously, Judi seeks out the essential *humanity* in her roles. In any drama worth the name, in her view, no character should be wholly evil or unnaturally good. And she sees it as her job to enlist the audience's sympathy or understanding for that character's human qualities, be they weak or noble. In *The Merchant of Venice* she believes that none of the characters exhibits sympathetic human behaviour. She feels that neither Antonio nor Shylock, Portia nor Jessica, Bassanio nor Lorenzo, does anything very commendable. Accordingly, she was mostly miserable throughout that production, never quite overcoming her regret at taking it on. Michael, too, shared Judi's feeling to some extent and the two of them worked with craft alone, not heart.

The Duchess of Malfi, John Webster's gory, vivid, poetic, Jacobean imbroglio, was Judi's personal choice for the 1971 Stratford season. And in the young, widowed Duchess, racked with torments and torture that revolve in a wheel of fire around her remarriage to her steward, she confronted a part which demands the steadiest of portrayals if it is to avoid a descent into melodrama.

Modern audiences tend to laugh at the accelerated pile-up of corpses with which Jacobean drama conventionally concludes and there is sometimes an inclination, on the other side of the footlights, to indulge this and play the material in a knowing, tongue-in-cheek way. At the other extreme, directors occasionally seek out a message for our times in the stark morality of the genre and slow down the rapid Jacobean mechanism in order to shift the emphasis from action to psychology, perhaps employing modern dress. A third possibility is to play the text straight and truly as if to a Jacobean audience, in the hope that the play will stand on its own merits come what may.

Such are the kinds of choices facing a company presenting Jacobean tragedy. The most natural option might be one which takes elements from each of the three basic approaches. In any event, a play like *The Duchess of Malfi* clearly needs a director's firmly guiding hand. Unfortunately, Clifford Williams — the director of that 1971 Stratford production — fell ill during the rehearsal period and the actors were left somewhat up in the air. As a result, the overall performance seemed to fall between all available stools. The company looked to be labouring hard against the odds and there was a tone of 'rewards for the workers' in the critics' appreciation of Richard Pasco as the Duchess' steward, Antonio, and Emrys James as her brother the Cardinal, as well as Michael, once more playing closely alongside Judi, as Ferdinand, Duke of Calabria — the Duchess' twin.

Judi herself negotiated all this uneven terrain with great determination and she was hypnotic. Having committed herself completely to the part of a woman whose passionate nature is fuelled both by pain and pleasure, she demonstrated her growing ability, this time in the midst of relative chaos, to bespeak a depth of many dimensions.

At the end of 1971 the RSC let its hair down and revived an old Stratford tradition of staging *Toad of Toad Hall* at Christmas. This was one of those pleasurable instances where the huge fun the cast is having is shared by the audience. Mike played Mole and Judi, to her utter delight, played a fieldmouse, a stoat and Mother Rabbit, who was pregnant — a highly significant piece of casting as it turned out.

The 1972 RSC tour of Japan took up virtually the whole of February. Three plays were featured: Judi was in *Twelfth Night*, Mike in *Henry V*, and the third was *Othello*. They were based at the Nissei Theatre in Tokyo, with some additional touring dates. Judi and Mike spent a lot of time in the company of Japanese actors, and in one memorable visit backstage at the Kabuki Theatre they gasped in wonder at a fat, little, bald man who was able to transform himself into an exquisitely beautiful young woman. They were invited by Keita Asari, the head of the Shiki Theatre Company, to his home in the Japanese Alps. The spectacular character of the snowy peaks was augmented that evening by an earthquake — through which the cast of *Othello* gamely continued their performance.

Judi consolidated her love of Japan and its people and she and Mike consolidated their family. It was in Japan that they found out she was pregnant. Judi wired London to inform the management that she would now only be available for a limited number of performances of *London Assurance* which was to begin a West End transfer soon after their return.

And so it was an expansive Judi Dench who opened at the New Theatre in April, her dresses gradually being let out further as her mobility slackened. But it was a welcome return so far as the press and playgoers were concerned. Irving Wardle wrote in *The Times* that 'on the second time round Boucicault's comedy exerts its spell as irresistibly as ever' and of Judi's performance as Grace Harkaway that it 'typifies the added detail and trapeze-artist timing which the production has developed.'

Judi remained in the cast until June, Sinead Cusak taking over her part. It was an exultant preparation for childbirth. As the pregnancy advanced Mike and Judi personalized the developing foetus with the name Finn and the days of Judi's bloom were also those of Finn's progress. Towards the end of September Judi was admitted to the Avenue Clinic in North London where Michael accompanied her to witness the birth of the child, and to announce at the apposite moment that it wasn't Finn but *Finty*. Michael and Judi's daughter, Tara Cressida, was born on the 24th of September 1972. She weighed seven pounds, ten ounces. And while Tara she may be officially, she has continued to be known to one and all as Finty".'

She was christened at the same little local church where her parents were married. The christening was an especially moving occasion for Barbara Leigh-Hunt: 'Judi and Mike were exceedingly generous in asking me to be a godparent to Finty, because they knew that I couldn't have any children. Judi said, "Darling, it doesn't matter about your not having children — you'll share Finty.

Finty had got off to a fine, loving start.

6   Good companionship

Judi's first professional engagement on stage after the birth of her daughter was in April 1973, when she returned to roots to play in *Content to Whisper*, by Alan Melville, at the Theatre Royal, York. This was a mistake which limped along for a few weeks. Michael also appeared, he and Judi having been signed by an old friend, Richard Digby-Day, then the artistic director at York. In the cast with them was Sidney Tafler.

After the first rehearsal, Michael, Judi and Richard Digby-Day went to a pub, looked at one another, and the first statement by one — 'I think we've made a booboo' — was readily acknowledged by all. But there they were and at least with Sidney Tafler in the company there would be plenty of laughs.

Judi had first seen Tafler on stage some months previously in *A Man for All Seasons* and she noticed that he was laughing all through the performance. And when she came to work with him he was exactly the same and the giggling passed, relay fashion, from one to another. He had a line, 'They say you were sitting with two officers . . .' which he constantly struggled to get out. He also used to place chewing gum on the underside of his desk, to the consternation of his colleagues.

The play itself was far from comic. It was a sombre piece about two prisoners trying to communicate from separate cells, and it exuded a grey, unexciting atmosphere. One night Judi jumped from Act One to Act Three and it took some quick thinking by Michael to rescue the situation and prevent Sidney Tafler being missed out altogether.

Judi, Michael and Finty stayed with Olave throughout the run and it was a time far more memorable for the emergence of Finty's first two teeth than for the efforts of her parents on stage.

*

Top: Judi (far left) in *Alice in Wonderland* at Miss Meaby's'. *Right:* Judi's first professional engagement, as Ophelia with John Neville (Hamlet) at the Old Vic, 1957.

Top: With John Neville in Sierra Leone during their West African tour, 1963. *Right:* The 'definitive Titania' in Peter Hall's 1962 Stratford production of *A Midsummer Night's Dream.*

Top: A first taste of Coward: Amanda in *Private Lives* opposite Edward Woodward as Victor, Nottingham 1965. ***Below:*** *Four in the Morning* (1965), Judi's first major film role for which she received a BAFTA award.

Top left: Judi (Lika) with Ian McKellen (Leonidik) in Arbuzov's *The Promise* at the Fortune Theatre, 1967. **Top right:** Receiving her Television Actress of the Year Award, with Eric Porter, 1967. **Below:** Viola with Donald Sinden (Malvolio) in *Twelfth Night*, Stratford 1969.

op: Judi and Michael's
edding, 5 February
971. ***Right:*** With Ian
cKellen in Trevor
unn's triumphant
roduction of *Macbeth*
t The Other Place,
tratford 1976.

Right: Laura, in the very popular television series *A Fine Romance*, 1981. *Below:* With Nigel Havers in *The Importance of Being Earnest* at the National Theatre, 1982.

Top: Discussing her role as Lady Bracknell with Peter Hall. ***Below:*** In Pinter's *A Kind of Alaska* Judi played Deborah, the victim of a strange sleeping sickness. National Theatre, 1982.

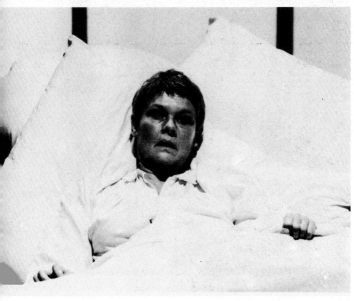

Marcia Pilborough in David Hare's *Wetherby*, 1985.

From the start of their marriage both Judi and Michael were keen to give their family life a broad base. And, although — to their subsequent regret — they have had only one child, their attachment to Olave and to Michael's mother and father has been a full, mutually enriching one.

Olave first met Michael's parents on her birthday in 1970, at a surprise party which Judi had organized for her. Judi, together with a couple of old friends, Herman and Edith Barr, arranged to take Olave for dinner at the Barque and Bite barge restaurant on the Regent's Park Canal. When they arrived, the staff — who were in on the secret — greeted them and asked if they wanted to dine on the upper or lower deck. Judi said, as if spontaneously, 'Why don't we try the top deck? We've never eaten there.' So, up they went and discovered a table of twenty-five people waiting for them, including Michael and his parents, Leonard and Elizabeth.

At midnight, quite by coincidence, there was a firework display on the opposite side of the canal, which Olave was convinced, despite denials, was part of her birthday celebrations. It was a happy, convivial evening, providing the firmest of foundations for the uniting of the Williamses and the Denches.

Having set up their own home, Michael and Judi saw their parents often. They invited them down regularly at Christmas and Easter, everybody at ease in each other's company. Every year on Easter Monday, whatever the weather (and sometimes it snowed), Judi would arrange a picnic in the country for the entire family. She had long nurtured an ideal of being part of a Continental kind of extended family household where young and old live under the same roof, so that when, one day over a drink in the Dirty Duck, Michael put the suggestion to her that they buy a house near Stratford for the family, parents and all, she found the prospect appealing in the extreme.

The idea met with instant approval from Len, Elizabeth and Olave. There was no apprehension about uprooting, at relatively advanced ages, from their home towns of Liverpool and York. In fact, Olave told Judi, 'It's just like all the dark clouds have rolled by.'

Each party was to make a financial contribution and Michael and Judi were entrusted with the task of looking for a suitable place. After a long and careful search they found a converted stable in the village of Charlecote, six miles outside Stratford. The enthusiasm of the elder generation held, and this choice was rapidly confirmed so that, in the early part of 1974, Olave, who was ready to move in advance of the others, took up residence in the Stable House at Charlecote.

Judi and Michael divided their time between Hampstead and Charlecote, while Len, Elizabeth and Olave were permanent residents in the Warwickshire house. It was an L-shaped building with eleven rooms, including a large sitting-room, study and dining-room. It had a much-loved garden, which Michael's father tended proudly, enhancing and developing its character with such features as a Japanese crab-apple tree, a tiny silver birch which grew taller than the house, a willow and a cherry tree which was a christening gift for Finty. During warm summer nights the five adults would commonly sit outside by the light of an oil-lamp talking into the small hours.

Duties were divided as equally as possible, though things didn't always run smoothly, and as the parents grew older a number of strains and tensions arose. But these were not fundamentally divisive and Judi's longed-for household unit was forged. The destinies of Elizabeth Williams and Olave Dench mingled. Elizabeth died in March, 1982, Olave almost exactly one year later. They were both buried in Charlecote Churchyard. The house was sold in 1984, Len moving in with Michael's brother, Paul.

It had been a domestic decade in which the happy times outweighed the stressful ones, and over which Judi looks back now with considerable satisfaction: 'Neither ma had to go into an old people's home. I would have deplored that. It has been wonderful for Finty to grow up with her grandparents. That was important to Michael and me. And the way our parents adapted was incredible. I'm terribly glad we did it.'

While looking for a family home near Stratford, Judi had been working back in one of her professional homes: Oxford. It had crossed her mind briefly to turn her back on the theatre, as least for the time being, and devote herself to her home and family. She and Michael had considered the possibility of a second child, which would have greatly extended her absence from professional circulation. But both were aware, Michael perhaps more consciously than Judi, that what life gave her and what she gave life was very largely bound up with acting. And of this realization, leaving aside the York interlude, Frank Hauser was to be the first professional beneficiary.

Something of a champion of East European writers, Hauser was planning to revive a play called *The Wolf*, written in 1912 by the Hungarian-born playwright, Ferenc Molnar. Frank Hauser adapted Molnar's text himself, in collaboration with Henric Hirsch, and produced an attractive, keenly observant comedy which achieved a success as surprising in its way as that of Arbuzov's *The Promise*, seven years earlier. After its opening in Oxford in September 1973, *The Wolf* transferred to the West End, firstly at the Apollo, then Queen's and finally the New London in Drury Lane — 'a horrible, cell-like theatre', in Judi's view.

The play was divided into three acts. In the first, a prominent Budapest lawyer is seen to suffer from comically paranoid jealousy as he is consumed by the appearance of his demure wife's former suitor. The second act is a dream in which the wife imagines her old admirer coming back to her as her lover in various guises, including those of a soldier and an opera singer. The final act comes firmly back to reality with an actual visit from the erstwhile dream hero. He is of course thoroughly humble, an awkward lawyer's clerk who spills the drinks. The essence of the play's appeal was that the undeniable humour of the story derived from genuine symptoms of the human condition. Its characters were three identifiable mortals stretched between desire and need, imagination and reality.

As usual, Frank Hauser extracted a detailed set of performances from his actors. Judi, as Vilma, the wife, found herself in a harmonious working relationship with her old Nottingham sparring partner, Edward Woodward, as the lover, and Leo McKern as the lawyer husband. Professionally, she was back on course, working with craft and filling the role of a woman who, most humanly, is more than she seems on the surface. It helped to be working with such a strict, precise director as Frank Hauser.

An idiosyncrasy of Judi's is that she rarely reads the book or the script before entering the rehearsals and will accept a part purely according to how confidently a director conveys his own interest to her. Knowing this, Frank Hauser makes a point, when directing Judi, of having a meal with her prior to the start of rehearsals and telling her the story in detail. That's part of his orderly method. He doesn't like loose ends and prefers to rehearse straight through from nine in the morning without a lunch-break.

Although Judi relies on directors probably to a greater extent than most performers, it is as a safety-net more than anything else. She responds best to a director who can create a stimulating climate for ideas to develop and risks to be taken but who, at the end of the day, is a rock-solid figure against whom the actors can lean and know he will be able to weld all the pieces into shape. In Frank Hauser Judi has always found that kind of solidity.

With her next director, Braham Murray, Judi felt no such security. This was in *The Good Companions*, a musical adaptation of J.B.Priestley's 1920 novel by Ronald Harwood, André Previn and Johnny Mercer. The medium aggravated Judi's uncertainty. In *Cabaret* she had been lulled by rehearsals generally unrepresentative of musical comedy. That show was ready-made, already a success in New York with Jill Haworth as Sally Bowles, the songs proven. But working from the ground floor of a musical involves a great deal of revision, rearrangement and frustration, as songs, dances, dialogue, music and scenery are all pushed around in permutation.

There is constant change; whole chunks of material, diligently learned, can be cut off at a stroke; and it all tends to take place in an atmosphere of pressure and anxiety, for when a musical flops, it crashes. It is invariably much more expensive to stage than the average dramatic production and the need to take money at the box-office is correspondingly much greater.

There was a connection with *Cabaret*, however, in that the producer of *The Good Companions* was Richard Pilbrow, in whose home Judi practised singing 'The Party's Over' for her audition. As on a previous occasion, Judi felt dreadfully exposed by the prospect of singing at audition and she asked Ronald Harwood, André Previn and Richard Pilbrow not to watch her, a request to which they responded by lying on the floor between the theatre seats. A pianist played and Judi sang, but in far too high a register. At the end of the song the heads popped up from behind the seats and Judi said, 'It's much too high.' André Previn agreed. He took over the piano and transposed the whole song, enabling Judi to sing again, more comfortably, and to land the part of Miss Trant.

Leading the company was John Mills, and other members of the cast included Christopher Gable, Malcolm Rennie and, to begin with, Celia Bannerman, who suffered more than most from the flux of rehearsal. As a 'non-singing' actress, she found it tough to adapt to the musical aspect of performance and decided to pull out after a preview in Manchester. Her replacement for London was Marti Webb, a performer whose strength was very much on the singing side. The company struggled to get it right in time for London but failed to satisfy Braham Murray, who felt they weren't giving of their best.

In the capital, the show opened at Her Majesty's Theatre in July 1974 to low-key notices. The prevailing view was that the liveliness and authenticity of Priestley's original novel had been flattened out to produce a safe, even, but unmemorable production. Michael Billington, in the *Guardian*, described it as 'dogged, dutiful' and 'characterless', although he praised Judi's performance as 'a touching portrait of a shy woman at large in an exhibitionist world.' In *The Times*, Irving Wardle suggested that 'Braham Murray's production does go down like some easily digestible dish for invalids. There are a few flashes of the harsh world outside, but for most of the time we are in a company of smiling lovable people, confronting problems that are certain to be overcome.' Harold Hobson, writing in *The Sunday Times*, was far kinder to the production as a whole and of Judi he wrote that she was 'as ravishing as a spring day'. The public were also more appreciative and *The Good Companions* continued into the following year.

During the run of *The Good Companions*, Michael went away for a couple of days' film location work in Switzerland. While he was there Judi persuaded a friend, the actor John

Barden, to stay at the Hampstead cottage to help her decorate a bedroom and the bathroom as a surprise for Michael on his return. Not only did they fully decorate the two rooms in two days but they also put down new carpets and Judi made some curtains. When Michael returned, she said nothing — just waited for him to go upstairs so that she could treasure the look on his face. She has sprung the same kind of surprise many times since then.

At this time Judi and Michael became friendly with John and Mary Mills. John and Judi had to sit together in a little Austin car waiting to go on stage and it became a kind of confessional in which they held long and therapeutic conversations. One day John said, 'I'm going to buy this car and put it in my garden, and when I feel all uptight I'm going to invite you down and we'll sit out in it together and talk.'

Once, John and Mary invited Judi and Mike to dinner at Overtons' restaurant, John informing Judi that their order needed to be telephoned through. At the beginning of Act Two, Judi was required to come on bearing a large clip-board, ostensibly for checking luggage. On that particular evening she had Overtons' menu attached to the clipboard with her and Mike's orders duly indicated, which she handed to an astonished John Mills.

For their 1975 wedding anniversary, Michael organized a dinner at the Connaught, keeping the venue secret from Judi. As they left after the show, John and Mary — who often came to the theatre to sit and paint in John's dressing room — asked Judi, 'Do you know where you are being taken?' 'No,' she replied. 'Well, have a lovely time anyway', they said in apparent farewell. But when Judi arrived at the Connaught, there they both were, sitting at the table laughing at the elaborate, affectionate surprise so typical of Mike and Judi's marriage.

Sir Arthur Wing Pinero died in the year of Judi's birth, 1934. He had been an actor for ten years before turning, more successfully, to playwriting. His acting no doubt stood him in good stead, for he was a master of theatricality, that full-blown use of wit and spectacle always so alluring to Judi. Pinero's dramatic technique is, in this respect, nowhere more heightened than in *The Gay Lord Quex* which he wrote in 1899, and which Sir John Gielgud decided to revive in 1975.

It concerns the wrong-headed attempts by a young female busybody to expose an aristocratic erstwhile rake, engaged to her foster sister. The dialogue is languid and amusing, and, with such exclamatory phrases as, 'simply heavenly!' and stage directions like, 'In a flutter of simple pleasure', Pinero might almost have had Judi in mind when writing.

In Gielgud's production, which opened at the Albery Theatre on 16 June 1975, Daniel Massey played the Marquis of Quex, Rosalind Shanks was Muriel Eden, the innocent foster sister, and Sian Phillips appeared as the Duchess of Strood, a calculating former mistress of Quex's. Judi played the aforementioned busybody — Sophie Fullgarney, manicurist to the aristocracy. She learned beforehand how to manicure to a professional standard, buffing, filing and tending nails with great expertise by the end of the run. The establishment over which Miss Fullgarney presided was brilliantly designed by Alan Tagg and stocked with elegant commodities from Crabtree & Evelyn.

Despite the theatrical pedigree of the writer, director and cast, the production didn't quite work, appearing more as the sum of its parts than a coherent whole. Judi's principal memories are of laughter external to actual performance (for which one friend in the audience, Ronald Eyre, tagged her 'The Colossus of Roedean'):

'After all the weeks of rehearsal and trying out different things, John would very much want to go back to the original way of doing it. He was divinely witty. He'd keep coming out with stories that were so good that you'd feel, "I never want these rehearsals to stop."'

'We rehearsed in the crypt of St James', Piccadilly. One day, two men came running out of the loo and dashed up the stairs, one screaming, among other things, that the other had taken his trousers! John could hardly rehearse for the rest of that day he was laughing so much. It was rather shocking in a way, but so funny.'

Later that year, Judi re-established the RSC connection, initiating a five-year association — punctuated by some rewarding excursions into television — which was to see her extend her capabilities beyond the scope of virtually every other actress on the contemporary English stage.

Her five-year alliance began brightly with a rousing production by Clifford Williams of Shaw's late comedy *Too True to be Good*. In this, Judi resumed a more specific professional relationship — that with Ian McKellen — which in itself would achieve a dizzying conquest within a year.

Shaw's stage direction for the opening scene of *Too True to be Good* begins, 'Night. One of the best bedrooms in one of the best suburban villas in one of the richest cities in England. A young lady with an unhealthy complexion is asleep in the bed. . . .' Out of this unpromising situation there develops what Shaw terms 'a political extravaganza'. Spread over three acts, in which the sick rich girl is burgled by the boyfriend of her bogus nurse and elects to join her robbers in flight to faraway places to flower as a liberated woman of action; the burglar is revealed as a cataclysmic preacher; and a blimpish general is upstaged by a T.E. Lawrence-like private soldier; it ends, after a parade of postcard characters, in an impassioned oration by the preacher who is gradually lost in a swirling sea mist which muffles his final words. In the earlier, uninterrupted part of his speech, he had declaimed to the audience that 'we have outgrown our religion, outgrown our political system, outgrown our strength of mind and character.' He is also the mouthpiece for a neat piece of self-conscious Shavian irony — 'what storyteller, however reckless a liar, would dare to invent figures so improbable as men and women with their minds stripped naked?' This was all assembled by GBS in 1932, when he was seventy-six and the world was still licking its wounds from the First World War, ignorant of the barbarous horrors to come.

With those horrors in hindsight, modern audiences tend perhaps to receive the play's political statements a little wearily, and the success of the 1975 RSC production — it transferred from the Aldwych to the Globe — was almost certainly attributable to the comic playing of the cast.

Ian McKellen played the central burglar/preacher character, while Judi eschewed the role of the liberated heroine (which went instead to Anna Calder-Marshall) in favour of 'Nurse' Sweetie Simpkins, the burglar's girlfriend who romps rumbustiously through the proceedings ending up in the arms of an earthily religious army sergeant (played by Joe Melia). It was a meaty role, played fully in the spirit of a production which sent spectators away entertained rather than edified.

In April 1976, John Barton's production of *Much Ado About Nothing* opened at Stratford. The two main roles of Beatrice and Benedick were allotted to Judi Dench and Donald Sinden. Shakespeare's play has proved almost notoriously adaptable, spatially and temporally, for many directors including, on this occasion, John Barton. His decision was to translate the Elizabethan Messina into the high noon of British Empire in India. Thus there was a real and recognizable officer class for Don Pedro and his followers to slot into; and in a browned-up and turbaned Dogberry, wrestling pretentiously with the English language, a similarly recognizable stage type who amused some and offended others. It also made for an unusual uniformity of setting, admirably concentrating the encounter between Beatrice and Benedick.

Judi and Donald rose to the opportunity and the challenge magnificently, sparking off each other in spiralling effectiveness. Judi phased and paced her performance carefully so that Beatrice displayed a believable progress from apprehension to acceptance. Both she and Sinden showed masterly control and timing, sharpening their bristling dialogue to the smoothness of a superlative double-act. Writing in the 1977 *Shakespeare Survey*, Roger Warren expressed the appreciation of critics and paying customers alike:

'All the great moments went off superbly, and all were related to character and situation: "Against my will (*pause*) I am sent (*pause; glower; then very emphatically*) to bid you (*then very fast, very loud*) come in to dinner!": Judi Dench underlined this by emphatically beating a small portable dinner gong. After this unappetizing invitation, Mr Sinden's triumphant "There's a double meaning in that" justly brought the house down. Again, Beatrice obsessively swept up the scattered flowers left over from the calamitous wedding to control her feelings as her dialogue with Benedick began; the business would no doubt work with a lesser actress — but this dry account can't begin to capture the way it was used, nor to communicate the life, command, control, and sheer human feeling of two superb actors at the height of their powers.'

Perhaps the chief strength of the production lay in Barton's establishment of credible antecedents for this society and its people. In happy coincidence, Judi and Donald both absorbed and conveyed this feeling to the full. Judi's Beatrice gave pointed emphasis to her reply to Don Pedro's observation that she has 'lost the heart of Signior Benedick':

'Indeed, my lord', she said, with open, deliberate phrasing, 'he lent it me awhile; and I gave him use for it — a double heart for his single one: marry, once before he won it of me with false dice, therefore your grace may well say I have lost it.'

From this clue, the relationship was given a history, with all the attendant signs of resentment, recrimination and guilt. In this *Much Ado*, Judi Dench and Donald Sinden made it abundantly plain that the word-play between Beatrice and Benedick was no idle banter.

In a magazine interview in 1974, Judi was discussing her adventures in Africa as Lady Macbeth, when her interviewer, Gareth Lloyd-Evans, asked if she had ever played the part in England. Her reply reads, in retrospect, as a very daring challenge to fate: 'No, and I would never be asked . . . Nor Cleopatra. That's not my scene. I wouldn't know how to approach them, actually.'

To date, Judi has still not played the sovereign of Egypt. But she has, stunningly, held — alongside her 'sovereign lord' — the brief, black occupancy of the Scottish throne. And in a matter of two years from that interview she had most decidedly worked out an approach to the lady.

It was Trevor Nunn who broached the question she'd assumed would never be asked. He was well aware that his choice for Lady Macbeth would raise eyebrows: 'Judi? Warm, round, sweet, charming, middle-class — how can Judi play the Ellen Terry, Sybil Thorndike figure of the mad scene, with hawk-like face and flowing robes?' To such a question Trevor Nunn had, of course, a ready answer: There was never any intention that Judi would play such a figure.

Ian McKellen was to play Macbeth and the production was to be a small-scale, intimate one in the RSC's new studio theatre at Stratford, The Other Place. Converted from a corrugated iron hut used by Michel St Denis in the 1960s as an actors' studio, this was established early in 1974, under the driving force of Buzz Goodbody, as the company's second Stratford auditorium, seating 140 people.

That same year Trevor Nunn had directed a highly metaphysical production of *Macbeth* in the main theatre at Stratford. Now, for the 1976 Stratford season, he turned to The Other Place. A more manageable, even domestic *Macbeth* was sought. The problem was to achieve this in such a way as to enhance the metaphysical aspect, not at its expense.

Those involved were strongly conscious of the magnitude of the challenge and assiduously set about getting to the heart of the play. It wasn't easy. After an early rehearsal, Ian, Judi and Trevor walked wearily from the theatre and Judi slipped and fell in the street *twice*. It seemed ominous. 'We won't be able to do this play, will we?' she sighed to Trevor, who characteristically rallied his players and steadily built up a rapport whose closeness was essential for his conception of the tragedy.

Nunn saw it as Shakespeare's great play about faith, in the same way as, say, *Romeo and Juliet* is about love, and *Othello* about jealousy. *Macbeth* demonstrates, *in extremis*, what can happen to people with the departure of their faith. Lady Macbeth is therefore seen at the outset to be motivated by her deep, loving faith in her husband, who is in turn sustained by his faith in his own invincibility, into which he has been led by the witches.

Judi remembers her starting point as 'wanting to find a *reason* for Lady Macbeth's behaviour, and I feel that it was because she was totally besotted with Macbeth. Not that she wanted it all for herself — to be queen — but for him. Having tasted blood he goes further and she draws back, and the rift between them begins. She is a creature to pity. Of course, it's her come-uppance but you should say at the end, "There but for the grace of God could go anybody" if you think ambition is that important.'

The foundations of Judi's portrayal were laid during a morning-long consideration by Trevor and herself of Lady

Macbeth's first soliloquy, which begins with her reading her husband's letter revealing the witches' startling prophecies. In particular, they strove to analyse the full implications of her statement that Macbeth's nature 'is too full o' the milk of human kindness.'

Taking the weight of tradition from their shoulders, the director and the performer concluded that they were, as Trevor Nunn recalls, 'dealing with a woman who didn't disdain her husband, who didn't think he was somebody to be manipulated or baited. She adored him close to idolatry. This took her to the point where she could not bear that his career should lack fulfilment, and then lamented that this extraordinary man had too much generosity, sympathy, vulnerability. How could he be helped? She had, for however long it took, to transform herself to give him that push, so much did she love him. Consequently the calling down of those spirits to infect her was something she had never conceived of before. It was done in a state of terror and thrill — entirely aware of the danger, but done, not for herself, but *only* for him, so that he might be fulfilled.'

Such were the seeds of the relationship at the core of an exciting interpretation. In performance, the acting area was virtually devoid of scenery and props; the whole cast were seated on boxes arranged around the edge of a circle. And there they remained until called upon to perform, for which purpose they would step into the circle, thereby appearing to undergo a kind of ceremonial transformation. Their scenes completed, their exits would take them back to the boxes in the semi-darkness outside the perimeter. And around and behind the actors sat the audience, one stage removed as it were, collaborators in the dark, intense atmosphere.

As the production developed, the circle seemed to tighten with the emotional pitch and closeness of the performance. This was a logical enactment of the play's pervasive imagery of blood and darkness. The impetus was maintained by having no interval. By the time it reached the RSC's London studio at the Warehouse Theatre in September 1977, all the strands were finely woven.

And when Judi came to the sleepwalking scene, the distance from Africa couldn't be measured in miles alone. The scene peaks at the following passage, with the distraught

Lady Macbeth observed by the doctor and the gentlewoman:

Lady Macbeth: Here's the smell of the blood still: all
the perfumes of Arabia will not
sweeten this little hand. Oh, oh, oh!

Doctor: What a sigh is there! The heart is
sorely charged.

Gentlewoman: I would not have such a heart in my
bosom for the dignity of the whole
body.

With Judi's performance, incorporating a sigh of such concentrated emotion, in that charged atmosphere one knew, as if for the first time, precisely what that gentlewoman meant.

What Judi aimed at here was to convey that this was not a woman simply disturbed, but, at this point, finally deranged, and that if she were to utter another such sigh it would certainly be her last.

The critical chorus of praise was extraordinary. The *Guardian*'s Michael Billington wrote, 'Instead of the usual broken-backed pageant, Nunn offers us a Satanic ritual in which evil is invoked, blossoms and is purged before our amazed eyes' and of the two principals: 'McKellen and Judi Dench as his Lady . . . usher us into the hair-raising, unmistakable presence of great acting.' Irving Wardle was equally breathless in *The Times* — 'a revival that compels you to reimagine the events step by step and a reminder that the test of great acting is not impersonation but revelation.' — expressing wonder that it was achieved under such humble conditions: 'What is the justification for main stage décor and mechanics when infinitely more powerful effects . . . can be achieved with rehearsal lights and few orange boxes?' He also noted Judi's gentle qualities, contrasting greatly with conventional perceptions of Lady Macbeth.

In *The Financial Times*, B.A. Young responded to the meticulousness of the production: 'There is something to think about from first to last'; while John Barber's *Daily Telegraph* review hailed the production as 'one of Trevor Nunn's supreme achievements as a director.' Robert Cushman wrote in the *Observer*: 'It is the best Shakespeare production I have ever seen, combining minute textual scrutiny with throat-seizing emotional power.'

One dissenting voice was that of Bernard Levin, the *The Sunday Times*' theatre critic: 'I can see nothing in Ian McKellen's Macbeth other than ranting and twitching, and he speaks the verse with inexcusable coarseness. Judi Dench, a marvellous actress on her day, veers from improbable whispers to impossible yells, with little of interest in between.'

But the general view was echoed in the public reaction, and the production transferred eventually to the Young Vic Theatre and was even televised. And though Judi, Ian and Trevor scooped awards (Judi was named Best Acrtress by the Society of West End Theatres), it was certainly, and importantly, a corporate triumph. In such conditions — a studio theatre, the cast ranged around the ceremonial circle — any imbalance in the performance could have dislocated the entire proceedings. Vitally, Ian and Judi received excellent support from John Woodvine as Banquo, Bob Peck as Macduff, Greg Hicks as Seyton, and all the others, among them Roger Rees, Ian McDiarmid, and — as the three weird sisters — Marie Kean, Judith Harte and Susan Dury.

Roger Rees played Malcolm. Judi was, he says, an inspiration: 'She had to get up off her box after everyone else had been on. And I remember sitting there as she read out the letter and did the incantation. I don't think she ever shirked it, even when she was frightfully ill, as she was at one period. It was wonderful to be so close to that performance.'

With such intense, tragic work to be done, the actors' mood behind the scenes was manic. The dressing-room at the Warehouse was fairly communal, the men separated from the women by a single partition over which flew pants, brassières and other items in a childish maelstrom.

The company laughed their way through a long season and Judi got them going in performance too. During the Young Vic run she bought a quantity of stick-on pink iridescent spots which she distributed among the performers each of whom was enjoined to stick one on his or her costume or person. The idea was to show the spot to as many people on stage as possible without the audience noticing. The winner — who turned out to be Duncan Preston, playing Angus — was the person whose spot was visible to everybody else in the cast. His prize, again courtesy of Judi, was an enormous pink spot mounted on cardboard.

Then there was the normal quota of hysteria-inducing, on-stage errors, as when John Woodvine entered the action with his orange-box seat attached to his costume, or when he walked on just before Duncan's murder, thinking he had missed an entrance.

One night the American film director, Fred Zinneman, was in the audience and there was a detectable shift in the actors' projection, towards him. A visit from Peter Brook had the same effect, the whole performance tilting in his direction.

But the lasting memory of that *Macbeth* is implicit in Trevor Nunn's summary of Judi and Ian's achievement. This was, he believes, 'to make the play genuinely tragic, not just melodramatic, about brutality and blood. There were times of quite amazing exhilaration in their work together. Shakespeare's words were the articulate, visible tip of the iceberg.'

In the opinion of Sir Peter Hall, Judi Dench has 'possibly the best comic timing in the theatre', an opinion endorsed by Bernard Levin in *The Sunday Times* theatre column of 20 November 1977, in which he described Judi as 'a comic actress of consummate skill, perhaps the very best we have.'

Levin's comment was made in an approbatory review of Trevor Nunn's production of *The Comedy of Errors*, by then transferred to the Aldwych after a satisfactory run-in at Stratford. The first performance there had been at the end of September 1976. Hard on the heels of *Macbeth* it demonstrated the breadth of the RSC's — and Trevor Nunn's — range of accomplishments as well as the extraordinary versatility, within that range, of Judi Dench. Here for the beholding in Stratford and London was an actress at the height of her considerable powers in tragedy and comedy *simultaneously*.

When Trevor Nunn had asked Judi to rejoin the company to play Lady Macbeth, and, among others, Adriana in *The Comedy of Errors*, the location was once more an Italian restaurant, this time in Hampstead, home territory for both parties, and at a sunny table outside. The setting was singularly appropriate, perhaps even inspirational, for the spirit of Mediterranean-style *al fresco* celebrations was at the heart of Nunn's new conception of *The Comedy of Errors*.

A number of RSC productions of the 1960s and 1970s were so fresh, so successful and so highly praised that they tended to cast shadows over any subsequent attempts to stage the same plays. A case in point, perhaps the most obvious, was Peter Brook's 1970 production of *A Midsummer Night's Dream* to which any subsequent version has fallen to be compared. And while Trevor Nunn was establishing one such legend in the shape of his *Macbeth* he was also grasping the nettle of another, namely Clifford Williams' production of *The Comedy of Errors* a decade earlier with Alec McCowen, Diana Rigg and Nunn's own wife, Janet Suzman.

What Trevor Nunn did in 1976 was to overturn pre-conceptions and make the play into a musical. He wasn't the first to do this, Rodgers and Hart having based their 1938 show *The Boys from Syracuse* on *The Comedy of Errors.* In Nunn's version, however, the songs were culled from Shakespeare's text, with music by Guy Woolfenden. Gusto was added by John Napier's set and Gillian Lynne's choreography.

The director explained his motives in an interview with John Higgins published in *The Times* in September 1976: 'I was a great admirer of Clifford's production. It was definitive in *commedia dell'arte* style, but after three highly successful revivals it's time to do something different. The play has never been of the slightest interest to the scholars, and rightly so. It's a work of no intellectual pretension, and my task must be to honour its intention, which is primarily to entertain. The play is beautifully constructed; it's the first modern farce . . . But a great deal of the verbal comedy is remote from us now . . . I decided to tackle the problem by reworking the difficult areas into songs for which the RSC's musical director Guy Woolfenden has written a score . . . I can't imagine the author in question objecting to some co-workers in the theatre trying to make his entertainment more accessible.'

Shakespeare's 'co-workers' certainly worked hard to achieve the desired effect, but it was a complex job and it took about a year, that is to say until its appearance in London at the Aldwych, before the summit was reached where cast and audience were able to bask so joyfully.

The stage was transformed into a fantastic and colourful Mediterranean bazaar where everything seemed to be on sale, from T-shirts and baubles through food and drink to the occasional member of the Ephesus populace, all in agreeable holiday fashion. The Antipholus twins were played by Roger Rees and Mike Gwilym, the Dromios by Michael Williams and Nickolas Grace. Luciana, sister to Judi's Adriana, was originally played by Francesca Annis, Pippa Guard later taking over. Richard Griffiths' comic potential was brought out in his portrayal of 'An Officer' of Keystone Cops dimensions, while the equally comical John Woodvine played Pinch with enormous zest as a clownish quack. On the last night, he inserted the old joke about not being a good doctor because he didn't have the *patients* by clamping his hand over Judi's mouth as she was about to speak her lines.

The song and dance routines gradually eased their way into the dialogue as the company sharpened up its timing. Judi dazzled in this respect; movement, pauses, expressions and business — notably with a well-aimed soda syphon — all coming together perfectly. Roger Rees again found close proximity to her performance to be an exhilarating, educative experience: 'She does a double-take like a humming-bird, so fast, so multiple; usually accompanied by a little hand on her chest as if to say, "It's nothing to do with me." It was a privilege to be near her Adriana.'

The exhuberance reached acrobatic proportions — most excitingly in Nickolas Grace's display of athletic stunts — without ever toppling the production's highly disciplined structure. Above all, Trevor Nunn had remained faithful to the life-enhancing spirit of Shakespeare's work, captured in the play's closing couplet:

> We came into this world like brother and brother:
> And now let's go hand in hand, not one before another.

For Messrs Nunn and Woolfenden this was a cue for a jubilant musical climax which had the cast coming down from the stage singing 'let's go hand in hand' and sending the audience home happy.

The RSC ended 1976 in Stratford with *King Lear*, the result of an unusual collaboration between three directors: Trevor Nunn, John Barton and Barry Kyle. Lear was played by Donald Sinden, his daughters by Barbara Leigh-Hunt (Goneril), Judi Dench (Regan), and Marilyn Taylerson (Cordelia). Tony Church was Gloucester; Bob Peck, Kent; Robin Ellis, Edmund; Michael Pennington, Edgar; John Woodvine, Cornwall; and Richard Durden, Albany. The Fool was played by Michael Williams in a manner for which he was much praised.

As with Lady Macbeth, Judi approached the part of

Regan in a spirit of determined refusal to see her as a totally evil, one-dimensional character. Indeed, the mainspring for the whole collaborative enterprise was an impulse to make the play *believable*. What was regarded as a 'pantomime' reading, with Cordelia interchangeable with Cinderella and Goneril and Regan with the Ugly Sisters, was to be studiously avoided. And the approach was even-handed. As Judi says, 'I bet I could find something pretty irritating about Cordelia!'

The company's motives were anything but iconoclastic towards what is after all one of the grandest works of art. Rather they were treating it consistently with the general RSC view — and the specific Judi Dench understanding — that Shakespeare is the great *humanist* writer.

In *King Lear* the gulf between the sexes is as vast and overpowering as in any literary work. Significantly there is no mother to bridge the chasm between this tempestuous and — most markedly in the Nunn/Barton/Kyle production — temperamental father and his three brotherless daughters.

With this background, Judi was concerned to show Regan as other than a merely manipulative, wicked woman. It was not an attempt at rehabilitation, there is no denying the evil of a woman who actively encourages the barbaric blinding of her host. But she wanted to show Regan's character as partly a reaction to her father, something which in performance she signified by a nervous stammer in his presence.

Trevor Nunn, at least, thought the idea and the interpretation brilliant, but it failed to impress on stage and Judi herself became increasingly uncomfortable in the role until eventually she dropped out, feeling 'badly beaten'.

The experience was not, of course, completely lacking in enjoyment, and it was fun having John Woodvine play her husband, as nasty a pair as Cornwall and Regan are: 'We actually found the blinding scene excruciatingly funny. This was because on the first night I suddenly saw John taking an eye out of a concealed paper bag. And when he said, "Out, vile jelly!" it made me laugh because I wasn't prepared for it, an eye being thrown out of paper bag. And the next night, just before we did that same bit I happened to glance up at the set and there was this eye stuck there from the night before. I thought, "before this run is finished that wall is going to be covered in eyes!"

'I had very much wanted the part but in the end resigned myself to giving it back. It's a terrible part to play; it starts downhill and proceeds further in the same direction.'

Judi's original concept had been bold and imaginative but the production as a whole was possibly a little over-wrought, the universal themes and powerful passions a bit constrained by a specifically Victorian setting, part military splendour, part Dickensian squalor. The successes of the production lay in individual pieces of acting, notably by Donald Sinden as a white-uniformed, cigar-smoking, tyrannical Lear, and Michael Williams as an old, infirm and poignant Fool.

The RSC's other nineteenth-century version of Shakespeare that season, *Much Ado About Nothing*, continued on its winning way when it transferred to the Aldwych in the summer of 1977.

Michael Billington, writing in the *Guardian*, called it 'one of the truest and most touching accounts of this play I can remember', and of Judi, with her 'overwhelming' Beatrice: 'I have never seen her better'.

Along with the transfers of *Macbeth* — first to the Warehouse and then the Young Vic — and *The Comedy of Errors*, two further plays which opened in the RSC's London season of 1977–8 were Ibsen's *Pillars of the Community* and Congreve's *The Way of the World*. In the first, Judi played Lona Hessel, in the second, she was Millamant. Both are key parts without being dominating, excessively demanding roles. And both are spirited moral anchors amid the flotsam and jetsam of hypocritical humanity.

Pillars of the Community had been consigned for many years to the scrap-heap of polemical melodrama. In fact there had been no professional production in London since that by Milton Rosmer in 1926, which interestingly featured Charles Laughton and later Felix Aylmer in the secondary roles of Rummel and Dr Roerlund. Half a century on, and a hundred years after the play had been written, John Barton made such neglect appear criminal. For here was a substantial drama, amply and compellingly showing Ibsen's deep-seated concern with the essentially false and unjust character of conventional bourgeois life, as well as more specific issues such as women's rights and the malpractices of unscrupulous merchant-shipping magnates (in the latter of which he was influenced by the English Member of Parliament, Samuel Plimsoll).

Ian McKellen played the main character, Karsten Bernick, the leading citizen in a prosperous little coastal community. He is an obviously successful man, a shipowner, whose house – in which the action is set – echoes with honest endeavour and moral precepts. But Bernick not only has a guilty past but also a fatal moral weakness with regard to the present conduct of his business. Lona Hessel is the disruptive life force, the breath of fresh air who, upon her arrival, symbolically pulls aside the curtains, and who brings back Bernick's past and dismantles the illusion of his present.

Judi found it satisfying to play a character who is disapproved of by those around her, an individual – whistling and wearing red boots – who strides into a prim and cloying society so ready to be scandalized. And although she was not this time on an equal footing with Ian McKellen, whose role was the important, pivotal one, there was once again a quick, instinctive understanding between them in rehearsal and performance.

Where Ibsen's tale is meticulously constructed and generally free of glib dialogue, Congreve's most celebrated play positively crackles with rapid-fire raillery with little or no regard for structure or plot. Though *The Way of the World* sparkles in places and entertains in parts, overall it is undeniably wanting and does nothing to challenge the verdict of the *Cambridge History of English Literature* upon this playwright: 'At no time in his life did Congreve learn to tell a story on the stage.' His appeal lies in the glittering surface qualities of *badinage,* costume, flourish and intrigue.

While Millamant is the focus of much attention, she is again not a commanding figure. She is a brisk, laughing butterfly of a character and really it was a romp for Judi. She 'enjoyed every single second' of the limited run of fifteen performances – at the end of which she was still trying to fathom the plot. Her lover, Mirabell, was played by Michael Pennington, and the presence in the cast of such arch jokers as Roger Rees and John Woodvine ensured plenty of on-stage fun and games.

This is not to say that the director, John Barton, allowed matters to slide into loose indulgence. Although the play is a farrago, it does have a satirical cutting edge and the RSC aimed to reveal a cross-section of an affected, acquisitive society. For the play to carry any moral force, though, the relationship between Mirabell and Millamant needs to have a steadiness which will offset the general flightiness.

In this respect some were convinced and some were not. The *Guardian*'s Michael Billington saw Mirabell and Millamant as 'people genuinely in love . . . Judi Dench plays Millamant as a woman in whom sincerity is bursting to get out . . . And this beautiful performance is well matched by Michael Pennington's Mirabell, which has an unusual gravitas and moral weight.'

John Peter, on the other hand, writing in *The Sunday Times*, described Pennington's Mirabell as 'a hunter . . . one whose feelings have been tainted by greed . . . There's not a trace of affection in the air. Judi Dench's Millamant is a dainty preying mantis.' But he too vouched for the quality of their performances — 'among the best I've seen in this theatre.'

Between April 1978 and April 1979, Judi made five television films. The stage versions, slightly adapted, of *Macbeth* and *Comedy of Errors* were rendered on the small screen and she appeared in three other major productions. At the end of this period she returned to the stage, and Stratford, to play Imogen in David Jones' production of *Cymbeline*.

If Lady Macbeth and Beatrice had been personal triumphs within triumphant productions, Judi's Imogen stood out as a personal success in a production generally held to be clumsy and inconsistent.

In the 1980 *Shakespeare Survey*, Roger Warren wrote that 'Judi Dench's Imogen was irresistible even in its tiniest details . . . but it lost some of its beautifully sharp-witted effect because even a great actress needs something to play to.' J.C. Trewin largely echoed these sentiments, declaring of Judi — 'the Imogen of our dreams' — that 'she conquered me so purely at the première that I was in danger of imagining David Jones' production to be better than it was.'

In *Cymbeline*, Shakespeare seems to be working out themes more economically and effectively employed in the last great romances which were to follow. A rich, poetic but untidy narrative, with sanguine and spectacular effects, it is notoriously problematical to stage. It is a long play with a rambling plot and its audiences need to be alert, receptive and non-sceptical; its actors, as Judi emphasized in a magazine interview at the time, alert and physically fit: 'I have to feel very well for *Cymbeline* now, because it's a really driving thing. For Imogen, the engine must be constantly ticking over.'

So it was a well-tuned Judi Dench who negotiated her way around such difficult passages as that in Act IV when Imogen awakens to confront a headless corpse, believing it to be that of her husband. In the event, the celebrated catch in the voice served wonderfully to arrest the catch of nervous laughter in the audience at the dumping of the corpse on stage.

Set on a simple, almost bare stage, designed by Christopher Morley, this was an unfussy, level-headed production but one which failed to surrender to the mystical, fairy-tale enticement of Shakespeare's verse and story. One critic, John Elsom of *The Listener*, concentrated his frustration on the verse speaking and the interaction between actors, writing of Judi and Ben Kingsley, who played Iachimo, that they 'were best when left alone to find their own readings of their lines without interruption either from the director or other actors.'

This was actually somewhat ironic since David Jones had in fact left the company in order to take up an appointment in America and they had fended keenly for themselves, working overtime in the knowledge that the proceedings needed tightening.

Besides Judi and Ben, the cast included Roger Rees (who played Posthumus), Bob Peck, Heather Canning, Patrick Godfrey, and Geoffrey Hutchings. Jeffery Dench, having already played his sister's uncle in *London Assurance*, was here cast in the title role as her father.

While Judi was appearing at Stratford in *Cymbeline* Michael was away in Newcastle for eleven weeks, but they managed to get to see each other most Sundays. Since that time they have consciously tried to arrange their working schedules to cause the minimum disturbance to family life. Each has vowed not to take on long runs abroad. For this reason Judi turned down the chance to go to America with the National Theatre company in 1983 in Pinter's *A Kind of Alaska* despite the almost guaranteed Broadway success and adulation it would have brought her.

One day at Stratford in 1979, during the run of *Cymbeline*, Trevor Nunn and Judi passed each other in the corridor. The following conversation ensued, Trevor speaking first:

'I've had an idea. I think we should revive O'Casey's *Juno and the Paycock* and I think you should play it.'

'Of course, I've *heard* of the play. Tell me about it.'

'I'm asking you to play a careworn, distressed, 42-year-old, working-class housewife.'

'Do you have a copy of the play?'

'Yes. I'll lend it to you.'

The following morning in the green room, Judi walked up to Trevor Nunn and said, 'The answer's yes.'

The part of the strutting 'Paycock', Jack Boyle, was to be taken by Norman Rodway, who was born in Ireland to English parents and who has a natural, easy Irish accent. Everybody else in the cast was Irish, several of them having acted together in Dublin. Judi's task was not only to integrate with that company but to convince as the centre of it. She wanted very badly to get this one right for Olave, whose own Dublin modulations were of course a guide — though not a model, as she came from a different class and background to Juno.

Judi feared she would be struggling at a disadvantage, an interloper among a group of Irish actors proudly performing a piece of their literary heritage. But she rapidly developed a tremendous affinity to the role. She was helped by a series of improvised conversations she had with Dearbhla Molloy, the young actress who played her daughter.

These were extra-curricular, unofficial. Part of the organized preparation consisted of various research projects which Trevor Nunn set for all the actors and actresses. Each of them was given some aspect of the play's historical and social setting to read about and then give a talk on to the rest of the company. Topics included such matters as the physical and living conditions of families in Dublin tenements in the 1920s; the Irish Civil War; and the employment situation among the men. Judi's project was on the nature and means of the payment of rent in apartments like that of the Boyle family and the domestic life of the women. It took a day and a half for everyone's findings to be discussed. This also helped Judi to feel assimilated into O'Casey's Irish world.

More particularly, the company created its own inner world and a family atmosphere developed, with no sense of hierarchy. Anybody felt able to say anything to anybody. Judi took on more and more of an Irish identity as time passed and, drawing on her lineage, joked with the rest of the cast as to who was the most Irish.

O'Casey's play, if sensitively produced, conveys a warm humanity at the heart of a world in ruins, though it is capable of melodramatic interpretation with Irish quaintness laid on thickly. Nunn's production, opening at the Aldwych in October 1980, a hundred years after O'Casey's birth, was never in any danger of falling into that trap. From the opening scene it was both poetic and precisely observed.

There was one moment when three or four of the characters on stage were called upon to look out through a window in the 'wall' facing the audience. The miming and the grouping involved in this action blended with the dialogue like the exquisite harmony of a string quartet combining at the peak of its powers in the finest music. Just a brief sequence, but an emblem of a great stage production.

The set, designed by John Gunter, was detailed and realistic, with a tenement skyline backcloth. The room in which the action mainly occurred was stark, shabby and faded but with the all-important hearth and armchair as symbols of the domain in which 'Captain' Jack Boyle could swaggeringly romanticize his manhood and pontificate about the 'world in a terrible state of chassis' with his acolyte, Joxer Daly (played by John Rogan).

In all this Judi was the hub, the mother figure who had to pull things together, cajole her husband, condole her neighbour, protect her daugher and mourn her son. There was lightness, in the form of lilting Irish conversation, impromptu singing during a party, and the playing of a mistakenly acquired gramophone, but all in the desperate context of poverty, street bloodshed and drunken escapism. Her achievement was that she appeared to occupy the central position absolutely naturally. She inhabited the role of Mrs Boyle as surely as Juno herself inhabited that tragic household.

As with her Beatrice, her character seemed to have antecedents. And even more than her Beatrice, perhaps even more than her Lady Macbeth or indeed anything she had ever done, Judi's Juno was *rooted* in the particular circumstances of O'Casey's tragedy.

It is frequently asserted that too much regard is paid to theatrical criticism in the press (it is also asserted with equal vehemence by some that the critics have no influence) and that directors and actors gear themselves up too much for first nights. Certainly the RSC has not been free of such an accusation. Actors, it is said, set too much store by good or bad notices, although many if not most actors will say that they don't pay any attention to reviews — rather like politicians who say they have no truck with opinion polls. Even so, the actor who doesn't collect his favourable press cuttings is a rare animal (Judi is in fact one such rarity).

There is no denying a degree of artificiality to hastily penned summaries of first-night impressions, and probably, with the very occasional exception, the individual critic's views don't count for much. But equally, where the general tide of professional opinion flows in one direction, there is no denying the boost or damage — to box-office and morale — felt by the company in question.

The Royal Shakespeare Company is not so reliant on good press notices as most. Apart from its subsidized status, its established reputation, the inevitable inclusion of 'star' names and its institutional standing with tourists in Stratford always ensure it an audience. But it still has to deliver the goods, and in an imperfect world the critics' published opinions are the measure of whether the transaction is adequate or faulty, superb or disastrous. Moreover, praise or blame are as feeding or fasting to the man or woman who chooses to earn a living by public display.

So, the company members were considerably buoyed up by the positive critical response to, for example, *Much Ado About Nothing, Macbeth* and *The Comedy of Errors*. For each of these productions the praise was high. Inevitably, though, there were reservations, qualms and dissensions among the views expressed. About *Juno and the Paycock*, however, all critics spoke with one admiring voice. For Trevor Nunn, it was his only production which he could remember receiving universal acclaim. For Judi Dench, it brought massive acknowledgement for her status as one of the great English actresses of the day.

In *The Financial Times*, B.A. Young wrote of 'a new voice, a new face, new movements, the familiar Miss Dench entirely submerged in the middle-aged Dublin housewife, victim of grinding poverty and a feckless husband. It is a triumphant success.' The *Guardian*'s Michael Billington responded to the by now totally matured quality of sheer humanity in her acting: 'Judi Dench's Juno is a wonderful blend of exhaustion and despair. Tiny gestures like a cynical lift of the eyes when the Captain starts his seafaring nonsense speak volumes; yet there is also in the very way she plumps the cushions, stokes the fire, or makes the breakfast the suggestion of a woman who finds what solace she can in domestic routine.'

John Elsom, writing in *The Listener*, praised the working of the various combinations which went to make up the production — between Judi and Norman, Judi and Dearbhla, and so on — and, by implication, the now highly polished professional combination of this leading actress and this director, whom he saluted as 'the best British director of our time.' In the *Observer*, Robert Cushman highlighted the transition Judi had made as an actress and focused on another piece of teamwork, this time with Marie Kean, who played the bereaved Mrs Tancred. Of Judi he wrote, 'underlying everything in her performance is an immense practicality; everybody's sweetheart is now everybody's mother. As for her last familiar lament, I doubt that any other actress could re-think or rephrase it to greater effect. It is a reprise, remember, and Marie Kean who does it the first time is a hard act to follow. Between them they give the play some of the grandeur of *The Trojan Women*.'

Byran Robertson wrote in the *Spectator*'s theatre column: 'I hope it will be clear by now that I am describing one of the great evenings in the English theatre ... Judi Dench's performance as Juno is beyond praise. Watchful, rueful, eager for hope, realistic, continually crushed by circumstances, Ms Dench commands our total belief but plays perfectly with the rest of the company.' Views, all of them shared by the public and by other professional colleagues, for whom James Fenton's conclusion to his *Sunday Times* review is accurate representation: 'Excellent stuff. Excellent!'

Judi was heaped with awards for her performance. She won the *Society of West End Theatres* Best Actress Award, the *Evening Standard* Drama Award for best actress, the *Plays and Players* Award for best actress and the *Variety Club* Actress of the Year Award.

Before the production of *Juno* had opened, Trevor and Judi, knowing this was a new departure for her, had decided to have lunch together, the day after the opening, to talk about it. In the event, in a tiny restaurant well out of the public eye, the mood was festive. Yet, as the plates were cleared away, Judi's eyes filled with tears. Trevor asked, 'What is it?' and she released the emotion of her realization that this major landmark of her career had been approached so impulsively on her part.

'I've never admitted this to you before', she told him, 'but when I said to you I'd do the play, I hadn't read it. I just went home and said to myself, "Trevor wants me to do this play, so I'll do it." An astonished Trevor Nunn was now in on the secret, shared by Frank Hauser and one or two others, of Judi's apparently whimsical 'method' of accepting parts.

It had taken a lot of dedicated but demanding labour for the *Juno* company to reach the standard it did, and the depressing situation of the play's events sometimes got to the performers. One day in rehearsal when Judi was feeling a little dispirited she asked Trevor to lift some of the gloom of the Dublin tenement by casting her in the bubbly, commercial production he was then piecing together with the composer, Andrew Lloyd Webber, a musical comedy based on T.S. Eliot's humorous collections of poems, *Old Possum's Book of Practical Cats*. Fed-up and tired, Judi asked Trevor if she could play 'one of those old cats that sits on a wall.' To her surprise he said, 'Yes, you can play that old cat' and a few days later rang her at home with a firm offer of two parts in the show — Jennyanydots, the Gumbie Cat who 'sits and sits and sits', and Grizabella.

Judi went to see Trevor and Andrew at Andrew's house, where he played her the score on the piano and they both told her the story line. With some apprehension about having to attend dance classes, she accepted. Dance was in fact to prove her undoing, though not in the way she might have envisaged in the early stages when choreographer Gillian Lynne used to say 'Brian and Judi, don't try this one.' 'Brian' was Brian Blessed, an old chum from *Z-Cars* days, when Judi had played a young criminal tearaway to whom Brian's character, PC 'Fancy' Smith, had indeed taken a fancy.

The principal dancer of *Cats* — as the show came to be called — was the ballet star Wayne Sleep. Judi was rehearsing with Sleep one Tuesday lunchtime in the Duke's Hall, Chiswick, having just returned from a poetry recital she had given with John Stride in the English speaking theatre in Vienna at the weekend. Suddenly there was a sound like a pistol shot and Judi felt an intense pain at the back of her right leg.

She was driven by Roger Bruce, the *Cats* company manager, to the Remedial Dance Centre in Harley Street where she was examined by the therapist Charlotte Arnold. She in turn referred Judi to a surgeon, Justin Howse. Roger drove her straight to Howse in Rickmansworth. He looked at the leg and told her, 'You've snapped your Achilles' tendon in half and I need to operate on it in the morning.' Judi asked him how long recovery would take and he said, 'Six weeks'. She burst into tears and was taken home by the indefatigable Roger Bruce.

The next day the operation was performed at the Fitzroy Nuffield Clinic. A day or so later Trevor Nunn and Andrew Lloyd Webber came to visit. They still wanted her to play Grizabella and promised to hold up production until she was ready to appear in a plaster. This was a jolly occasion and the press were on hand to record it, a picture of a smiling Judi, Andrew and Trevor appearing in the dailies.

Judi was discharged after two weeks and went back to rehearsals. She worked on her song, watched a studio run-through of the show and then went off to Charlecote for a recuperative weekend. The following Monday morning she went to the New London theatre, where *Cats* was to be staged, for the choreography of the opening number in which the cast all clamber up ramps. Judi took a step up the ramp and fell, cutting her knees. She knew then that she wouldn't be able to do the show.

She went to the dressing-room, collected her things and, without saying a word to anyone, took a taxi home. She told Michael that she couldn't go on with it, and with his encouragement she rang Roger Bruce. A little later Trevor phoned back and Judi's withdrawal from *Cats* was official.

Michael was about to return to Paris where he was filming *Enigma*, whose director Jeannot Szwarc, hearing the news about Judi, suggested to Michael that he brought Judi and Finty with him. Apart from anything else this would mean Judi would be out of London when *Cats* opened without her. It was a grateful if subdued Williams family who flew off that week to France.

Judi did then receive one very good piece of news. She was offered a part in *Smiley's People* the television series based on John Le Carré's book and starring Alec Guinness, a personal idol of hers. She was out of plaster but her leg hadn't really healed. Soon after the French trip she was rehearsing for another television play with Anton Rodgers, who, happening to glance down at her leg, said 'Judi, you've absolutely no right to be here.' She turned her head to see a trickle of greenish matter along the back of her ankle.

Since her discharge from the clinic Judi had been attending the Remedial Dance Centre for sessions, including laser treatment, with Charlotte Arnold, and that was where she went from the television studio. The festering was not a good sign and Charlotte Arnold sent Judi back to Justin Howse. He took one look and said he'd have to open up the leg again, she could continue with the present television play with Anton Rodgers but *Smiley's People* was out.

That evening Judi and Michael went to a reception given by the Stars' Organization for Spastics. She felt very low. They met John and Mary Mills who took them out to the St James' club for dinner, which cheered Judi a little.

The next morning she was about to leave for rehearsal when the telephone rang. It was Justin Howse. He said,

'Look, I've been up all night worrying about this. I think you ought to come in today.'

So she had to ring the director of the TV play, Jon Amiel, and tell him she'd have to drop out unavoidably. Anna Cropper stepped in at short notice and the play, a kind of surreal drama called *Preview*, was saved.

Judi entered the Nightingale BUPA clinic in Lisson Grove where she stayed for five weeks. She was scheduled for another operation but the night before it was due to take place, her wound burst open like a boil. Justin Howse came to see her and said what had happened was miraculous — the trouble had cleared itself. It was now just a question of a gradual healing process with Judi lying with her feet suspended.

She sewed, read and slept a lot and watched the Wimbledon tennis championships on the television. She had a stream of visitors and was allowed out one night for a surprise birthday party for Michael which she had organized at the Cavalry Club. The nurses would bring her tea and biscuits at one o'clock in the morning, and during the daytime Charlotte Arnold would come in and give her exercises and physiotherapy. This continued after Judi had left the clinic.

Once *Cats* had opened and firmly established itself, Judi felt better about the whole business. Eventually, on 9 September, she went along to see the show. It was frustrating to sit in the stalls and she was itching to join in, but she loved it. Her understudy, Myra Sands, had taken over the Gumbie Cat and Grizabella was played by Elaine Page. Alec Guinness had telephoned to express his sympathy for her injury, some powerful television drama lay ahead and there were overtures from the National Theatre, where her old boss Peter Hall was in charge. Life wasn't so bad. Some lines from an altogether different poem by the author upon whose work *Cats* had been based might almost have been addressed to Judi:

You are invulnerable, you have no Achilles' heel,
You will go on, and when you have prevailed
You can say: at this point many a one has failed.

8 National matters and private concerns

When Peter Hall telephoned Judi early in 1982 to ask her to appear in *The Importance of Being Earnest* she suddenly appreciated the old cliché about the heart sometimes 'skipping a beat'. Hers did just that, she says — 'it stood still for a moment. When he said *The Importance* I thought that he was talking about Gwendolen. I couldn't contemplate the possibility that he was asking me to play Lady Bracknell.' But Lady Bracknell it was, offering Judi a potentially controversial début at the National Theatre.

Michael was away at the time of Hall's phone call and Judi, having indicated her qualified agreement, needed some weighty encouragement to dispel her misgivings. She spoke to Peggy Ashcroft, who told her she was mad to do it, and to Trevor Nunn, who thought it a wonderful idea.

The main obstacle was, of course, the profound imprint of Edith Evans upon the play. Peter Hall was anxious to erase this as far as possible to look afresh at Wilde's classic. And, like Trevor Nunn with *Macbeth* he was conscious that his decision to cast Judi of all people in such a role would be criticized: 'People are always comfortable with received opinions. Lady Bracknell is in her forties from the evidence of the text. Judi was obvious casting. Edith Evans was quite a young girl when she played her first. She went on playing her for years until people thought of her as a battleaxe in her seventies with a 19-year-old daughter.'

Peter Hall steered Judi towards his concept of the play. Hers would be a decidedly young Lady Bracknell, vying with her daughter. In this line of thought, her statement that she despises illness is linked to the phenomenon of the absent, ever-ill Lord Bracknell, for him to be dismissed beyond her interests, which instead lie in the company and concerns of the play's young men.

A new company was assembled for the production: Nigel Havers and Martin Jarvis as Algy and Jack, Zoe Wanamaker and Elizabeth Garvie as Gwendolen and Cecily, Anna Massey and Paul Rogers as Prism and Chasuble, and it was to play in repertory with three short pieces by Harold Pinter, gathered together under the title of *Other Places*. These were to be staged at the Cottesloe, the National Theatre's small auditorium, with Peter Hall again directing.

Two of the three playlets were new: the slight, tricksy *Victoria Station* and the main work *A Kind of Alaska* in which Judi was offered the key part. For once, she read the script, and it captivated her. She read it through at a sitting and accepted the part immediately. It was a most exacting role and rehearsals would be a strain; but first she had to cope with those, hardly less demanding, for the Wilde play.

It took many rehearsals for Judi to still her trepidation. Each time something didn't work smoothly Judi would address Peter Hall along the lines of, 'This is why I'm not right for the part', and he could calm and reassure her, until one day he reacted differently, replying, 'I never want you to say that to me again.' And she never did.

At one crucial stage he gave her a fortnight off and she, Michael and Finty went camping in Scotland. It was a rather alarming proposition, two weeks complete break from the working ambience, but it enabled her to relax and to come back better equipped psychologically for the role. She took a copy of the play with her and built up an image of Lady Bracknell for herself. With the influence of her remote Argyllshire surroundings, she was able to refine that image to a sharp definition: her model for Lady Bracknell was to be Margaret, Duchess of Argyll.

With Judi cast as Lady Bracknell, the National Theatre production of *The Importance of Being Earnest* — opening at the Lyttleton in September 1982 followed by an autumn provincial tour — was awaited eagerly. There was a high demand for tickets in anticipation both of a cherished, familiar piece and of an unfamiliar treatment of it. Theatregoers found it hard to envisage lovable Judi Dench in the role of the modern stage's most fearsome gorgon. They wondered how her relatively youthful Lady Bracknell would shape up to convention. As Robert Cushman, the *Observer*'s theatre critic, put it, 'Really, we were there to hear how she would say "a handbag".'

Actually, it was said with a somewhat quieter astonishment than that of Edith Evans in John Gielgud's famous filmed version. Judi incorporated her retort into a more generalized, though still haughty interrogation of Jack. Playing it, Judi was very aware of the audience's tense air of expectation: 'After the line, people in the audience would say "ohh" disappointedly and shuffle in their seats making it pretty obvious that they felt it had hardly been worth coming.'

Although there had been a couple of recent stagings of *The Importance* which had restored a long-forgotten fourth act, Sir Peter opted for the standard three-act version. The play's cast-iron structure and epigrammatic dialogue proved resistant to an all-out naturalism and the production could do no more than dampen down some of the Victorian excesses and yield to the inherent comic sparkle of the piece.

But there was no desire to reject the essential spirit of the play. What Hall did was to individualize the younger characters in particular, supplementing their familiarly polished exchanges with recognizable human traits. Thus, awkwardness, anxiety or aggression, for example, were treated as real, not feigned for effect. It was a difficult balance — the gains in human interest often resulted in corresponding losses in theatrical entertainment — but Wilde's dramatically concise wit was ultimately communicated.

As for Lady Bracknell, her renowned loftiness was channelled into Judi's expert way with words. Her apparently total command of situations reflected her command of the language rather than inbred self-importance. The famous barbs and arrant aphorisms in tribute to the trivial rolled off Judi's tongue at a cracking pace. Her disdain was not all icy; it issued from a woman of some sensual warmth, indicated by such details as the placing of her hand on Algernon's knee as she spoke to him.

This flesh-and-blood humanity was the source of the one quibble in an appreciation by the critic whose comments

about Judi's very first professional performance had so injured her: Richard Findlater. In the intervening quarter of
a century he had come to acknowledge fully the subtlety
and stature of that once raw Ophelia.

Reviewing *The Importance of Being Earnest* for *Plays
and Players* magazine, Findlater wrote, 'For Judi Dench's
performance as Lady Bracknell I have almost nothing but
praise, in abundance . . . She is formidably funny, with
finger-tip control of nuclear comic energy; needing only to
remove her spectacles when she comes to the notorious
hurdle of the handbag line. Here is a definitive Lady Bracknell in her own kind, to match Dame Edith's in power, if
not in extravagance, and perhaps to surpass it in humanity.
With a touch *less* humanity, she will be just about perfect.'

A Kind of Alaska was inspired by a book by Oliver
Sacks called *Awakenings*, a curiosity in that it won for
Sacks the 1974 Hawthornden Literary Prize despite being
in essence a medical book. Its subject matter was the
spread of a strange sleeping sickness earlier this century
which kept its victims in a perpetual coma when it didn't
kill them outright. Fifty years later a drug was developed
which suddenly released the surviving sufferers.

In Pinter's play Judi played Deborah, a woman in her
forties who fell prey to such a disease while a teenager and
who now faces the trauma of recovery. Paul Rogers played
her doctor, Anna Massey her sister.

Passionately committed to the role, Judi was nonetheless
very frightened by *Alaska*. As the rehearsal stage passed
into the preview stage, Judi all but broke down one evening
as the director was giving the actors their notes. Distraught,
she appealed to him, 'Peter, you've got to help me' and he
succeeded in calming her down, telling her to relax in the
knowledge she was tackling it in the right way.

But there were times during performance when both
Judi and Peter felt she had lost her grip on the part,
though she always got it back. She was partly inspired by
a fatalistic notion that came to her on the first night at a
point where Deborah rises from her bed to cross the room
very gingerly towards a table. As she was making this
difficult manoeuvre across the stage she thought about *Cats*,
her snapped Achilles' tendon and her hospitalization. 'This

is why that happened to me', she thought, 'because, like Deborah, I had to learn to walk again. Somehow we don't realize how remarkable a thing it is to be able to walk.'

She believed, accurately enough, that had it not been for her enforced withdrawal from *Cats* she would not have been able to perform this part as well as she did. That she did perform it well, and indeed that it was an all-round success, was indisputable. Both the *Standard* and *Drama* magazine, the journal of the British Theatre Association, named her Best Actress in their annual awards for 1982, while Paul Rogers and Anna Massey picked up *Drama* prizes for Best Supporting Actor and Actress. Pinter's play won the Best New Play award, a rare accolade for a one-act drama.

All the greater, therefore, was Judi's astonishment, anger and resentment when she, Paul and Anna later became casualties of the much publicized row between Sir Peter Hall and Harold Pinter. It was planned to record a video of the National's production of *A Kind of Alaska* and on the strength of that Judi signed only a limited, four-month contract for her next stage play, *Pack of Lies*. However, with the publication in 1983 of Peter Hall's diaries, a rift occurred between the writer and the director of *A Kind of Alaska*. Pinter objected strongly to Hall's diary references to the break-up of Pinter's marriage to Vivien Merchant and his subsequent coming together with Lady Antonia Fraser. Working projects on which the two men were to collaborate were abandoned, including the *Alaska* video.

Harold Pinter wrote to Judi telling her they would not be going ahead with the original plans. Peter Hall remained silent. A video was eventually made but with a new cast and crew. Judi's role, Deborah, was taken by Dorothy Tutin, who herself wrote to Judi regretting the situation.

Judi has yet to get over her dismay at such 'cavalier, casual and perfunctory' treatment. It is probably the only episode in her entire theatrical career about which she feels any strong and lingering bitterness.

Working at the National put Judi in the interesting position of being able to compare it from the inside with the RSC. At first she certainly found them two very different places

— 'as different as Stratford is from London. In Stratford the theatre is the focal point with very little to distract you from it. In London you are pulled all ways and it's quite difficult to have that kind of togetherness where you don't just come to the theatre, get ready and go on, but you arrive well before time, settle yourself and see how everyone is.

'At the National it is like a little city within a city. Three auditoriums and so many people. You can't get to know everybody and create that company thing. But on your own production you can build up an inner company sense — as we did on *Importance* and *Alaska*.

'I like the building very much. I think it's perfectly easy to find your way around. The Cottesloe, though is quite deceiving acoustically. It's not as small as you think, and in *Alaska* I had a lot of difficulty.'

Now that the RSC too has its own concrete temple in London, such comparisons are perhaps even more pertinent: 'I think the Barbican Theatre is terrific inside and the piazza is marvellous, but I have to say that I don't like the building. The National doesn't give you as cold and "concrete" a feeling as the Barbican does. I like anything that is warm. Concrete is a non-sympathetic surface and the Barbican is a concrete jungle. But I do like the theatre and it was very exciting to do the acoustic tests there with Michael and Ian McKellen and Alan Howard.'

The 'company thing' Judi enjoyed during *The Importance of Being Earnest* and *A Kind of Alaska* was fortified by the provincial tour, on which she found a close friend in Anna Massey. But the happiness of those productions was marred for Judi from the outset by her mother's illness.

Judi had watched Olave gradually deteriorate after Reg's death, which had exacted an enormous emotional toll. This, coupled with the natural effects of advancing years, had clipped the wings of an exceptionally active and spirited woman. Her eyesight had steadily faded and all the knitting, appliqué work and reading she was wont to do had been abandoned.

She was born at the end of the nineteenth century and, as she and the twentieth century progressed into their seventies, she developed a tendency suddenly to go blank in mid-conversation. This culminated in a stroke which paralysed her right side and removed her power of speech, just at the time that Judi was embarking upon her work with the National Theatre.

Though weighed down, Judi was able to maintain a disciplined attitude, not merely in the theatre but also in the London Weekend Television studios, where she and Michael were filming the comedy series, *A Fine Romance*. It was there, on Tuesday 15 February at around 6 p.m. just as they were to record an episode of the show, that Judi and Mike received a call from Warwickshire. Olave was dying. Judi dug deep into her professional and spiritual reserves to go out and face the audience and make them laugh. It was the hardest thing she had ever had to do, but it didn't show.

Immediately after the recording, Judi and Mike sped up the motorway towards Charlecote to be at Olave's bedside. Jeff had already been there a few days and they sat with her each day until eventually she died on Sunday 20 February, at lunchtime. She was eighty-four.

Prior to that time Judi had an inordinate fear of death. Despite her conviction that there exists 'a divinity which shapes our ends', she could never bring herself to contemplate the ending of any human life. Even talk of the possibility of an after-life upset her greatly. On one occasion when she and Olave were having dinner in Stratford with Joseph McCulloch, Judi cried throughout the meal because the conversation had turned to the subject of after-life.

Her feelings in this regard had to some extent been moulded by the experience, some years earlier, of losing a disproportionate number of young friends and acquaintances through death. Three young men she had been brought up with in York, all doctors' sons, had died within a short time of each other, John Mackenzie of leukaemia, Anthony McGarrigle in a car crash on his way home from a cricket match, and David Platts on manoeuvres with the Green Howards in Germany. Each had barely passed the age of twenty.

With her mother's death, much more than her father's, Judi was forced to face the unavoidable. She had been present throughout the final days and hours and had actually seen her mother die. And with her passing, Judi experienced a hard, sobering feeling that 'the last buffer has gone and now I am the buffer.' Her presence at the bedside and at the funeral and the shared ordeal of grief all overcame Judi's fear because death was no longer the unfair and shocking unknown:

'Since I saw my mother die, this terrible fear has eased. It is frightening and painful but in a way I'm more able to take it. I would have hated her to die without me being there. She knew Jeff and I were there. Peter arrived just before she died and of course had to deal with the medical side of both parents' deaths, and that's much worse.

'After she went — peacefully — Michael said, "I now know the meaning of *and gave up the ghost*." At the funeral I was totally aware that the spirit of my mother was nothing to do with the corpse in that coffin and I was hugely comforted, although I miss her in amazingly painful ways. I find I miss my parents much more deeply as the months go by, and my childhood has become so vivid. I suppose I'm going through a process that many, many people go through.'

Michael confirms that Olave's death brought 'a major reckoning' for Judi in that 'before that, she simply wouldn't discuss death at all', and recalls her reaction when his mother died, almost exactly a year before Olave:

'I should think Jude's grief was even greater than mine because she was grieving on my behalf as well. Her capacity for grief is enormous. I don't think I've seen anybody cry like Jude cried when her own mother died. Perhaps it's because it goes so deep that she doesn't dwell on things of a sad nature.'

Judi's family feelings grew even stronger during this period. To be with them, she unhesitatingly turned down the National Theatre's American tour with *Importance* and *Alaska*, in whose company members she found staunch support. Anna Massey, in particular, became a solid companion when called upon, much as Frank Hauser had, almost twenty years before, when Reg had died. Peter Hall was significantly impressed with Judi's professionalism in the circumstances: 'I knew about her mother's illness and death but Judi is an extremely professional lady, not a creature of moods or indulgence of her own ego.'

The work went on. As did the honours. She won a *Plays and Players* award for her performance and in July 1983 she made a poignant trip home to receive an honorary doctorate of letters from the University of York, to add to the similar recognition accorded her by Warwick University five years earlier.

In 1983, following their successful television teamwork in *A Fine Romance*, Judi and Michael were asked by the production team of Michael Redington, Bernard Sandler and Eddie Kulukundis to appear together in a rather more complex drama, this time on the stage of the Lyric Theatre, Shaftesbury Avenue. This was *Pack of Lies* by Hugh Whitemore, based upon actual events connected with the so-called Portland spy ring of the early 1960s.

At the centre of this was Gordon Lonsdale, who communicated secret information to the Russians via a radio transmitter maintained and operated by an American couple, Peter and Helen Kroger, in an innocuous-looking house in the Middlesex suburb of Ruislip.

Judi and Michael played Barbara and Bob Jackson, neighbours of the Krogers across that Ruislip street, and in real life the parents of journalist Gay Search. The theme of the play, originally conceived by Whitemore for television, is betrayal, not so much in terms of espionage as in relation to friendship, though of course the two are linked, loosely in the spirit of E.M.Forster's celebrated assertion that, faced with a choice, betrayal of one's friend is worse than that of one's country.

The Krogers befriend the Jacksons — the childless Helen Kroger showing special fondness towards the Jacksons' teenage schoolgirl daughter — with a transatlantic breeziness that threatens at times to overwhelm the self-deprecating, slippered-and-cardiganed Jacksons. The very incongruity of the friendship somehow makes the dowdy, dutiful Mrs Jackson value it all the more.

It is disrupted, however, when British Intelligence detects the Krogers' involvement with Lonsdale and ingratiates itself into the Jacksons' home, using it as a look-out post. Bob and Barbara are forced to accept that their friends might be traitors. (All this was put to them in terms of the most refined old-world politeness in Richard Vernon's sharp portrayal of the intelligence chief, Stewart.)

Not only do the Jacksons have to deal with the possibility of the Kroger's treachery but they in turn have to deceive and dissemble to them. It is a double sorrow by which Barbara Jackson is eventually broken.

Besides being teamed with Michael, Judi was reunited professionally in *Pack of Lies* with Barbara Leigh-Hunt, who played Helen Kroger, and Clifford Williams, who directed. Peter Kroger was played by Larry Hoodekoff and the other parts by Elizabeth Bell, Eva Griffith and Penny Rider. A coincidental footnote to the story lay in the fact that when the real Helen and Peter Kroger were arrested in 1961, they were standing outside the Old Vic Theatre looking at a poster advertising *A Midsummer Night's Dream* — with Judi Dench as Hermia and Barbara Leigh-Hunt as Helena.

Barbara Jackson was a difficult character for Judi to enter into. Describing her problems in this regard, she holds up her thumb and forefinger, placing them less than an inch apart to indicate the narrowness of scale in which the character speaks and moves. Mrs Jackson would never, for example, sit with her hands open. And the considerable emotional strain is borne without any natural, easy release. When the truth dawns, Mrs Jackson has to be seen to be devastated but with the shock waves registering internally. Judi tried various ways of doing this during the preview run at the Theatre Royal, Brighton, ranging from absolute immobility to animated sobbing, all the time patiently and reassuringly encouraged by Clifford Williams. They eventually settled on shocked stillness but continued to vary the approach.

The intelligence service's release of the facts of the case to the Jacksons with all the attendant suspicions, is very gradual. To convey this effectively requires skilful dramatic techniques. One device employed by the writer is the use of monologues, whereby each character steps outside of the action to give a personal recollection of the events depicted.

In one such monologue, Mrs Jackson recalls the first sighting, by the woman intelligence officer posted in her home, of the spy Lonsdale, and the house from which, to Barbara's horror, he was apparently emerging:

'I looked out as well . . . *Helen's* door was open — the man appeared.' The sense of weary shock invested by Judi in that word 'Helen's' seemed so very appropriate that, although few people if any in the audience could have known a comparable moment in their own lives, most would have identified with Barbara Jackson's reaction to it as articulated by Judi Dench.

In the main, the play was favoured by the press. Michael Coveney of *The Financial Times* praised 'a remarkable evening: decent in sentiment and, in Clifford Williams' adroit production, powerfully and surprisingly substantial', while the *Daily Mail*'s Jack Tinker called it 'intriguing and ingenious'. Judi received her almost customary paean of tribute (reflected in yet another brace of best actress awards, from *Plays and Players* and the *Society of West End Theatres*) and Michael was also nominated for a Best Actor award. They were now an acknowledged and market-able pairing, a source of delighted satisfaction to Judi, whose modesty about her personal success remains un-dimmed despite nearly three decades of richly-praised achievement. Michael, too, revels in the combination and the thrill of 'racing alongside a thoroughbred'.

It gave an extra edge to their continued appearances to-gether on the poetry recital platform. With such experience they were hardly unused to playing alongside or opposite each other. As recently as October 1981, they were in Shaw's two-hander, *A Village Wooing* for a handful of benefit performances at the little local theatre in Hampstead, the New End. This was directed by Frank Hauser, who also com-piled an anthology piece about the year 1933 which Judi and Mike performed as a support to Shaw's 'comediettina'.

At times the strain of playing Barbara Jackson told on Judi. A doctor was called in more than once and he ex-horted her to rest but she resisted his advice and remained in the cast, without replacement, from the play's opening in October until May when she left to take up other commitments.

Despite the emotional and physical fatigue, Judi felt a professional duty to go on before a public which was filling virtually every house. But in any event she was incapable of simply switching off and relaxing to doctor's orders. As Barbara Leigh-Hunt, a close witness to the pressure Judi was under in *Pack of Lies*, remarked: 'Judi can't rest. She lives every minute of every day. If she's got a spare two hours, she'll do more in those two hours than most people will do in two weeks.'

Having initially experienced such difficulty in taking on the role of Barbara Jackson, once into it Judi became totally immersed. To some extent she brought to Mrs Jackson's pain something of her own pain at the loss of her mother. In the circumstances she spent a lot of time meditating on her personal attitude to human anguish:

'In private life you either keep it to yourself — and sometimes have a breakdown as a result — or you tell somebody, though probably not your nearest and dearest. If I were that worried about something I wouldn't tell Michael, because I know it would worry him. I might unburden myself to Susie [Bodmer] who'd give me good, practical advice.

'I don't think I'm breakdown material, though I did begin to wonder during *Pack of Lies*. Because of the nature of the play, nothing happens except the breakdown of the family. Nothing extraordinary — they're extremely ordinary people — therefore if you don't simulate a breakdown, the play's emotional content is not conveyed. So I had to do it and it got me down a lot. The company was remarkable. Everyone was very jokey and that got me through. But it was very, very taxing. To comfort myself I had to think when the curtain came down that if we were doing *Cymbeline* we'd only be about half-way through and I'd still have to wake up and find my husband's headless body beside me!'

During the run of *Pack of Lies*, the house at Charlecote was sold, Michael's father moving in with his other son Paul and his wife, who had themselves been living in Charlecote for some time, filling the gap left by the deaths of the two mothers.

While looking for a new home in the country, once again focusing their attentions on Warwickshire, Michael and Judi saw advertised in a magazine a splendid-looking unspoilt seventeenth-century house in Surrey, not far from their friends the Bodmers. They decided to combine a visit to Susie and Gerald Bodmer with an inspection of the house. Set in its own grounds in a quiet village, it had five bedrooms, a magnificent open fireplace in the hall and a huge kitchen. Outside, there was a small swimming pool, and a Sussex barn which the owner had actually had transported from Sussex and rebuilt.

In all, it was rambling, comfortable, solid and unpretentious. It seemed a bit too expensive at first, but Mike and Judi fell in love with it and, egged on by Susie Bodmer, they bought it, and, once they had each completed their stints in *Pack of Lies*, spent weeks through the summer of 1984 knocking the place into shape.

Hampstead still provides the base, Charlecote the memories, but now that the family have put down roots in such surroundings, the new country home is likely to prove for Judi — now fifty, at the top of her profession, the mother and the 'buffer' — as rich in association as Heworth Green.

In November 1984 the Royal Shakespeare Company presented *Mother Courage and her Children*, Bertolt Brecht's 'chronicle play of the Thirty Years' War', written in his Scandinavian exile in 1938 and 1939 with all the impetus of outrage and despair at Hitler's spoliation of history and of Germany. It was an exciting vehicle for Judi Dench's return to the company and her first performance on the stage of the Barbican Theatre.

Although the play is a long, well-modulated, anti-war harangue, a sense of triumph at the production's close was not an irreverent sentiment, for this was an artistic triumph, Courage being an unforgettable addition to the list of Judi's greatest roles and Judi herself surely joining the ranks of the great Mother Courages, including Therese Giehse and Helene Weigel.

Even the RSC administration had certain marks of triumph about it, emerging just a little battle-scarred from the production trail. The company had applied to the Brecht estate late in 1982 for the rights to perform *Mother Courage* and was granted them, allowing stewardship for a certain length of time.

Soon afterwards, the Oxford Playhouse, along with the Triumph Apollo production company, applied for a licence to stage the play, having secured Glenda Jackson for the lead. In the meantime, the RSC director Howard Davies had asked Judi to play the part. (He approached her while she was playing Lady Bracknell, thus presenting her with another opportunity to ring the changes in her career.)

The RSC refused to countenance an Oxford production, reasoning that it would be too close geographically to its own theatres — the management was especially concerned about the possibility of a London transfer by Triumph Apollo — but not revealing the identity of its Mother Courage.

The Oxford company reacted bittery and, with Glenda Jackson, conducted a publicity campaign against the RSC, which stood its ground, pointing out that a licence had been granted for a production in Glasgow. For sound commercial reasons, the RSC was not prepared to risk the stealing of its considerable thunder. One can therefore only speculate on the effect of Glenda Jackson's and Judi Dench's rival Mother Courages cheek by jowl in the London theatre.

Much has been made of Brecht's attempt to dampen any sympathetic response to the resourceful, scavenging heroine of *Mother Courage and her Children*. For him, her amoral acquisitiveness is part of the flow of oil which lubricates the great war machine. Yet she offers a titanic challenge for an actress: on stage constantly, a mother struggling against harsh adversity who loses her three children who have been brought forth to the point of action only as a result of her tigerish protection.

In fact, the audience's sympathy is *needed* to make the play work dramatically. And the nightly ovations for Judi Dench constituted a loud declaration of sympathy. Her Mother Courage was not just a profiteer, but a caring parent; not a piece of political fabrication but a human being.

Judi's human warmth was apparent from the start. Chirpy and cockney under a shock of red hair and an enormously heavy greatcoat, she used her body possibly more expressively than ever before. Although her voice conveyed due assertiveness and grit, her movements spoke volumes — a Marceau-like shrug, at times an almost Groucho Marx-like walk, and, memorably, the dropping of her head in order not to betray her anguished recognition of the corpse of her son.

At the end her fight against weariness was something genuine — the sheer hard work involved was staggering. (And this was combined with her appearance as Amy O'Connell in John Barton's studio production of *Waste* by Harley Granville Barker at The Pit.) A great deal of energy was taken up by continuously having to rattle open and closed the various flaps on Courage's caravan-like cart which John Napier had designed to revolve around an awesome set, fringed with smoke and light and a troupe of musicians playing George Fenton's sinewy score.

With robust support from Stephen Moore, Trevor Peacock and Zoe Wanamaker (as Kattrin, Courage's mute daughter), Judi strode the stage — joking here, cajoling there, and of course performing the Brechtian songs (with lyrics by Sue Davies) — like a music-hall star. And, like the very best of music-hall stars, and *pace* Brecht, she expressed her character's foibles in basic human terms with which audiences can identify. As T.S.Eliot wrote in explanation of the 'uniqueness' of the most famous music-hall star of all, Marie Lloyd, 'It was, I think, her capacity for expressing the soul of the people.'

9   Big screen, small screen

That an actress of such rare ability as Judi Dench should have had no real film career to speak of is perhaps remarkable. Mysterious even, given that the industry recognized her as 'Most Promising Newcomer' in 1965 for her performance in *Four in the Morning*, her third film. Since then, contemporaries like Glenda Jackson and Vanessa Redgrave have achieved far greater big-screen prominence.

Judi herself has only recently begun to feel comfortable in the movie medium. Whether this is a cause or an effect of her patchy record to date is difficult to say. What does seem clear, though, is that, whatever misgivings or disappointments she has suffered over this in the past, she has lately arrived at a stage of life where regrets have apparently been eroded by calm, happy acceptance — the perfect quality for the camera.

In this respect, as in so many others, her personal and professional values have coincided. She admires and aspires to economy in acting much more than she ever used to. When Judi appeared in *Hamlet* in 1957 she employed as many signs and devices as she could muster to tell the audience Ophelia was mad. Now she is concerned to pare down her technique as far as possible — to get it 'leaner and leaner and leaner'. And if she discovers a gesture to indicate something — such as madness — about a character, she will use it just once, never flaunt it, and reject it altogether if it doesn't fit naturally into the overall characterization.

In the cinematic context her respect has grown for such old stars as Greta Garbo and James Stewart, and more recently Al Pacino or Dustin Hoffman, who show so few signs of effort on the screen, who have 'worked it all out to a point where they *do* hardly anything — the camera can pick it all up in their eyes.'

To be fair, Judi's attitude to film performers isn't always so analytical. Like so many members of the profession — in contrast to the popular image of the actor or actress as a preening, self-important prima donna — she is frequently star-struck. And when American performers like Paul Newman or Kirk Douglas have, on occasional visits to London, called at her dressing-room after watching a performance, she has reacted with an almost schoolgirl mixture of glee and bashfulness.

Added to what she would describe as a lack of naturalistic technique in earlier days, Judi would ascribe the low-key quality of her film career to her physical appearance. It hasn't been the adulation, the fan letters or the printed praise of her looks that she has taken to heart. Instead, she remembers what she was told at her first film audition a couple of decades or so ago: 'Miss Dench, you have every single thing wrong with your face.'

'I know the way film people look at you,' she says, 'and my appearance is not what they're after. Though there did seem more opportunity in the era of post-kitchen-sink realism — I very nearly got *A Taste of Honey*, but Rita Tushingham just pipped me.

'I haven't really been asked many times. I don't regret not doing more. I don't miss films where they want you to walk into a room just looking the part. In television you can wear a wig; you can look unlike yourself. After all, our business is acting. It angers and bores me when people in the film world just look at you and say, "Oh no, you're not right. Sorry."

'But I do admire good film actors very much. What they can do on a couple of takes is extraordinary. That's not me. Good film actors, I'm sure, do have their complete performances included, but you have to get to that stage of skill. I'm not good at sitting about. Your performance is not whole but made up of bits. The editor and the director have the final say.

'I don't like the instant commitment of film. You do it and that's it. In the theatre you can fool people, change, alter. Make people believe you're tall or whatever — another person. But there's something so frank about film acting.'

Recently, however, Judi has grown less afraid of frankness, in the process revealing, according to film and television director Stephen Frears, with whom she has made *Going Gently* and *Saigon − Year of the Cat*, cinematic qualities akin to those she admires in others: 'She conveys a balance − some inner thing whereby all the parts fit together and I know that if I shoot her, it'll be quite clear what I'm trying to say. You look through the camera and it's easy. Like a sunset. You could do it in five minutes.

'It's a harmonious quality. She has actually to do nothing. She radiates power. Actors have this quality at different stages. I imagine it's to do with her marriage, or her child, or the age she is. Whatever it is, clearly Judi didn't have it when she was young.'

Peter Hall, on the other hand, who directed Judi in a film version of *A Midsummer Night's Dream*, believes Judi could have had a successful cinema career from the start. That she hasn't is, in Hall's view, 'to the lasting discredit of the film industry, such as it is . . . had we had a film industry with a sense of talent instead of a sense of glamour, in 1958 she should have become a film star. She's got the popular touch. She was an extremely attractive young girl. We've always been very bad about women in films.'

Judi's first feature film was *The Third Secret*, starring Stephen Boyd, in 1964. The director was Charles Crichton. It was a thriller and Judi's contribution was neither extensive nor distinguished. She had a scene with Richard Attenborough, set in an art gallery of which her character was the proprietor, wherein she had to protest, 'Oh no, oh no, oh no!' as Attenborough stalked her. This was cut by the censor, who felt it was too torrid for a family audience.

Despite the momentousness of the event − her first film part − Judi has to this day never seen *The Third Secret*. Nor has she yet caught up with her couple of scenes in her second film, *A Study in Terror*, which itself hardly lives in the memory.

This was a Sherlock Holmes picture, directed by James Hill with John Neville as the famous sleuth and Donald Houston as Doctor Watson. At one point Judi was called upon to sing 'Bread of Heaven' to an audience of down-and-outs containing John and Donald as Holmes and Watson in disguise, an experience she describes as 'a tricky moment of my life'.

Judi's first full-length acting role in the cinema came in 1964 with *Four in the Morning*, which she was asked to do by the director Tony Simmons. He employed five main performers — besides Judi there was Norman Rodway, Joe Melia, Ann Lynn and Brian Phelan — splitting them into two groups, each improvising a script from a given situation.

The film started out as a drama-documentary about the work of the London river police, who are seen fishing the body of a young woman from the Thames. She is not identified but has on a raincoat of a kind worn in the film by both Judi and Ann Lynn.

Simmons rehearsed Judi, Norman and Joe completely separately from Ann and Brian, and two different sets of circumstances were created, both seen to be taking place simultaneously during the early hours of one morning.

All the rehearsals Judi was involved in took place in a house in Deodar Road, Putney, on the river. There was plenty of atmospheric noise: trains, buses and aircraft roaring past continuously. Opposite, there was a dumping site for river waste. The constant flow of transport regularly prompted Joe Melia to amuse everyone on the set with a comic rendering of 'Wagon Wheels'.

Four in the Morning, with its ad-libbed, *vérité* style, was much praised — at least, in Europe. Some of the British critics were rather less enthusiastic. *The Times* found it 'difficult to see why' it had been so acclaimed across the Channel. Richard Roud, in the *Guardian*, commented: 'From beginning to end, I just don't believe one word of it. You may.' There was, however, a critics' prize at Cannes, and Judi's BAFTA award — news of which was phoned through to her at Nottingham, where she was playing St Joan — seemed to have set her on the road to film fame and fortune. Instead, she has come to call herself, with rueful amusement, 'the newcomer who never arrived.'

*

'A cliché-ridden script does not help this unassuming film about a professional burglar and his way of life. But Tom Bell has a compelling screen presence as the hero, and the film, like all directed by Charles Crichton, has a certain grace and freshness in its treatment which are appealing.'

Such was *The Times*' reviewer's summary of the next film in which Judi appeared: *He Who Rides a Tiger*, in January 1966. She enjoyed working again with Charles Crichton, the director of her début film, *The Third Secret*, but had the unfortunate experience of not being paid fully, one of the producers having appropriated a chunk of the money.

As one who has always liked to prepare herself mentally for a performance by spending time beforehand taking in the atmosphere of the theatre and dressing-room, and whose personal dynamics favour the uninterrupted execution of a role, Judi found the adjustment to film tremendously hard. In *He Who Rides a Tiger* she played Tom Bell's girlfriend 'in a wig that looked like a hat' and found herself playing searing love scenes with him on the grass at 8.30 a.m. in Godalming on the first day, 'when I'd barely said, "how do you do?" to him.'

In an interview shortly afterwards she described this as an 'absolutely shattering experience, especially as I don't look my best at that time of the morning. When I've just got up I look frightful. They couldn't even see my eyes to make them up. It was awful. So you see I don't really know about films.'

It was three years before Judi's next film appeared, and it was one firmly rooted in theatre, in which medium in that intervening period she had extended her range from St Joan to Sally Bowles.

Peter Hall's film of *A Midsummer Night's Dream*, produced by Lord Birkett, was actually made towards the end of 1967. The intention was to reproduce, with necessary adaptations, the spectacular stage version of 1962, with costumes by Lila de Nobile, in the Warwickshire countryside setting of Compton Verney. As the finance was later in forthcoming than anticipated, the actors found themselves wet and shivering where they had expected conducive sunshine.

The company experienced another problem once they began shooting, in that the outdoor staging failed to recapture the effect of the Stratford scenery and costumes, wherein the immortals had flitted like butterflies. Through the camera they simply looked like a bunch of people dressed up and playing before a rural background. So, to achieve a fusion, the original costumes were abandoned in favour of scant, aboriginal coverings. As Titania, Judi wore a coating of green dust, patches of imitation tree bark and a girdle of brown net and ivy leaves.

Peter Hall explained his aims and motives for the film thus: 'I'm trying to do it completely without illustrative scenes — there are no shots without dialogue. If you're doing Shakespeare it must be Shakespeare — there's no point in purely pictorial "cinematic" scenes. What we're doing is using the camera to make 'Shakespeare more ambiguous — and more human.'

It was generally felt that he failed. In his review in *The Times*, John Russell Taylor demolished the film, calling it 'frankly terrible on almost every conceivable level.' Exempting Sebastian Shaw as Quince, Russell Taylor thought the actors either 'downright miscast', referring here to 'Judi Dench's school-prefect Titania', or apparently 'put hopelessly off their stroke' by the way in which the film was made. Perhaps the sharpest barb, given this was a filmed version of a Shakespeare play made by a leading theatrical director, came in his suggestion, 'not that Mr Hall has a misguided or eccentric conception of the play, but that he seems to have no communicable conception of it at all.'

Looking back, the director himself would still take issue with that, declaring himself 'actually quite proud' of *A Midsummer Night's Dream*. As for Judi, she certainly didn't feel as happy about the enterprise as she had when playing the part on stage, and this was another of the films she could not bring herself to face on a screen.

Judi's next two films were inconsequential and, while her stage career was continuing to develop and expand, her screen one seemed to be petering out (the early seventies was also a fairly quiet period for her on television). Parts were still being offered but none strong enough to lure her from her resolve to cut down on film work after Finty was born. Shortly after Finty's birth in 1972 Judi did appear briefly — appropriately enough holding a babe in arms — in *Luther* starring Stacey Keach, released in 1974. That same year she was in *Dead Cert* directed by Tony Richardson.

Based on a thriller novel by Dick Francis about horse-racing, *Dead Cert* was an unremarkable sub-Hitchcockian project, which also featured Michael Williams. It was filmed on Hayling Island in glorious sunshine. Judi and Mike, both of whom had been keen to work with Richardson, enjoyed themselves thoroughly staying at the Hotel Commodore, being well looked after by the financial backer, Rex Saluz, who would bring them a drink by the hotel pool each morning, and, not least, going to see the horses at Josh Gifford's stables.

It is in the recent blurring of the distinctions between the media of cinema and television that the flourish and promise of Judi's screen career can now be located. In the past few years she has acted in several notable and powerful filmed dramas for television, her career in which dates back to April 1959 and John Wiles' thriller, *Family on Trial*, which had Andrew Cruickshank in the principal role.

Judi had not long returned from the Old Vic American tour and the offers of broadcasting work — she also appeared in a radio play, *Lucius Junius Brutus* with Sir Donald Wolfit — represented an early chance to establish a broad base. She received a boost, too, from the considerate and helpful attitudes of Cruickshank and, perhaps, surprisingly, Wolfit.

All television drama was live at that time, a prospect which would now fill most actors, including Judi, with dread. But since there was no other way then she tended to be no more nor less nervous than she was on stage. In fact television drama was in those days much closer allied with the theatre than the cinema.

In 1960, this alliance led to some confusion for Judi and some other performers. It was then that the BBC launched its ambitious *An Age of Kings* drama series, based on Shakespeare's English history plays. Judi found herself playing Katharine in *Henry V* at the Old Vic at the same time as she was rehearsing the part for the television series. Simultaneously she was faced, in the same role in the same play, with two different directors: Peter Dews and Michael Langham; two different Henrys: Donald Houston at the Vic and Robert Hardy — who felt himself the very incarnation of Henry — on the screen; two different designers; costumes and sets of cuts — in short, two different performances.

The same thing happened with *Richard II*, in both versions of which Judi played the Queen: to Alec McCowen's stage Richard and opposite David William on the television:

'They were very different. Had they been remotely the same it would have been even more complicated! It made for a stimulating experience — got me past the tiredness barrier and stood me in good stead when much later I was doing *A Fine Romance* by day and *The Importance of Being Earnest* at night. I think it actually enhanced the evening performances.

'I'd gone about it the right way round — theatre then TV — so for the studio I scaled down from working in large auditoriums. So many these days go the other way round and it's irritating when you can't hear them in the theatre. You get TV-sized performances on the stage.'

In between *Family on Trial* and *An Age of Kings*, Judi's television work comprised that single episode of *Z-Cars*, in which she played Peter Woodthorpe's unruly girlfriend; the six-part serial, *Hilda Lessways*; and *Pink String and Sealing Wax*, a play with an Edwardian setting by Roland Pertwee.

Hilda Lessways, based on Arnold Bennett's novel, gave Judi her first main television role. Her director was Peter Dews, who was also responsible for *An Age of Kings*, and the cast included Eileen Atkins, Violet Carson, Bernard Hepton and Miranda Connell.

In one episode, following the end of a particular scene, Judi had to run across the studio changing her clothes on the move for a close-up shot through some banisters. Being live television, she didn't have time to put on a skirt. Fortunately the cameraman did his job properly, showing her above the waist only, wearing a high-buttoned blouse.

Another ended with the dubious character of George Cannon proposing to Hilda. As the credits went up, Judi was called to the telephone. It was Reg, who said, 'Darling, you were absolutely terrific, but mummy and I think you ought to know the man's a cad!'

Pink String and Sealing Wax, which was broadcast in February 1960, is now remembered chiefly by Judi for the fact that she had to eat on camera: 'In rehearsals I'd been miming, and when it came to it they put out real bacon and eggs and I couldn't say a word.'

Major Barbara, which was transmitted by Granada in October 1962, was directed by Stuart Burge, a skilled theatrical director. This made Judi feel much more comfortable than she normally did in a TV studio. Brewster Mason played opposite her as Undershaft, as he would do again eight years later at the Aldwych Theatre. Adolphus was Edward Woodward, who managed accidentally to hurl a drum stick at Judi's head in the opening shot.

After initial rehearsals in London, the programme was made in Manchester. For Judi, this involved a considerable amount of travelling as she was appearing with the RSC in Stratford at the time. One night, after shooting in Manchester, the cast went off for a meal to a little seaside hotel in Morecambe, run by a friend of Stuart Burge's. Afterwards Brewster Mason gave Judi a lift south. Rather romantically she had arranged to meet Tom Fleming at midnight outside Lichfield Cathedral, where he arrived in his Sunbeam Talbot in plenty of time to drive Judi back to Stratford.

However, Brewster's car had a puncture, and midnight came and went in Lichfield without Judi. Eventually a taxi passed the spot where the erstwhile Undershaft and daughter had come to grief and where Brewster Mason, feeling quite unlike a tycoon, was changing the wheel. Judi took the taxi to Lichfield, where she arrived long past one o'clock to discover that Tom had been picked up by the police for loitering.

The play itself got a tepid reception from the critics. The *Guardian*'s Mary Crozier found it 'in this day and age a most peculiar play', while *The Times*' Olympian com-

ment was 'The most arguable casting was that of Miss Judi
Dench as Barbara: she has to perfection the golden girl
quality, the hockey captain under the uniform, but as yet
she lacks the incisiveness and authority which Barbara
should surely have, at least intermittently. Barbara is a
little bit of a prig, not wholly and uncompromisingly
heroic, but perhaps it was felt that would be to compli-
cate matters unduly for the mass audience.'

From Shaw to Ford Madox Ford, and *Parade's End*,
adapted into a dramatic trilogy by John Hopkins and
screened towards the end of 1964. Judi played the part of
Valentine Wanop, a suffragette, and the director was Alan
Cooke, whom Judi remembers as having very little sense of
humour.

'We were filming on a golf course and Annette Robertson
and I had to run and take a golf ball and hide it. Alan
Cooke was remonstrating with us to be aware of the
import of this, saying, "I don't think you realize what
you're doing. Pinching their balls makes them very, very
cross." He never batted an eyelid – while we were in fits.'

Professionally, she felt pleased with the trilogy – 'all
in all, a very good piece of work.' And it certainly seemed
to have some effect, with questions asked in the House of
Commons by Tory MPs complaining about 'questionable
material' and 'continuous socialist party propaganda'.

By this time John Hopkins, with original material as
well as adaptations like *Parade's End*, was establishing himself in the first team of television writers. Within a short
time he could lay claim to the captaincy. Writing with
feverish commitment he devised a quartet of plays, under
the collective title *Talking to a Stranger*, which poignantly
and powerfully dramatized the strains in a family where,
typically, communication had seized up. Each individual
play dealt with the same situation – a middle-aged
woman's suicide – but from the viewpoint of a different
member of the family: the suicide herself, her husband,
son, and daughter. Margery Mason was engaged to play the
mother, Maurice Denham the father, and Michael Bryant
the son, Alan.

The part of Terry, the daughter, was the key one. She
was based on John Hopkins' own view of himself, some-

thing of an anguished rebel, and her prototype had appeared years before in *Z-Cars*, played by Judi. Hopkins very much wanted Judi to play Terry. His director, Christopher Morahan, preferred Eileen Atkins. Hopkins' wishes prevailed and Judi was sent a script. But when she'd read it she thought it too difficult and turned it down. John Hopkins then rang her, urging her to accept. He promised her that he would sit outside in his car while the programmes were being made, and be available for consultation (a promise which he kept). So Judi agreed and not only overcame Morahan's reluctance but gave a performance which was earmarked for distinction from the moment it unfolded.

The home to which the character of Terry, at the end of an affair, bitter, defensive and pregnant, had paid a rare visit, was like an emotional torture chamber, something movingly conveyed by the quartet of actors and the quartet of plays. Originally screened on BBC 2 in October 1966, *Talking to a Stranger* made a successful transition to BBC 1 and won a wider audience. It was loaded with praise and awards — Judi was named Television Actress of the Year by the Guild of Television Producers and Directors. It was memorable, original work by everyone involved; the complex thread of feelings in the story kept carefully taut by Christopher Morahan (who, having perhaps got less than his share of recognition, was to receive due acclaim as a television director several years later for the ITV series, *Jewel in the Crown*).

It was Judi's first major achievement on television and gave her much cause for satisfaction. She received a lot of letters from the public including one from a woman about the same age as Margery Mason's character who, inspired by Judi's performance, had resumed talking to her daughter after years of silent hostility. Judi also forged lasting friendships with her three fellow principals. They had become — perhaps appropriately — like a family, Maurice Denham in fact bearing more than a passing resemblance to Judi's father. A sincere, solid person herself, Judi sets great store by such feelings of community within the acting world:

'People who are not in the theatre think of it as affectation — everybody calling everybody else "darling" and not meaning things. What attracts me about actors is that they *do* mean things. And their lack of class consciousness. When one of them is in trouble everybody rallies round with support like steel. Occasionally you get somebody pulling against others, but it's rare. People in the theatre are of the most constant and the most concerned.'

It was to be some time before Judi would lend such a commanding presence to the television screen. Between January 1968 — when she appeared as Helen in an ITV 'Playhouse' presentation of Frederick Lonsdale's comedy, *On Approval* with Robert Stephens, Maggie Smith and Moray Watson — and April 1978, when the RSC's *The Comedy of Errors* was televised, her appearances were sparse in number and content.

She was in *The Funambulists*, by John Moxon, a clever play along the lines of *The Firescreen* in which she had appeared at Oxford. Francis Matthews played a jealous husband who employed a detective (Peter Barkworth) to follow his wife. Originally innocent, the wife has an affair with the detective.

She worked with Francis Matthews again in an episode of a series called *Detective*, starring Alan Dobie, whom Judi was called upon to rescue by jumping into a wintry sea.

In *The Teachers* she found herself ostracized by the rest of the cast as a joke for arriving two days late on account of other work in hand. In *The Days to Come*, a futuristic H.G. Wells piece with Dinsdale Landen, she wore a most unlikely diaphanous costume. This prompted a letter from a woman in Surrey, a psychiatrist, angrily listing the parts of Judi's anatomy she claimed to be able to see through the costume:

'She named them — words I'd never heard of. I sent her a telegram saying, "Psychiatrist, heal thyself." '

Judi also received some nasty correspondence in the wake of *Neighbours*, a two-hander in which she played opposite a black actor, Calvin Lockhart, with whom she had worked before in *Talking to a Stranger*.

Around this time Judi did some voiceovers for commercials. One, for Players' cigarettes, was withdrawn because it was 'too sexy'. Later she did an After Eight Mints ad, again voice only.

ATV's screening of *The Comedy of Errors*, translating Trevor Nunn's stage production from the Aldwych, was thrilling for those who had seen it in the theatre, if only because it acted as a reminder of that uplifting experience. For those who hadn't seen it before, the television version, firmly theatrical right down to shots of an eager audience, was possibly a little remote — 'simply a superb stage production filmed' as Nancy Banks-Smith wrote in the *Guardian*. On the other hand, Clive James welcomed it in the *Observer* as 'easily the cleverest, and probably the best Shakespeare production I have ever seen on the box.'

That same year, 1978, the director David Jones took Judi out for a drink and told her about a book by Aidan Higgins which Harold Pinter was adapting for television. It was called *Langrishe, go down*, an elliptical atmospheric and erotic tale, set in Ireland around a country house called Springfield, occupied by two reclusive sisters, one of whom is seen to have a passionate affair with a young German while the other pines mysteriously.

The atmosphere and location David Jones was seeking were enough to sell it to Judi and so she went over to Ireland to play the part of the lover of Otto, the German, played by Jeremy Irons.

Everybody worked expertly and thoroughly on the production, which was broadcast in September 1978. Pinter's script, Jones' direction and the camera work by Elmer Cossey, combined to produce a steamy lyricism, full of supercharged performance (Jeremy Irons acquired his part in *The French Lieutenant's Woman* and consequent stardom as a result of his work in *Langrishe*).

Higgins' story is set in County Kildare, but they couldn't find a suitable house for Springfield in Kildare. Then, one evening, around dusk, at the end of a long search they came across a place in Waterford. It had no summer house — for the lovers' trysts to take place — but was otherwise perfect: somehow venerable and mysterious, with overgrown gardens containing a long-neglected tennis court. As Judi recalls, it seemed to exist solely for the purpose of *Langrishe*:

'It actually turned out to be called Springfield House. It was so eerie. The atmosphere was so strong. One day there was a gigantic thunderstorm. It was bewitching. The building was razed to the ground after we'd gone. Apparently the land was needed for a factory.

'Mike brought Finty over for a long weekend and said he'd never do it again. He felt outside this personal, intimate company that we had become. I was thrilled to see them but was so enmeshed in it and it was awkward for him. The same thing happens at Stratford — you create an enclosed unit and outside partners do feel awkward.

'I lost a lot of weight for the part so I felt very good. I got down to eight stone ten. This was because I had to run through the fields with nothing on, which I was extremely frightened about. But — despite the stern, moralizing letters it provoked — it was all done in such a sensitive way. I'll never forget it.'

When *Macbeth*, based on Trevor Nunn's memorable stage production, was broadcast by Thames Television in January 1979, its players did not altogether feel the same as they had about the earlier *The Comedy of Errors* adaptation. They had gathered to watch *Macbeth* at Trevor Nunn's home, and afterwards all had a drink as an antidote to anticlimax. Perhaps the novelty of adaptation had worn off, or perhaps by then they felt surfeited with the production. Nevertheless, the critical approval was almost as roaring as it had been after the opening at The Other Place in 1976.

Sean Day-Lewis of the *Daily Telegraph* thought that 'the logic of [Trevor Nunn's] thinking clearly pointed to the television screen and the brilliantly taut Thames recording of his Other Place production,' a view put somewhat more extravagantly by Herbert Kretzmer in the *Daily Mail* in his statement that '*Macbeth* might have been written for television.'

Peter Fiddick, in the *Guardian*, wrote of a 'triple triumph', alluding to the director's vision of the play's progress from stage to screen, and felt that 'Ian McKellen's Macbeth and Judi Dench as Lady Macbeth came to the screen with all the weight of experience behind them and it showed from the first word to the last.'

The Listener's review was written by its theatre critic, John Elsom, who expressed reservations. He admired the straightforwardness of the adaptation (produced by Philip Casson) and again found the two central performances 'remarkable', but thought that the atmosphere had been lost and also that 'certain effects jarred', demonstrating that what is effectively theatrical in one medium can be awkwardly stagey in the other.

But the most negative reaction of all came not in a review as such but in Auberon Waugh's 'Another Voice' column in the *Spectator*. Having, perhaps whimsically, referred to Trevor Nunn as 'silly, over-excited and intellectually under-endowed', Waugh recalled the stage production, in which he saw Ian McKellen's Macbeth as 'half-baked' and Judi as 'extraordinarily implausible', and went on to dismiss the idea of a television production as misbegotten, the Bard belonging properly in the theatre, or just possibly on the printed page. Waugh's views were couched in customarily humorous style, but were hardly calculated to please.

In the preparation of Judi's next appearance in a televised version of a stage play — *A Village Wooing* shown on 17 April 1979 as part of ITV's *Plays for Pleasure* series — lay a disaster of the scale you would be forgiven for imagining attended *Macbeth* had you read Waugh's *Spectator* diatribe.

Directed by David Cunliffe, Shaw's late two-hander featured Richard Briers with Judi. The *Daily Telegraph* described Judi as 'delightfully resourceful', while the *Guardian* thought the 'delectable Dench' had never before shown 'more sure a sense of comic seriousness. This was . . . a definitive performance.'

The 'delectable Dench's' own recollection tells a rather different story: 'It was a hideous experience. Wonderful in rehearsal — we did the run-through and all the stage hands and technicians laughed. It was so lovely — then when we went up to do it I lost my nerve. I went completely to pieces. That old actors' thing. I was in such a state I couldn't remember any of my lines. They just kept

re-shooting. David Cunliffe and the editor must have had a
terrible time, as must Dickie Briers waiting for his big Act
Three. Poor Dickie. He was very professional. I don't
expect he'll ever work with me again. Absolute torture!

'Perhaps that's why I was so keen to do it again at the
New End with Frank Hauser — I wanted to lay that ghost.'

In between the Shakespeare and the Shaw, Judi was in
an unusual drama for BBC Television which won an international 'Emmy' award and reunited her with Tony
Simmons, the director of *Four in the Morning*, the film for
which Judi had been voted 'Most Promising Newcomer'
some fourteen years before.

On Giant's Shoulders was a BBC 2 Play of the Week, first
broadcast in March 1979 and transmitted on BBC 1 three
months later. It was based on a book by journalists Marjorie Wallace and Michael Robson which was itself derived
from extensive research carried out by Marjorie Wallace for
the *Sunday Times* in its campaign on behalf of thalidomide-
damaged children. One of these children was Terry Wiles,
limbless, dwarfed and partially sighted. *On Giant's
Shoulders* was his story, adapted from the book and
Marjorie Wallace's subsequent screenplay by William
Humble and Tony Simmons, a moving account of his
adoption against all odds by a brave, unconventional,
doughty couple. Judi played Hazel Wiles, the mother;
Bryan Pringle was Len Wiles, the father; Terry Wiles played
himself.

It was an exceptionally difficult undertaking. Not only
were the professional actors working with somebody, in
Terry, for whom the sad story was real life, but the people
Judi and Bryan were portraying, Hazel and Len Wiles, were
present throughout.

Judi and Bryan were extremely nervous as they drove
from London to Huntingdonshire together to meet the
Wileses and chewed their way through a huge quantity of
sweets. Whey they arrived at the house and were shown in
through the hall, Judi heard a loud voice declaring
emphatically, 'Well, I know *you*. I've seen *you* on the
television.'

It was Terry, and in one bold stroke he had blown away
all of Judi's apprehension. He was then seventeen, with a

deep voice — which wasn't heard in the recording as his part was dubbed. He was a cheerful, cheeky and affectionate boy and Judi grew very fond of him:

'We had lots of parties, which Terry loved. He loves dancing — which means you hold him, and he's very heavy. He was mad about crosswords and we'd do them every day. He lives in California now. A smashing boy. I never saw him depressed once.'

In her performance Judi displayed flashes of that dowdy world-weariness later to be employed so successfully on the stage in *Pack of Lies*. Alongside her, Bryan Pringle was colossally sympathetic as the patient, persevering, dedicated father.

In 1980, Thames screened *Love in a Cold Climate*, a serial based on Nancy Mitford's book of the same name and another of her novels, *The Pursuit of Love*. The adaptation was by Simon Raven. The programme makers wanted both Judi Dench and Michael Williams to be in the cast and they were sent scripts separately — Michael was playing in Newcastle at the time. And when he rang Judi to tell her he'd received the script, the coincidence inclined them both to accept, so that Michael eventually played Davey while a slightly surprised Judi was Aunt Sadie — Lady Alconleigh ('I thought I'd be playing one of those girls, not their mother'). Both were quietly, unspectacularly successful.

Love in a Cold Climate was directed in an effective, concise fashion by Donald McWhinnie, always finishing off rehearsals quickly and early (one actor, Job Stewart, once timed his contributory presence at a rehearsal at eight minutes), and involved quite an amount of location work. Michael and Judi had Finty with them for part of their travels and even brought along one of the family pets, a hamster, which managed to bite one lady at the Golden Valley Hotel in Cheltenham.

Lord Merlin was played by John Moffatt, with whom Judi and Michael spent a lot of time, often picnicking in Cotswold cornfields. On one occasion, John, Judi and Selena Carey-Jones were taken, in costume, twelve miles between locations in the chauffeur-driven car used in the series. And in the midst of it all, a ten-week technicians' strike gave the actors an extended break on full pay.

A year after *Love in a Cold Climate*, Judi appeared in a BBC 2 'Playhouse' production which similarly strove for authenticity of detail; this time, however, the authentic details of grim, tragic reality rather than those relating to light comic fiction. *Going Gently* by Thomas Ellice, based upon a novel by an American professor of English called Robert Downs, was set in a hospital ward and concerned the suffering and deaths of two cancer patients.

When Judi was offered the part of the ward sister, she saw the obvious artistic value of the piece (although her agent raised his eyebrows at the casting of the comedian Norman Wisdom in one of the main roles) but her instinctive revulsion from the subject of death held her back. She was eventually persuaded and humorously helped through it by the director, Stephen Frears.

For his part, Frears was extremely keen for Judi to take on the role, having earlier overcome what he now calls 'an appalling, stupid prejudice' against her, dating back to the 1960s when he was working at the Royal Court Theatre in London. In those days the team at the Court tended to regard the RSC as the establishment, and therefore the enemy.

'We were absolutely on principle against anybody who worked at the RSC', recalls Stephen Frears, 'and Judi was top of the hit list, being so firmly identified with them.'

Later he 'grew out' of his prejudice, helped no doubt by seeing Judi as Lady Macbeth, and when he saw a picture of her in *On Giant's Shoulders* in which he was struck by how radically she had changed her appearance, he was convinced that 'she must be very good indeed.' Then he made *Going Gently* with her, which he describes as 'a piece of cake — it became apparent to me how powerful she was as an actress.

'I probably made *Going Gently* because there had recently been deaths in my family; and thinking of Judi I might well have been looking, deep down, for somebody you would be prepared to die in front of, or entrust your life to at a very private moment. Somebody whom you could even insult in those circumstances.'

The part of Sister Scarli was actually quite a small one in comparison to the roles of the salesman (played by

Norman Wisdom) who at first can't accept the seriousness of his condition, and the irascible professor (played by Fulton Mackay) who faces up to his plight all too boldly.

Yet Judi built a memorable character almost out of nothing (she did consult her nurse friend Susie Bodmer), indicating depths of emotion behind her bluff matter-of-factness. She formed a bridge between the two main characters, whose own situations were heavy with irony. This was nowhere more apparent than in the line uttered by the salesman to the professor when the former has come to feel the sharp isolation of having a family with whom he shares no real closeness: 'It's easy for you — you've got nobody.'

Filmed on location at the King Edward Memorial Hospital in Ealing, West London, *Going Gently* was a brilliant piece of work, quite exceptional in the coherence of its component parts. There were moments of theatricality — like Mackay's character's excursions round neighbouring wards with a whisky bottle — which were given a wholly appropriate context by telling shifts of emphasis between lighting, dialogue and even costume, consistently achieving a comic or a touching accuracy.

The play had such a muscular artistic strength that it was tempting to look for a lesson or a message in it, whether about the administration of the health service, dignity in death, or whatever. But in the end the message was that there was no message: that we are all, after all, helpless and human. *Going Gently* certainly possessed one of the elements of true tragedy — the investment of distressing material with an elevating quality through the potency of its sheer creative force.

In his *Guardian* review of Richard Eyre's production of *The Cherry Orchard* for BBC 1 in October 1981, Peter Fiddick wrote: 'Twenty years ago *The Cherry Orchard* came to the stage of the Aldwych in a glowing new production by Michel St Denis. It was a triumph of the exciting theatrical discovery of the day, something called ensemble acting. I can see it now with Judi Dench in her selfless corner as the younger daughter, Anya.

'Can this really be her now, sad behind the smiling eyes,

lonely through the gravity, grand in rich furs as Madam Ranevsky?'

It could and was. When Richard Eyre, whom she knew well from her Nottingham Playhouse days, telephoned her to offer her the part, Judi's first thought was that she was too young. But she considered it further and concluded that she was ready to tackle it and could 'still have another go in a few years time.' It was a decision that probably helped her make up her mind about the offer of Lady Bracknell which Peter Hall was to make a few months later.

Richard Eyre brought together a strong cast for *The Cherry Orchard* on television, including Paul Curran, Suzanne Burden (as Anya), David Rintoul, Tim Spall, Anton Lesser, Anna Massey (who as the governess Carlotta frequently disappeared during rehearsals into a room to learn conjuring from The Great Kovari), Bill Paterson (as Lopakhin), Frederick Treves, and Harriet Walter. He used a version of the text by the gifted modern playwright, Trevor Griffiths, with whom he had also worked at Nottingham.

Judi gave her Ranevsky more girlish qualities than is conventional (as she would do subsequently with her Lady Bracknell), making her very obviously affected by the break-up with a lover in Paris. In an interview published in the *Radio Times* in the week of transmission, Judi summed up her sympathetic feelings towards Madame Ranevsky's lot at the end of the play:

'The outlook is grim. She'll go back to the bounder in Paris, of course. Yasha [her valet] is extraordinarily intimate in many ways. He's not a very pleasant man. I think in Paris Yasha had seen her in extraordinary circumstances, when the door had been bolted against her, when she had been up all night crying, before she got herself together. And he is in charge of the pills. That is a curious insight. She'll drink a lot I expect.'

She still wants to have that second crack at the part, and establish even more definitely than she felt able to at the time, 'that mixture that Ranevsky is of foolishness and naivité and disappointment.' As she said in the *Radio Times* interview quoted above, 'There is that tiny border-line which they all seem to walk between crying and laughing all the time. On the brink. I understand that frightfully well.'

Shortly after the first episodes of the situation comedy, *A Fine Romance* — during which sadness and laughter would later come closer together than ever — had been shown on London Weekend Television in November 1981, Judi was asked by somebody she met socially if it had been her first television work.

It was a remark which underlined the fact that she and Michael were taking a step out of the sphere of 'minority taste' into a larger public arena.

He had been filming in Greece when she received a copy of a script for the show, written by Bob Larbey. Its theme was the gauche courtship between Laura, an unmarried 37-year-old translator, and Mike, a bachelor of around the same age who runs a landscape gardening business. Laura's younger, more glamorous sister, Helen, and her husband Phil are accessories, concerned to get Mike and Laura together.

Judi read bits and laughed. She found the people and the situations identifiable. She phoned Michael in Greece and told him about it — she'd been offered Laura and he'd been offered Mike. She was keen and he decided to accept, purely on her recommendation mainly, he says, because he felt homesick (later when a second series was offered, it was Judi who was abroad and homesick — in Bangkok).

And so, soon after Michael's return from Greece they began work on *A Fine Romance* which eventually ran for twenty-six episodes. Helen was played by Susan Penhaligon, Phil by Richard Warwick. It quite quickly became successful. Its unfussy, low-key style, well acted, drew the laughter of recognition at familiar and believable awkwardnesses. Judi's popularity was suddenly widened dramatically. People constantly pointed out her and Michael in the street, and wondered if, even assumed, they were like Laura and Mike in real life. The readers of *TV Times* voted Judi 'the funniest woman on television.'

At first, Judi didn't feel at all at home playing Laura. She became tense, the studio audience frightened her — she was always nervous of being introduced as herself before each recording. Technically, it took her some time to adjust to playing to camera with an audience of up to 700 people watching from a different direction.

Michael found things easier in this respect and was able to give Judi moral as well as professional support, until eventually their instinctive playing together lifted the programmes out of the commonplace.

Susan Penhaligon and Richard Warwick felt themselves lifted, too, and a very jolly company spirit was created. Beforehand, Susan Penhaligon had been somewhat in awe of Judi:

'She was one of my favourite actresses. I'd always looked up to her. And when I came to work with her I couldn't open my mouth at first. I hadn't expected someone so unaffected by all the acclaim. Someone so giggly and easy-going. And frightened, just like me.

'In *A Fine Romance* I've watched her go from a moment of grief into pure comedy *effortlessly*, without losing any reality, and truthfulness. She makes *you* feel that it is true. She's totally believable. There's not a moment of insincerity. And she also hits the right note for each scene. Exactly.

'It's difficult to describe such a big talent when you think of this ordinary person coming through the door at rehearsal and chatting about clothes, wallpaper and losing weight, or what she's going to do with her hair.

'She was generous to me as a younger actress. A number of occasions she'd come up to me and say, "How about doing it like this?" And she'd give me a little bit of business which would make it work much better. Judi is the sort of person that, if I was in trouble or my private or professional life was going badly, I would ring her up. One day I came in and was near to tears about something. After lunch she came back with a great big bottle of expensive perfume for me. I count myself extremely lucky to have had the opportunity of working with her and knowing her. I have never heard anyone say anything derogatory about her. She's a giver. So warm and generous. *A Fine Romance* was the most enjoyable job I've ever done.'

The director of that first series was James Cellan Jones, an experienced drama director — one of the reasons why Judi accepted the part — and a man of waggish humour.

One of his apparently humorous suggestions was for Judi to sing the title song, the famous old Jerome Kern/Dorothy Fields number, after which the programme was named. In any event, she played along, it was recorded and went out over the titles with each episode.

A second series was made, directed by Don Leaver, with the cast the same as before, and this brought still more fans — and fan mail. Judi and Michael spent a lot of their time reading and replying to correspondence. More than ever, people regarded Judi's and Michael's personalities as interchangeable with Laura's and Mike's, believed they actually *were* Laura and Mike. Michael received frequent invitations to open new garden centres.

In the 1984 BAFTA awards Judi was named Comedy Actress of the Year for her performance as Laura.

As classical actors, Michael and Judi sometimes found themselves having to rebut the charge that they had lowered their standards by appearing in such a lightweight and popular series as *A Fine Romance*. Judi almost delighted in such accusations, refusing as ever to allow herself to be categorized. Michael also found it more than worthwhile to be able to work closely with his brilliantly gifted partner, setting them up for grander things: 'Our *technique* of working together came to fruition in playing the leads in *A Fine Romance*. It manifested itself in *Pack of Lies*. We don't even have to look at one another now.'

They were also pleased that a new public was attracted to the theatre, a large proportion of the audience for *Pack of Lies* undoubtedly consisting of unaccustomed theatre-goers who'd got hooked on *A Fine Romance*.

The financial rewards were not to be sneezed at either: Michael and Judi once worked out that the number of people watching any one episode of *A Fine Romance* would fill the Aldwych Theatre for approximately fourteen years.

In *Saigon — Year of the Cat* Judi was directed again by Stephen Frears, who had enthusiastically offered her more work after *Going Gently* but she had held out for 'something glamorous'. Then, after watching *The Cherry Orchard* on television, Stephen rang her and exclaimed, 'Your shoulders!' and said he would be sending her a script by David Hare.

Judi was excited by this opportunity, so subtly different from the establishment image which, to her irritation, still lingered, and affording a contrast from her recent work. She would play the part of Barbara, an English woman who is the assistant manager of a bank in Saigon in the closing days of the Vietnam War, just prior to the American evacuation.

Before Frears was taken on as director, it had been intended to offer the part to Julie Andrews or Jean Simmons.

Outwardly, Barbara is very English and conventional, but, with the help of Judi's voiceovers on the soundtrack, it becomes plain than she has a secret, passionate side to her. She meets and falls in love with a young American from the CIA. They are parted amid the confused *melée* of the American departure.

It not being possible to film in Saigon itself, the film — made for Thames Television at a reported cost of around £2 million and entered in the London Film Festival — was shot over eight weeks in Bangkok, in order to capture as much of the Eastern atmosphere as possible. Judi's co-star was the American actor, Frederic Forrest, and among the rest of the cast was an old mate, Roger Rees. He went sightseeing with her, something which helped prevent her from feeling too lonely and homesick, though Finty did manage to fly out to join her during the last fortnight of filming. For most of the rest of the time she walked, drew, read — John Fowles' *Daniel Martin* and a book of Somerset Maugham short stories — and made many phone calls to Michael in England.

The casting of Judi in *Saigon* had a certain amount of shock value. Not only were viewers seeing this apparently upright and well-mannered woman, Barbara, making love to a rather risqué young American, but they were also watching nice, decent Judi Dench playing bed scenes with the unconventionally charming Frederic Forrest.

To Stephen Frears, this was 'part of the fun . . . I think that *Saigon* showed "the other side" of her. It would be interesting to do more things on this "other side". I suspect that's what she likes doing. Since I'm not interested in filming Chekhov or Shakespeare I wouldn't expect to use those overt qualities of hers.'

One reason why Judi was so pleased to take on this role was that she had great confidence in Stephen Frears: 'A paragon — he's so clever and imaginative. He sets up each shot in sequence very carefully. He never stands still for a moment. He says he always looks for the marvellous shots in great films and remembers those shots. Stephen's a tremendous film buff. Always wondering how Francis Ford Coppola would do it. "What would Francis do now?" he'll say.'

Certainly, *Saigon* was not without its Hollywood moments, most notably perhaps in the first meeting between Barbara and her American lover. Judi was standing in front of Frederic on a verandah, and carried on a conversation with him without looking round, as he came over cool, dynamic and puffing cigarette smoke, *à la* Bogart.

Frears himself was especially pleased with Judi's performance in that sequence: 'The ability to stand there, naturally, and not think it odd to have a conversation with a man standing behind you; *that* requires imagination.'

It was all part of a process of discovery for the director: 'She's better than anyone else and more interesting than anyone else, more skilful. Her qualities on film really haven't been touched. I just love photographing her. She's so expressive, a very clear image, very visible.

'You can't imagine what it's like for somebody who hasn't been fully explored on film finding out what it's like to be lit and photographed properly and at the same time to have twenty-five years of night after night on the stage behind you. Watching that was wonderful.'

Not that everything went just right as far as he was concerned: 'There were a couple of speeches where you can hear that RSC voice. I can remember hearing it and not knowing what to say to her because what I really felt was, "You're using your old voice and I don't like it." I couldn't think of anything to say so I said nothing and it stayed in.'

The impact of *Saigon — Year of the Cat* was softened by being shown on ITV at the same time as the BBC were screening *An Englishman Abroad*, Alan Bennett's highly-regarded film about Guy Burgess, starring Alan Bates and Coral Browne and directed by John Schlesinger.

It was also a partial victim of its own advance publicity, many people expecting more action, fantasy and romance to match the exotic location and lavish expenditure.

Nonetheless, however perfunctory the sentiments and however downbeat the action, it was all conveyed naturally, watchably and occasionally hauntingly. And, as Stephen Frears avers, Judi has now developed a captivating screen presence, much stronger than in the past.

It could well be that Frears' excitement about Judi's new potential and his feeling that she is shedding a back-log of negative factors about filming, indicate more and greater film work for her in the future:

'I can see that she must have had a thing about films. It'd been so miserable. She'd been badly cast and directed, by which I mean that she wasn't put in something where her talents could be used, though Tony Simmons did her justice in *Four in the Morning*. Her heart and best qualities were so firmly in the theatre. I suspect her heart has slightly shifted.

'She surprised me one time when I re-shot a scene because I'd done it badly. She said, "I've never met anyone who went back and re-shot a scene just because he got it wrong the first time." I couldn't believe it. It's the most elementary thing. It must happen on all films. Her knowledge of films must be very, very small.

'She plays the text very loyally. But I like the bits in between, when you can just photograph the light on her face. She has real cinematic qualities. She reminds me slightly of Celia Johnson — who had a run of about four films.

'It's worth writing about an English middle-class woman right now because there's someone who can do it well. David Hare writes about middle-aged women. When he wrote *Plenty* for the stage he couldn't find the right actress in her forties and Kate Nelligan played it in her twenties. Now he's tremendously excited to have found an actress of the right age.'

Interestingly, Judi's most recent film appearance was in David Hare's *Wetherby*, released in March 1985, in support of another middle-aged actress, Vanessa Redgrave. Twenty-seven years after Central, with much distinguished and classical stage work behind them, the two former fellow students found themselves working together for the first time in the unlikely setting of a highly contemporary movie with Judi playing a really quite modest part.

Clearly she felt no sense of rivalry with Vanessa and accepted the role enthusiastically on the strength of having already felt at ease with David Hare's material in *Saigon*.

David Hare himself, who directed as well as wrote *Wetherby*, a cool, intelligent but edgy and violent film about the fragility of small-town professional life, certainly felt no suggestion of rivalry between the two actresses. There were one or two preconceptions, however, which were quickly swept aside:

'It was put to me I'd be working with Vanessa the supreme emotional actress and Judi the supreme technical actress. I find this completely false. Judi has just as much emotional depth as Vanessa. It has simply been unexplored by British film makers.'

There weren't many scenes between the two of them and Hare later regretted he hadn't written more. But the question of competition never arose. In David Hare's view Judi is simply 'one of the least concerned actresses about reputation and status that I know.'

10   Anatomy of a natural

When Judi played Ophelia at the Old Vic in 1957, her first professional engagement, she was paid seven pounds ten shillings a week. Later in the season, when the company went to the Edinburgh Festival, her weekly pay was increased to seventeen pounds, which felt like 'real money'. Her rent was just under three pounds a week, she was a young single girl, her future was uncertain.

Since then, in getting to the top of a profession notorious for its hordes of unemployed members, she has spent only three weeks out of work and has passed her fiftieth birthday financially and emotionally secure, happily married with one daughter, two houses, several pets and an OBE. The dazzling accoutrements of film stardom have so far passed her by but she has upheld an admirable integrity on the stage, despite an almost reckless willingness always to look for range-broadening challenges.

It has been this general desire to spread her wings and be different, rather than any aspiration towards particular roles, that has impelled Judi's career to date. And while Sir Peter Hall, for example, laments the fact that Judi has never played Cleopatra, and Michael Williams thinks it a great pity that she hasn't been called upon to play Rosalind in As You Like It, Judi herself has neither heavy regret nor burning ambition.

The fact is, she has succeeded. Where other actresses would be spreading their talents dangerously thinly by taking on Adriana and Lady Macbeth, Millamant and Barbara Jackson, Juno and Beatrice, Judi has combined exceptional breadth and depth. And where others have built reputations keeping firmly within one sphere of acting, Judi has distinguished herself across the board. In the words of Peter Hall, 'She's one of the few English

actresses who can actually play a peasant or a queen . . .
she's tried and done everything and really knows her job.
The magic is something to do with craft, and with the kind
of person she is — because I don't think acting is imitation,
but finally reveals to the audience certain things about the
actor. Judi's enthusiasm, impetuosity, warmth, extraordinary sense of humour, generosity, selflessness, integrity,
honesty (they all sound too good to be true but they're
quite real) come through to an audience.'

Hall sees Judi as such a sunny personality that he believes
it is hard for her to play an unpleasant person. He felt her
Lady Macbeth showed so much 'feminine sunshine' that it
was difficult to accept the flintier tragic side from her.
Nonetheless he would like to see her tackle 'a really mean
woman with almost no redeeming virtue — I'd like to see
her project that black side which exists in all of us.'

The intriguing part of that statement is the reference to
the existence of a black side *in all of us*, with its implicit
testimony to Judi's ability to strike some universal human
chord. It is almost as if this extremely sympathetic actress,
with whose obviously generous qualities audiences invariably wish to identify — 'everybody's sweetheart' and
'everybody's mother' as the critic Robert Cushman has
referred to her — might, in the process of enacting on stage
the dark, primitive side of human nature, achieve some collective exorcism.

Interestingly, Peter Hall's sentiments are echoed, indeed
amplified, by the film director Stephen Frears. He had
intended making a film with Judi as a mass murderess but
was unable to secure the rights to the book upon which it
was to be based:

'It's her *power* I find so exciting. Normally this would
be used as a power for good but I don't think of it all like
that. I think of her as much more interesting as a villain
than a heroine. She should have made a film with Hitchcock. She'd be wonderful as a passionate poisoner.

'I admire her capacity to deal with things. She rolls her
sleeves up and scrubs the floors, which I like. It's a pioneering, Jean Arthurish quality. You can imagine her dealing
with any crisis. What was interesting about the nurse in
Going Gently was the tough side, the fact that she could

face up to it all. And her physical presence. I liked her *fore-arms* in *Going Gently*. You can imagine her punching somebody.'

Frears is one of the directors Judi most likes working with, confident in the belief that he will give meaning and structure to her purely instinctive approach. But he regards her claims to rely absolutely on directors as 'nonsense — it all comes from her. You just hang around and edit the good bits. She always pretends she's insecure, but she's so skilful and able she can't really be.'

Peter Hall finds her fertile, humorous, provoking, exhausting: 'She's one of those great actors who bring a lot out of a director. It's no good just sitting there with Judi and saying "lovely". She wants to know; she wants to be challenged, to be made to think. She wants to be stretched. All great actors I've worked with have wrung me dry.'

Not passive then, nor needing to be carried, but requiring a sense of certitude from her directors. Trevor Nunn's view is that 'she has a healthy suspicion. She's not so reliant on directors that she'll do anything asked, however batty or flying in the face of the text or taste. I think she's privately circumspect about ideas. She turns down a lot of offers. But having elected to do something she does grow un-happy if there is indecision.

'I've known Judi to be very unhappy during one or two rehearsal periods at the RSC under the control of col-leagues, and want to talk to me about it as artistic director of the company. And the unhappiness grows as she feels the indecisiveness and is being asked to make a number of crucial decisions about the role — she is not that kind of actress.'

There is no doubt that Judi Dench is an actress who can metaphorically fly — provided she has a push. As her hus-band puts it: 'She depends for her independence on the opinions of others.'

Certainly one reason why Judi has produced her best work on the stage is that she needs a *reaction* to her per-formances, which a theatre audience provides best of all. Though acutely shy of appearing in even the smallest of gatherings as herself (she has been known to stand outside quaking before entering a room with a party going on) Judi is not at all reticent about playing a part in front of several hundred people at a time.

That is not to say she never suffers from nerves on stage — in some ways she is more nervous now, knowing all the pitfalls, than she was during her earliest professional years — but that is a nervousness to do with getting things right, not with actual appearance.

On the other hand she does like to 'personalize' her acting, in that she finds it easier to sharpen and define her performance, to put, in her own words, 'the barb on the arrow', if there is somebody she knows sitting in the audience — 'otherwise you're firing at an amorphous mass.' At one time she used to look out into the audience and pick an individual spectator at whom she could direct her performance.

In an interview published in *Plays and Players* in 1979, Judi gave an amusing insight into the degree of awareness that an actor has of his audience: 'The audience is absolutely paramount in making you feel good or bad at the end. Audiences have no idea how important they are. They're always amazed to know we can hear them cough . . . sometimes you know that a whole section of the audience — because somebody has a great big cough or blows their nose — has lost a line or two. And sometimes it's very important. Once I was playing Portia and a little girl in the front row unwrapped a Mars bar and ate it all through "The quality of mercy is not strain'd." That's all I'll say about my performance.'

The point of greatest contentment for Judi in her professional life derives from the contractual business of being offered and accepting a part. Thereafter she always says she finds rehearsals a strain, performance a hard grind, and completion of a run, with the disbanding of the company, a time of regret.

Intelligent without being intellectual, painstaking without being academic, her mode of preparation once she has passed the 'glorious moment' of accepting a role is grounded in instinct and the subconscious.

She has no special rules for preparing for a part although she does actually follow a pattern. She avoids reading or research (the only exceptions being for *Juno and the Pay-*

cock and *Cats*, where detailed research was part of Trevor Nunn's rehearsal programme), partly to avoid preconceptions: 'One's instinctive reaction to something can be very valuable. I think sometimes you blur that by reading about a character or reading what other people have said about it. It's better for me to have those blank white pages to work on.

'You can't draw it all from yourself, so you have to be able to observe people. Then your "inner camera" stores away the information. I work out very early on what I'm going to look like. I usually do a drawing. And I suppose the all-seeing eye looks around at people and paintings for a bit of inspiration. Ideas come from all sorts of sources. Alec McCowen and Michael each looked at the monkeys in Regent's Park before playing the Fool in *Lear*.

'A lot of the preparation is subliminal. You find you just can't work out how to play the role and then, suddenly, it all comes together, like it did when I went to Scotland for a fortnight in the middle of rehearsals for *The Importance of Being Earnest*. Something had worked itself out by the time I'd got back.'

Judi sees the subconscious mind as a kind of super-efficient filing system. She would contend that her observation of somebody's physical characteristics is mentally indexed ready to be imitated in a subsequent, suitable context, or, more specifically, that the influence of seeing Dorothy Tutin in *I Am a Camera* or Peggy Ashcroft as Imogen or Barbara Jefford as Viola, ran deep and was ready to be mined for her own performances in *Cabaret*, *Cymbeline* and *Twelfth Night*.

In common with all actors, Judi's own personal nature is also an obvious influence upon her playing, and the fact that she is a caring, sensitive but optimistic person undoubtedly lends strength to her acting. For Judi, private life can feed professional life but not vice versa. She says the energy from being emotionally charged personally can be channelled into playing a character. Thus, Judi Dench's emotional reaction to her mother's death could bring something extra to Deborah in *A Kind of Alaska* or Barbara in *Pack of Lies*, but neither Deborah nor Barbara could alter the private Judi Dench. So far as she is concerned, a strong emotional performance is basically 'just tiring'. The role does not 'take over'. At the end of the evening, exhausted though she may be, she will be utterly herself.

A phrase often used by Judi in rehearsal is, 'I'll get that up at home', by which she means that, rather than continue to experiment, probe and analyse under rehearsal conditions, she will allow her subconscious mind to work out that particular bit of the role while she gets the supper or does the crossword. This sometimes means that she wants to bring a rehearsal to an early close which Trevor Nunn, for one, is happy to let her do:

'She is one of the very few people I would trust to do that. What she means by, "I'll get that up at home" is, "If I do it any more I will be doing something untrue, I will be continuing to do something that I haven't digested. What we've done is to ask a lot of questions. Now I've got to be left alone and maybe in two days' time I'll know what that means to me." So when Judi says, "Can we stop there?" I trust that completely.'

Judi is drawn to certain directors and companies because she knows that rehearsals will be conducted in an uninhibited atmosphere of collective questioning and unpretentious hard work, where the play is continually kept alive, with a dynamism carrying it well beyond the first night.

She always does extensive physical work, being greatly concerned to get right the movement of her characters, and performs a sequence of vocal exercises before each appearance. Her voice, celebrated for its distinctive and expressive qualities, is far from invulnerable. During the first weeks of *Mother Courage* at the Barbican, Judi regularly lost her voice in between performances and had to sleep for two or three hours a day to restore it.

She develops a routine for each play, which invariably involves getting to the theatre early and one or two little superstitions like refraining from whistling. When she played Lady Bracknell she always took a bath beforehand. And when her dressing-room is orderly, with the inevitable array of good-luck cards arranged panoramically around the walls and her mirror, with make-up, costumes and all the other paraphernalia carefully in place, she is ready to launch into performance.

Her love of build-up, of continuity, is perhaps the central reason why she feels most comfortable working in the theatre, where there is no quest for a once-and-for-all performance to be put away 'in the can'. Judi loves constantly working at a part, honing, re-defining and developing it. Best of all she likes to be working on three or four plays at the same time, as at the National or the RSC, because 'it keeps you on your toes and you make continual fresh starts.'

To a film director like Stephen Frears, this deep, concentrated craftsmanship is fascinating, mysterious and admirable: 'It never seems to me that her routes to her ends are straightforward. In the minutiae of doing a scene, on the professional level it's perfectly clear, but deep down she's making complicated decisions and they're immensely interesting.

'When she works with me I don't get the feeling she's thought about the part at all. But I'm not going to help her, I'm not going to tell her what to do. She's always saying, "I don't know what to do" at such and such a moment. I say, "You'll find out" — and she finds out at a much more complicated level than that of the audience's response. She makes a simple decision, then generally goes away and sleeps for a bit. Then she does it with such authority that it appears as though there is no other way.'

Directors and actors are united in praise of Judi's work. Frears sees her as our best actress — 'she makes you feel good, that all things are possible. She's so malleable and so strong' — while Sir Peter Hall enthuses over her 'watchability', in that the eye is drawn to her whenever she walks on stage, and her gift of 'self-mockery' in the tradition of great English actresses like Ellen Terry, Edith Evans and Peggy Ashcroft.

David Hare is excited by her combination of 'supreme technical ability and extraordinary emotional depth and simplicity.' To demonstrate the extent of her technical skill he gives the instance of a complicated group discussion scene in *Wetherby*, during a rehearsal for which Judi asked him how she should express the word 'yes', what it meant exactly at that point.

He replied, 'It means "no" ' and she was able to say it straight away in precisely the way he'd conceived it. Hare believes that her basic technical expertise is what enables her to take off into the furthest emotional areas: 'It gives her freedom. Most actors can say a line five ways. Any one of a hundred ways are available to her.'

Barbara Leigh-Hunt is particularly impressed by the way Judi has 'bridged the gap between being a juvenile actress, in the old commercial jargon, and more mature roles. A lot of actresses of Judi's type, some very talented, who would play the Ophelias, Juliets and Perditas — young, pretty girls — never do bridge the gap.' As evidence of Judi's achievement, Barbara Leigh-Hunt cites her immediacy and openness with the public, and her generosity and receptivity towards her colleagues, views endorsed by Richard Pasco, Miss Leigh-Hunt's husband, who has worked with Judi many times.

Judi's own spouse, Michael Williams, is plainly astounded by his wife's talents, her 'emotional well so deep', her speed of thought — 'if you can keep up you feel rather good' — and her capacity for giving stunning first-night performances.

Roger Rees is one actor for whom Judi has been an enormously beneficial influence, even though he concedes that 'there are things about Judi's work that people could dislike — maybe the voice, the energy, the adulation — I can understand that.

'I think I do certain vocal things which I've inherited from Judi. I don't mean the immortal crack in the voice but there's a certain kind of speaking with the breath, extending vowel sounds.'

Both Roger Rees and Peter Hall see in Judi an ability to combine masculine and feminine attributes, something which Hall again feels links her with the likes of Terry, Evans and Ashcroft: 'They have all been superb as Shakespearian heroines. All have a curious boyish quality as well as being intensely feminine, which makes them so wonderful in Shakespeare. They all have a "dancing wit" quality. There are others: Vanessa Redgrave has it; Dorothy Tutin; but they're fairly rare.'

Joe Mitchenson is another who brackets Judi with Ellen

Terry and Peggy Ashcroft ('I'm sure Peggy herself is strongly aware of the inevitable comparision. They are very akin'), describing them as 'natural' actresses who are 'always for real'. In this respect he also likens Judi, perhaps surprisingly, to an altogether different kind of actress, the late Margaret Rutherford: 'She always had to treat her characters as very real people.'

Among Judi's contemporaries there are few direct comparisons to be made. She is very much her own person, whose mighty versatility has been stretched into areas where other actresses would be reluctant to tread, and the names commonly mentioned — Glenda Jackson, Vanessa Redgrave, Diana Rigg, Maggie Smith — are usually compared simply in terms of status in the 'Who is Britain's leading actress?' kind of discussion.

Judi herself likes to watch Eileen Atkins and has electric memories of Coral Browne as Gertrude in *Hamlet* and of course of Barbara Jefford and Dorothy Tutin. Working recently with Anna Massey at the National was also an exciting revelation.

The supreme quality for Judi is professionalism. She strives for it herself and it is what moves her most of all in watching performers. She chooses an unlikely example to illustrate this. Several years ago she was taken to see Danny La Rue in *Come Spy with Me*, in which, dressed as a woman, coiffeured and made up in the usual glamorous manner, he sang a duet with the late Gary Miller.

They sang one verse and Danny went off, leaving Gary Miller to sing a verse alone. Then, right on cue, Danny returned as himself, dressed in tails, no make-up, false nails or eyelashes, and the two men sang the remaining verse and chorus together. Though within the realm of undemanding entertainment, it was an accomplished piece of technique and it made Judi burst into tears. She wrote a fan letter to Danny La Rue and they became good friends. He was a guest at her wedding, proving very popular with Judi's nephew and nieces, who clambered over Dame Peggy to get Danny's autograph.

Conversely, one of Judi's pet hates in the theatre is lack of professionalism, 'holding others to ransom' she calls it. 'There are certain things we all know are homework and some people take up other people's time to sort it out then and there.' She hates the casual approach, remembering her early days at the Vic when the company would be formally attired for the first reading, the women in dresses and high-heeled shoes.

As for rehearsal, so for performance: 'I don't like self-indulgence on the stage. We can all be accused of it at times. And I get maddened by inaudibility. There's absolutely no reason for that. It's carelessness.

'I don't like somebody who spends a long time indulging himself saying, "To be . . . or not . . . to be." I'm tired by then and lost. John Gielgud said the third time he played Hamlet was the best because by then he was able to present that speech in an arc. The equivalent of John is Frank Sinatra. I don't care for someone like Tony Bennett who sings, "I . . . left . . . my . . . heart . . . in San-Fran-cis-co." It's to do with speaking — songs need to be spoken. I love the sound of Binnie Hale, Fred Astaire, Lotte Lenya. I've always maintained that if you listen to Frank Sinatra it will teach you something about speaking Shakespeare.'

Another thing Judi took to heart during her early years was the fact that discipline — or lack of it — in a company, stems from the top, and she is a most determinedly professional leader of a company. Judi is always concerned about the whole company, its environment and welfare. She invariably knows and acts on details like people's states of health, birthdays, the name of the stage doorkeeper, and so on.

She is especially keen to ensure that the entire company pulls together to become so familiar with each other that everyone can make a fool of himself: 'Unless you can make a joke at your own expense I don't believe you can act; shed that necessary final layer.

'It's embarrassing to appear foolish in front of people you don't know. The more you know people, on the other hand, the more you know the way they work, the more prepared you are to go "too far". And then you can always be pulled back. It's a terrible thing to leave it without having pushed it far enough.'

Peter Hall regards Judi as a very positive influence, humorous and professional, making sure everyone has a good time, though 'she expects people not to waste time, to be punctual, and to get on with it.' Trevor Nunn describes her as 'a natural company leader. No artistic director was ever as potent as a leader from within a company. Judi's professional standards, punctiliousness, optimism and spirit are exemplary. There can be nobody within a company led by Judi Dench who can say, "I'm not doing that, because there's a senior member of the company not doing it."'

Judi's thorough, professional attitude is one she tries to impart to the students she teaches from time to time, mainly at the Actors' Centre in London. Her message is: 'Learn as much as you can about every aspect of the theatre, not just acting. Learn how you make a wig or a costume or a prop or how to light something. It's only by seeing that all the parts are working that you can be sure the whole is well.' One drama school, the Mountview, named its studio theatre after Judi, and from time to time she does some judging there.

She is as concerned to apply professional standards to her lessons and lectures — another recent outlet was to some American students on a drama course at Balliol College, Oxford — as she is to her stage and television performances or indeed to her poetry recitals.

These have continued almost unabated since Nottingham in 1965, and most Sundays she shares a platform with Michael, or such other leading actors as Richard Pasco, Barbara Leigh-Hunt or Roger Rees, and musicians Robert Spencer and Jill Nott-Bower, usually for charity. In the 1960s she inaugurated a series of readings at Westminster Abbey and since then she has read thousands of verses by hundreds of poets, always remembering those evenings of jazz and e.e.cummings at Nottingham.

Part of Judi Dench's attractiveness as an actress lies in the probability that she has no idea that she is so very good. And, like an eager youth apprenticed to a diamond cutter, she works hard and enthusiastically at her trade without ever quite appreciating the full value of her raw material — her talent. Michael Williams, closer to her than anyone, believes, 'she doesn't have any real recognition of how great her talent is.'

The only one of her performances in which she permits herself to take pride was on the radio with Peggy Ashcroft in a play by Susan Hill where both actresses were given long monologues. Judi heard it by accident when she was in hospital with her Achilles' tendon injury and didn't recognize herself at first. Radio's higher degree of anonymity appeals to her greatly, even though her appearances in this medium have been comparatively sketchy — though here too, she has demonstrated her versatility, with roles ranging from the classical to a bizarre underwater opera in which she and Norman Rodway had to wear snorkels and goggles.

There is no trace of arrogance in Judi's work, a fact which combined with her natural warmth and her shortness of stature, puts her at a disadvantage in any role calling for imperiousness or *hauteur* — a quality which, nonetheless, she has been able to convey effectively through, say, Beatrice (for whom it is incidental) if not quite comprehensively as Lady Bracknell (for whom it is fundamental).

Judi's grandeur is of a weightier kind: the dignity she conveys on stage — as Juno or Lady Macbeth, or, to a lesser extent, Barbara Jackson or Mother Courage — is built on weakness or suffering, often imbuing her characters with a touch of nobility.

After all her years in the theatre — and this is again an attractive part of her professional make-up — Judi still does not feel secure as an actress, or indeed wholly as a person. Her shyness, she says, can make her 'conventional, dull and very unadventurous'. She is unduly sensitive to criticism and in constant need of approval and support. Her greatest fear, expressed more frequently before a camera than on the stage, is of being exposed as inadequate, of 'somebody saying, "She's no good. She can't do it. Get her off the set."'

She says she doesn't know what her strengths and weaknesses are on stage, but off stage claims a ready familiarity with her failings: 'I wish I didn't have such a butterfly mind — which I see in Finty, now. I can concentrate only for so long on one thing, though I don't find it hard to learn a part. I find it very, very easy. It drives Mike mad.

'I'm always hoping that I look different. It's a lifelong

battle. When we did the film of *Saigon*, I had it so much in my mind what I looked like and then saw the rushes and was appalled. So I do go through life in a bit of a fantasy. I don't face up to realities.'

This last statement is one with which Michael concurs: 'It is an extraordinary part of Jude's personality that she shies away from reality. It's difficult getting her to understand the realities of everyday expenditure, money in the long term, like insurance. I have to sit her down to explain any financial problems and get her to look at them in an objective way, just as I do with scripts.

'When it comes to the crunch and she has actually to do it, has to understand, say, a financial problem, she's marvellous. But initially she doesn't want to know about the basic realities of getting down to work.

'She hardly ever gets pessimistic or depressed. If Jude has got a fault at all, it's that it has to be Christmas every day for her and all those around her.'

Judi's devotion to her friends is legendary, and in turn she depends upon their constancy. And her circle of friends is positively equatorial. While she is in regular touch with Susie Bodmer — with whom she is always exchanging cards and telephone calls and with whose family Judi, Michael and Finty nowadays spend their Christmases — and others in various walks of life, including Charlotte Arnold, her erstwhile physiotherapist, a large body of her close friends are, naturally enough, theatrical people, among them Alec McCowen, John Moffatt, Wendy Toye, Pinkie Kavanaugh — whom she was with at the Old Vic, Lee Montague and his wife Ruth; Bryan Pringle and Annie, his wife; Anna Massey; David Hare; Barbara Leigh-Hunt and Richard Pasco; directors Hauser, Frears and Nunn; actors McKellen and Rees; and her agent, Julian Belfrage.

The link is humour — 'I can't think of *any* of those I would call my close friends who haven't got a definite sense of humour' — with diverse other factors in permutation. Barbara Leigh-Hunt, for example, points to an astrological connection:

'We're both Sagittarians (Judi's a year older and gets cross because each year there are five days when she's *two* years older!) and both think and act along the same lines. Often we independently buy the same things for ourselves or our houses. One time Jeff Dench rang and spoke to me for twenty minutes which I thought strange until suddenly the penny dropped. He thought I was Judi.'

Barbara Leigh-Hunt has also observed Judi's need to be surrounded by people. 'I think Judi finds it hard when, rarely, she is not the centre of attention. She's used to being the life and soul of the party and she plays it to a great extent. But she does it to keep other people and the atmosphere happy.'

Judi was one of the two witnesses at Barbara's wedding. The other was Richard Pasco's uncle, to whom Judi has since always referred as 'the other bridesmaid.' Judi's outfit contained three buttons, each of which popped off throughout the ceremony which was thereby halted three times as the registrar stopped to pick them up for her.

Magazine and newspaper interviewers frequently say of Judi that she is not at all 'actressy'. Similarly, other actors and actresses often refer approvingly to her 'plainness' or 'ordinary' or 'down-to-earth' qualities. Such comments have created something of a myth. The truth is that Judi's manner and bearing are emphatically those of an actress and she is about as plain as a gazelle. She *is* demonstrative, extrovert and excitable but in a genuine way — her 'darlings' are for real.

Unfortunately, terms like 'actressy' or 'actorish' have come to mean false, insincere and affected. Quite simply, Judi is not and does not consider herself to be too grand for the ordinary, day-to-day aspects of life. Her demeanour can be as hotly theatrical as the next person's, but there is nothing showy or calculated about it. She has nothing to prove. Actressy she is; affected she isn't.

She is a fatalistic person who believes that 'we sometimes get what we need rather than what we want,' and that it is 'much better to sit back and see what unfolds' than to burn energy striving for goal after goal, quaintly referring to 'the man with the bucket of ice-cold water waiting round the corner to soak you just when you think you are riding high.'

The only regret she admits to is that she didn't have a second child. At one stage she and Michael discussed adoption, and made one or two tentative enquiries. They considered the possibility of a Vietnamese child and enlisted the help of Mervyn Stockwood, the former Bishop of Southwark, but it was not to be.

She and Michael have shown great kindness at times of stress to many people, Joe Mitchenson and the actress Polly James among them. Judi's brother Peter, whom she sees about three or four times a year, describes her as 'utterly kind with never a nasty word. She has just not changed over the years, though in the best possible way she's got a lot more extravagant — we can never pay for a seat or a meal.

'She rides all the troubles — she doesn't let on. You know she's sometimes worried about a part, but that's all. She doesn't talk an awful lot about her career.'

'A little powerhouse' is what Roger Rees calls her, and certainly it's hard to imagine anybody crowding so much, so fulfillingly, into one life. Amid a score of consuming pastimes she sews at every available moment and has a queue of people wanting one of her renowned rude cushions which have four-letter words artistically embroidered upon them. Satisfied recipients to date include Nigel Havers, David Hare, Anna Massey and Stephen Frears.

An avid collector of a variety of objects and ornaments, Judi describes herself as an inveterate hoarder who has inherited this trait from members of her family, most notably her father's eldest brother Will:

'He used to keep everything. One day he put in an entire bathroom for somebody on a Sunday. They said, "Will, where on earth did you get all the things from?" "I had them by me," he said. Once we were all painting — Will was an RA — on a picnic at Bosham. We had lobster. Uncle Will was painting in oils and he was eating with a palette knife he had just been using on his painting. I was frightfully impressed. He saw me looking and broke off one of the lobster's red whiskers, put it in his top pocket and said to me, "You never know when you might need one of those." '

Through the years Judy has organized picnics galore. She also loves cooking and giving dinner parties, which sometimes overwhelms Michael, a rooted meat-and-two-veg man — 'He hates it when I sneak wine into something. He says it should be in the glass. I'm always inflicting things like salmon mousse on him and seeing him sigh.'

Judi herself appreciates wine in the glass, too, as well as in the casserole. She loves champagne and hates spirits. She never smokes, however. On her eighteenth birthday her parents gave her a pigskin case, full of cigarettes with a lighter to match but she never enjoyed smoking and has found it uncomfortable in parts like Sally Bowles in *Cabaret* and Amanda in *Private Lives*.

She swims, cycles and paints whenever she can and involves Michael and Finty in all these activities, cherishing the occasions when the family is collectively absorbed. Once, all three of them were on holiday at Windermere concentrating very hard on painting a little group of islands there, the Lilies-of-the-Valley, and so preoccupied were they that none of them noticed a large cow sidle up to them, until it fell over a log and caused the ground to shake.

Animals are another family passion. At any one time an assortment of cats, dogs, hamsters and guinea-pigs may be found in and around the home. They also own two otters at the Zoo. Once, in Hampstead, after a few drinks in celebration of a wedding anniversary, Judi went up to bed while Michael went out to check the pet hamster.

After a while he appeared and announced sorrowfully, 'The hamster's broken its leg. The bone is sticking out through the fur.' Judi went to look and cried in confirmation, 'Oh Michael, the bone is sticking out right through the fur.' In desperation they called the vet. It was now well past midnight and they were both distraught. When the vet arrived early the next morning he reached into the hamster's cage and promptly removed the offending 'bone' — which turned out to be a Sugar Puff stuck to the hamster's fur.

A romantic couple — he has sent her a red rose every Friday for years — who 'cannot bear' to row, Mike and Judi do sometimes have their differences. Occasionally they don't see eye to eye on political matters, whether internally at the RSC or in the world at large. Michael is a firm supporter of the Liberal/SDP Alliance, Judi a more recent convert — just in time to vote for her local SDP candidate in the 1983 General Election. Previously she'd voted Labour, never Conservative.

She has given her name to a number of causes over the years. She was a signatory to the December 1984 large press advertisement calling for support for the families of striking coal-miners, and is a vociferous opponent of VAT on theatre seats.

Among the various charities in which Judi takes an interest, Help the Aged, the Wings Fellowship Trust and the Pre-School Playgroups Association are favourites. In 1968 she flew out to Israel to film a Christmas Day Appeal for Christian Aid, which raised £37,000. It was shown at peak viewing time on BBC 1 and the TV critic of *The Scotsman* wrote that it was the highlight of Christmas Day viewing. Olave went with her and the experience left a vivid impression:

'We stayed on for a while after the filming was finished. We were at Tiberias eating St Peter's fish. It was a glorious evening until suddenly out of the calmness an enormous storm rose up. In the morning you could hear all the cocks crowing and you think of the story of the denial in the Bible, everything happening so quickly. And then on the hill above Bethlehem I pulled up this round thorny plant, exactly like in all those pictures of the crown of thorns.'

Religion is an area where Judi and Michael have arrived at a working accommodation. The Mount's influence remains and though Judi goes only rarely to meetings nowadays, she is probably closer than ever to that Quaker inner peace. And while Judi takes Finty to meetings and talks to her about Quakerism, Michael has taken it upon himself to introduce her to Catholicism and the two of them go to mass together. Both Judi and Michael are consciously creating a basis from which Finty can eventually choose her own path.

The latter end of 1985 saw Judi coming increasingly before the cameras and extending her repertoire into the writings of some of the most celebrated authors of the past century or so.

John Barton's production of *Waste*, Harley Granville-Barker's once notorious play about political scandal, came out of the hothouse atmosphere of the RSC studio theatre at the end of March and into the proscenium arch of the

Lyric, Shaftesbury Avenue on May 24 with Sara Kestelman and David Waller joining the cast. Judi continued her role as Amy O'Connell, whose early death enabled Judi to leave without waiting for the curtain call and so get home regularly at a reasonable hour.

Just before the West End opening Judi flew to Florence for a fortnight to play the cameo role of the British Italophile, Eleanor Lavish, in James Ivory and Ismail Merchant's film of E.M. Forster's *A Room With a View* with Maggie Smith and Denholm Elliott. Next came *The Browning Version* for BBC TV, under the direction of Michael Simpson, in which Judi played opposite Ian Holm, with support from Michael Kitchen and John Woodvine. She then became more familiar with the work of *The Browning Version*'s author when she appeared in the *In Praise of Rattigan* series of readings at Chichester and the Aldwych with Denis Quilley, Robin Bailey and Christopher Cazenove.

On July 8 Judi performed a scene from *Private Lives* with Ian McKellen at the special request of the Queen Mother, as part of that royal lady's birthday celebrations on Radio 4. That same month Judi gave recitals as part of the City of London Festival and with Michael at a cluster of beautiful venues on the Channel Islands.

The first half of August was a domestic time in which Judi passed her driving test at the first attempt and went up to York for the wedding of her nephew, Simon. Then came four weeks in Sri Lanka for the filming of a 90-minute BBC drama adapted by Trevor Bowen from Noel Coward's short story *Mr and Mrs Edgehill*. This was directed by Gavin Millar, produced by Alan Shawcross, and had Judi working with Ian Holm for the third time in a year. It is the story of an unlikely couple from London living in the Samoan Islands during World War Two and finding themselves suddenly burdened with a national and diplomatic job. Judi was allowed time off in the middle for Finty's birthday, taking the 17-hour flight back to the UK.

She then did another play for BBC TV, taking the part of Mrs Alving in Ibsen's *Ghosts* with Kenneth Branagh, Natasha Richardson, Freddie Jones and Michael Gambon, and found it to be one of her most difficult tasks to date.

*

The road from ancient York to the new Barbican has been a long but fairly smooth one and Judi Dench has trodden it firmly. Few actresses, given so many accolades, can have been so attentive to the feelings of others, few can have been so wide-ranging, so comprehensively respected within the profession and outside.

Somehow Judi doesn't fit the description of 'star'. A star is inevitably remote, aloof even, from the public, whereas Judi's great strength is her ability to reach audiences directly and profoundly. In the best sense of the word she is a *natural*.

It's not that she doesn't have to sweat for her living — she does more than most — but she does bring to her art the marvellous advantage of being Judi Dench, the doctor's daughter with a natural sympathy and retentive consciousness, whose vividly happy childhood provided the supplest and most solid of springboards.

Number 54 Heworth Green was a house that rang with laughter, which for Judi has always been the main route to the human heart, whether in practical jokes with friends or in the professionally humorous playing of an Adriana or a Beatrice.

Judi Dench is surely a genius among actresses. She may lack the natural grace of some or the stark presence of others, but whatever she does, her audience believes her. As Sir Peter Hall says, 'Very few people can hold a candle to her. There are a few — there always are. She is one of the great actresses of our time. What more can I say?'

Appendix

The stage roles of Judi Dench 1957—85

		Opening date
Old Vic 1957—61		
(incorporating tours to United States, Belgium, France, Yugoslavia and Italy)		
Hamlet	Ophelia	Sept. 57
Measure for Measure	Juliet	Nov. 57
A Midsummer Night's Dream	First Fairy	Dec. 57
Twelfth Night	Maria	Apr. 58
Henry V	Katharine	Jul. 58
The Double Dealer	Cynthia	Aug. 59
The Merry Wives of Windsor	Anne Page	Dec. 59
As You Like It	Phebe	Sept. 59
The Importance of Being Earnest	Cecily Cardew	Oct. 59
Richard II	Queen	May 60*
Romeo and Juliet	Juliet	Oct. 60
She Stoops to Conquer	Kate Hardcastle	Nov. 60
A Midsummer Night's Dream	Hermia	Dec. 60
(and walk on parts in King Lear and Henry VI)		
Royal Shakespeare Company 1961—2		
The Cherry Orchard	Anya	Dec. 61
Measure for Measure	Isabella	Apr. 62
A Midsummer Night's Dream	Titania	Apr. 62
A Penny for a Song	Dorcas Bellboys	Aug. 62
Nottingham Playhouse 1963		
(incorporating tour to West Africa)		
Macbeth	Lady Macbeth	Jan. 63
Twelfth Night	Viola	Jan. 63
Lyric, Shaftesbury Avenue 1963		
A Shot in the Dark	Josefa Lautenay	May 63

*The production opened in November 1959 but this was when Judi took over from Maggie Smith.

Oxford Playhouse 1964—5

Three Sisters	Irina	Apr. 64
The Twelfth Hour	Anna	May 64
The Alchemist	Dol Common	Jan. 65
Romeo and Jeannette	Jeannette	Feb. 65
The Firescreen	Jacqueline	Mar. 65

Nottingham Playhouse 1965—6

Measure for Measure	Isabella	Sept. 65
Private Lives	Amanda	Oct. 65
The Country Wife	Margery Pinchwife	Jan. 66
The Astrakhan Coat	Barbara	Feb. 66
St Joan	Joan	Mar. 66

Oxford Playhouse 1966—7

The Promise	Lika	Nov. 66
Rules of the Game	Sila	Dec. 66

Palace Theatre 1968

Cabaret	Sally Bowles	Feb. 68

Royal Shakespeare Company 1969—72
(incorporating tours to Japan and Australia)

The Winter's Tale	Hermione and Perdita	May 69
Women Beware Women	Biana	Jul. 69
Twelfth Night	Viola	Aug. 69
London Assurance	Grace Harkaway	Jun. 70
Major Barbara	Barbara Undershaft	Oct. 70
The Merchant of Venice	Portia	Mar. 71
The Duchess of Malfi	Duchess	Jul. 71
Toad of Toad Hall	Various	Dec. 71

Theatre Royal, York 1973

Content to Whisper	Aurelia	Apr. 73

Oxford Playhouse 1973

The Wolf	Vilma	Sept. 73

Her Majesty's 1974

The Good Companions	Miss Trant	Jul. 74

Albery 1975

The Gay Lord Quex	Sophie Fullgarney	Jun. 75

Royal Shakespeare Company 1975—80

Too True to be Good	Sweetie Simpkins	Oct. 75
Much Ado About Nothing	Beatrice	Apr. 76
Macbeth	Lady Macbeth	Sept. 76

The Comedy of Errors	Adriana	Oct. 76
King Lear	Regan	Dec. 76
Pillars of the Community	Lona Hessel	Aug. 77
The Way of the World	Millamant	Jan. 78
Cymbeline	Imogen	Apr. 79
Juno and the Paycock	Juno Boyle	Oct. 80

New End, Hampstead 1981
| A Village Wooing | Young Woman | Oct. 81 |

National Theatre 1982–3
| A Kind of Alaska | Deborah | Oct. 82 |
| The Importance of Being Earnest | Lady Bracknell | Nov. 82 |

Lyric, Shaftesbury Avenue 1983
| Pack of Lies | Barbara Jackson | Oct. 83 |

Royal Shakespeare Company 1984–5
| Mother Courage | Courage | Nov. 84 |
| Waste | Amy O'Connell | Jan. 85 |

Index

Achard, Marcel 46
Ackland, Joss 34
Adams, Polly 47, 49, 52, 53
A Fine Romance 134, 136, 150,
    163-165
A Kind of Alaska 8, 120, 129,
    131-132, 133, 135, 174
Alchemist, The 53, 56
Alice in Wonderland 9
A Man for all Seasons 96
A Midsummer Night's Dream 14, 26,
    28, 35, 36, 40, 41, 42, 43, 112,
    137, 145, 147–148
Amiel, Jon 127
An Age of Kings 149, 150
Anderson, Mary 75
An Englishman Abroad 167
Andrews, Harry 30
Andrews, Julie 166
Annis, Francesca 113
Anouilh, Jean 57
Ansermet, Ernest 33
A Penny for a Song 45, 46
Arbuzov, Alexei 55, 65, 99
Arden, John 24
Arms and the Man 47
Argyll, Margaret, Duchess of 129
Arnold, Charlotte 125, 126, 127,
    182
Arnold, Matthew 64
A Room With a View 187
Asari, Keita 94
Ashcroft, Peggy 17, 19, 37, 40, 91,
    128, 174, 176, 177, 178, 181
Asherson, Renée 23
Ashmore, Peter 23
A Shot in the Dark 46, 52, 53, 54,
    73
Astaire, Fred 179
Astrakhan Coat, The 63
A Study in Terror 145
As You Like It 34, 170

A Taste of Honey 144
Atkins, Eileen 62, 150, 153, 178
Attenborough, Richard 145
A Village Wooing 138, 157
Awakenings 131
Aylmer, Felix 116

Bailey, Robin 187
Baker, George 52, 53
Banks-Smith, Nancy 155
Bannerman, Celia 101
Barber, John 109
Barden, John 101, 102
Barkworth, Peter 154
Barr, Hermann and Edith 97
Barton, John 74, 78, 79, 83, 105,
    106, 114, 115, 116, 118, 142,
    186
Basie, Count 31
Bates, Alan 168
Beckett, Samuel 24
Bedford, Angela 10
Beggar's Opera, The 23
Belchamber, David 11
Belfrage, Julian 17, 21, 68, 69, 182
Bell, Book and Candle 18
Bell, Elizabeth 137
Bell, Tom 147
Benedictus, David 89
Bennett, Alan 167
Bennett, Arnold 33, 150
Bennett, Tony 179
Benson, Tony 23
Benthall, Michael 23, 24, 25, 26, 27,
    28, 29, 30, 32
Berlin, Irving 69
Berry, Cicely 21, 22
Billington, Michael 101, 109, 116,
    118, 123
Birkett, Lord 147
Blackley, Elizabeth 9
Blatchley, John 41, 42, 59

Blessed, Brian 125
Bodmer, Gerald 52, 139, 140
Bodmer, Susie (Taylor) 52, 139, 140, 161, 182
Bogarde, Dirk 54
Bogart, Humphrey 167
Bolam, James 17
Boucicault, Dion 87, 95
Bowen, Trevor 187
Boyd, Stephen 145
Boys from Syracuse, The 113
Brake, Patricia 43
Branagh, Kenneth 187
Brecht, Bertolt 70, 140, 141, 142
Brennan, John 91
Bridge, Peter 67
Briers, Richard 157, 158
Brook, Peter 45, 111, 112
Brown, John Russell 37
Browne, Coral 25, 168, 178
Browne, Martin 25
Browning Version, The 187
Bruce, Brenda 76
Bruce, Roger 125, 126
Bryant, Michael 152
Bryden, Ronald 77
Buck, David 40
Burden, Suzanne 162
Burge, Stuart 151
Burgess, Guy 168
Burton, Richard 18
Bury, John 42
Byrne, M. St Clair 29
Byrne, Patsy 40

Cabaret 12, 67, 68, 69, 70, 71, 72, 73, 74, 100, 174, 185
Caesar and Cleopatra 4, 8
Cairncross, James 47, 49, 54, 68, 81, 82, 90
Calder-Marshall, Anna 104
Calvert, Phyllis 3
Canning, Heather 119
Carpenter, Edward 89
Carey, Jenneth 40
Carey, Liz 40
Carey-Jones, Selena 159
Carson, Violet 150
Casson, Philip 157
Catley, Gwen 68, 70, 71
Cats 125, 126, 127, 131, 132, 174
Cazenove, Christopher 187
Celebration 85
Cenci, The 33

Centrelivre, Mrs 87
Chekhov, Anton 54, 167
Cherry Orchard, The 26, 39, 40, 41, 72, 161, 162, 165
Christie, Julie 17
Church, Tony 43, 114
Clements, John 19
Clurman, Harold 52
Collier, Patience 40
Colquhoun, Robert 16
Colson, Kevin 73
Come Spy With Me 178
Comedy of Errors, The 112-114, 116, 118, 122, 154, 155, 156
Compton, Fay 34
Congreve, William 116, 117
Connell, Miranda 150
Content to Whisper 96
Cook, Juliet 27, 28, 29
Cooke, Alan 152
Cooper, Rowena 17
Coppola, Francis Ford 167
Corbishley, Tom 89, 90
Cossey, Elmer 155
Country Wife, The 63
Coveney, Michael 138
Cowans, Theo 71, 72
Coward, Noel 60, 61, 187
Craig, Michael 67
Crichton, Charles 145, 147
Cropper, Anna 127
Crozier, Mary 151
Cruickshank, Andrew 33, 149
Cuckoo in the Nest 4
cummings, e.e. 63, 180
Cunliffe, David 157, 158
Curran, Paul 162
Cusack, Sinead 95
Cushman, Robert 109, 123, 130, 171
Cymbeline 22, 118, 119, 120, 139, 174

Daneman, Paul 27, 30, 47, 49
Daniel, Jennifer 18, 19, 20
Daniel Martin 167
Davies, Gareth 71
Davies, Howard 141
Davies, Sue 142
Dawson, Anna 17
Day-Lewis, Sean 156
Days to Come, The 154
Dead Cert 149
De La Tour, Frances 62

De Musset, Alfred 57
Dench, Bessie 7
Dench, Betty 8
Dench, Daphne 7, 39, 56, 91
Dench, 'Gampy' 8
Dench, Jeffery 1, 3, 4, 5, 6, 7, 9, 11, 14, 15, 74, 84, 88, 119, 134, 135, 183
Dench, Kathleen 8
Dench, Louise 39
Dench, Olave 1, 2, 3, 4, 5, 6, 7, 8, 9, 10, 11, 13, 14, 15, 16, 19, 28, 30, 31, 54, 56, 58, 71, 82, 83, 86, 91, 92, 96, 97, 98, 120, 133, 134, 135
Dench, Peter 1, 3, 4, 6, 7, 8, 10, 11, 39, 55, 56, 90, 91, 135, 184
Dench, Reginald 1, 2, 3, 4, 5, 6, 7, 8, 9, 10, 11, 13, 14, 15, 16, 19, 28, 30, 31, 51, 52, 54, 55, 56, 86, 133, 135, 151
Dench, Simon 7, 56, 187
Dench, William 14, 184
Denham, Maurice 152, 153
Dennen, Barry 73
De Nobile, Lila 147
Desert Song, The 68
Detective 154
Devils, The 45
Dews, Peter 150
Dexter, John 23
Digby-Day, Richard 96
Divided Self, The 77
Dobie, Alan 154
Donald, James 23
Dotrice, Roy 40
Double Dealer, The 33, 34
Douglas, Kirk 144
Downs, Jane 31
Downs, Robert 160
Duchess of Malfi, The 88, 93, 94
Duffy, Patrick 51
Duncan, Frank 38
Duncan, Miss 9
Dunham, Joanna 38
Dunlop, Frank 46, 50
Durden, Richard 114
Dury, Susan 110
Dyson, Ann 78

Eagle in a Cage 86
Ebb, Fred 69
Edinger, Leland 'Dingo' 11
Eliot, T.S. 78, 124, 142

Ellice, Thomas 160
Elliott, Denholm 187
Ellis, Robin 114
Elsom, John 119, 123, 157
Enigma 126
Evans, Edith 30, 32, 34, 128, 130, 131, 176, 177
Evans, Tenniel 4
Everett, Rupert 17
Eyre, Richard 161, 162
Eyre, Ronald 62, 87, 88, 103
Family on Trial 33, 149, 150
Farrell, Pat 51
Faust 4
Feldman, Marty 71, 72
Fenton, George 142
Fenton, James 124
Fiddick, Peter 156, 161
Fields, Dorothy 165
Findlater, Richard 25, 29, 131
Finney, Albert 41
Firescreen, The 53, 57, 66, 154
Firstborn, The 14
Fleming, Tom 41, 42, 151
Fogerty, Elsie 17, 21, 23
Ford, Ford Madox 152
Forrest, Frederic 166, 167
Forster, E.M. 136, 187
Four in the Morning 55, 143, 146, 158, 168
Fowles, John 166
Francis, Derek 29
Francis, Dick 149
Fraser, Antonia 132
Frears, Stephen 145, 160, 165, 166, 167, 168, 171, 172, 176, 182, 184
French Lieutenant's Woman, The 155
Freud, Sigmund 77
Fry, C.B. 18
Fry, Charis 18, 19
Fry, Christopher 14
Funambulists, The 154

Gable, Christopher 101
Gabriel, John 3
Gambon, Michael 187
Garbo, Greta 143
Garrick, David 87
Garvie, Elizabeth 129
Gascoigne, Jill 47
Gay Lord Quex, The 102, 103
Gershwin, George 69

Ghosts 187
Giehse, Therese 140
Gielgud, John 30, 37, 40, 41, 85, 103, 130, 179
Gifford, Josh 149
Gigli, Beniamino 20
Giles, David 4
Goater, Miss 6, 7
Godfrey, Derek 27
Godfrey, Patrick 119
Going Gently 145, 160, 161, 165, 171, 172
Goldsmith, Oliver 35
Good Companions, The 100, 101
Good King Charles' Golden Days 23
Goodbody, Buzz 88, 107
Goring, Marius 42, 45
Gowon, General 82
Grace, Nickolas 113, 114
Graham, Colin 45
Granville-Barker, Harley 142, 186
Griffith, Eva 137
Griffiths, Richard 113
Griffiths, Trevor 162
Guard, Pippa 113
Guinness, Alec 126, 127
Gunter, John 121
Guthrie, Tyrone 46, 51
Gwilym, Mike 113

Hale, Binnie 179
Hall, Peter 39, 41, 42, 43, 44, 68, 79, 87, 112, 127, 128, 129, 130, 131, 132, 135, 145, 147, 148, 162, 170, 171, 172, 176, 177, 179, 188
Hall, Willis 85
Hamlet 24, 25, 26, 29, 30, 31, 33, 37, 44, 46, 143, 178
Hammond, Kay 19
Hands, Terry 75, 78, 87, 88, 92
Hardwick, Paul 40, 43
Hardy, Robert 150
Hare, David 21, 166, 168, 169, 176, 178, 182, 184
Hare, Robertson 45
Harris, Julie 46, 52-53
Harte, Judith 110
Hartley, Rachel 15
Harvey, Laurence 30
Harwood, Ronald 100, 101
Hauser, Frank 53, 54, 55, 56, 59, 66, 99, 100, 124, 135, 138, 158, 182

Havers, Nigel 129, 184
Haworth, Jill 100
He Who Rides a Tiger 147
Healy, Patsy 54
Helpman, Robert 27
Hendry, Ian 17
Henry V 18, 30, 31, 82, 94, 150
Henry VI 29
Henry VIII 30, 74
Hepton, Bernard 150
Hewitson, Ian 43
Hiawatha 4
Hicks, Greg 110
Higgins, Aidan 155
Higgins, John 113
Hilda Lessways 33, 150
Hill, Adrienne 27, 35
Hill, James 145
Hill, Susan 181
Hippo Dancing 19
Hirsch, Henric 99
Hitchcock, Alfred 171
Hitler, Adolf 140
Hobson, Harold 27, 92, 101
Hoffman, Dustin 143
Holm, Ian 40, 42, 43, 187
Hoodekoff, Larry 137
Hope-Wallace, Philip 42, 52, 70
Hopkins, John 33, 64, 90, 152, 153
Horn, Roderick 21
Houston, Donald 34, 145, 146, 150
Howard, Alan 21, 44, 61, 133
Howerd, Frankie 26, 35
Howse, Justin 125, 126, 127
Hudd, Walter 'Dickie' 17, 18, 23
Humble, William 158
Humphrey, John 27
Hurt, John 54, 55
Hutcheson, David 69
Hutchings, Geoffrey 119
Huxley, Aldous 45

I am a Camera 19, 67, 174
Ibsen, Henrik 116, 117, 187
Importance of Being Earnest, The 26, 34, 128, 129-131, 133, 135, 150, 174
Ingham, Barrie 76, 88
Innocent, Harold 31, 61, 62, 63
In Praise of Rattigan 187
Irons, Jeremy 155
Isherwood, Christopher 67, 73
Ivory, James 187

Jackson, Glenda 141, 143, 178
James, Clive 155
James, Emrys 79, 92, 94
James, Polly 184
Jarvis, Martin 129
Jeans, Ursula 55
Jefford, Barbara 18, 19, 23, 25, 27, 28, 30, 31, 32, 33, 34, 42, 69, 174, 178
Jewel in the Crown 153
Johnson, Celia 168
Johnson, Pat 6
Johnston, Bill 20, 23
Jones, David 118, 119, 155
Jones, Freddie 187
Jones, Harry Jebb 1
Jones, James Cellan 164
Jones, Johnson 1
Jones, Otto 1
Jonson, Ben 56
Juno and the Paycock 2, 120-123, 124, 173
Justin, John 34

Kander, John 69
Kavanaugh, Pinkie 182
Kay, John 14
Keach, Stacey 149
Kean, Marie 110, 123
Kedrova, Lila 72
Kemp, Jeremy 20
Kern, Jerome 165
Kestelman, Sara 186
King Lear 16, 34, 35, 114-116, 174
Kingsley, Ben 119
Kitchen, Michael 187
Klemperer, Otto 33
Kovari, The Great 162
Kretzmer, Herbert 156
Kroger, Peter and Helen 136, 137
Kulukundis, Eddie 136
Kurnitz, Harry 52
Kyle, Barry 114, 145

Laing, David 11
Laing, R.D. 77
Landen, Dinsdale 154
Langham, Michael 35, 36, 40, 150
Langrishe, go down 155, 156
Larbey, Bob 163
La Rue, Danny 178
Laughton, Charles 116
Laurenson, James 55

Leaver, Don 165
Le Carré, John 126
Lehmann, Beatrix 23
Leigh-Hunt, Barbara 24, 26, 27, 28, 29, 33, 35, 36, 40, 55, 67, 91, 95, 114, 137, 139, 177, 180, 182, 183
Lenya, Lotte 179
Lesser, Anton 162
Levin, Bernard 110, 112
Little Glass Clock, The 19
Livesey, Roger 54, 55
Lloyd, Marie 142
Lloyd-Evans, Gareth 77, 106
Lloyd Webber, Andrew 124, 125
Lockhart, Calvin 154
London Assurance 87, 88, 94, 119
Lonsdale, Frederick 154
Lonsdale, Gordon 136, 138
Look Back in Anger 24
Love in a Cold Climate 159, 160
Lovers, The 19
Love's Labours Lost 84
Lucius Junius Brutus 149
Luther 149
Lynn, Ann 146
Lynn, Ralph 45
Lynne, Gillian 113, 125

Macauley, Pauline 63
Macbeth 47, 48, 49, 50, 51, 82, 106-111, 112, 115, 116, 118, 122, 128, 156, 157
Macdonald, Kay 14
Mackay, Fulton 161
Mackenzie, John 11, 134
Macshane, Ian 65, 66
Magill, Ronald 62, 63
Major Barbara 41, 88, 92, 151, 152
Malcolmson, Christopher 12, 13
Malleson, Miles 34
Mander, Raymond 37, 71, 84, 85
Marshall, Susie 12, 13
Marshall, Wilson 6
Mason, Brewster 78, 92, 151
Mason, Margery 152
Massey, Anna 129, 131, 132, 133, 135, 162, 178, 182, 184
Massey, Daniel 103
Masteroff, Joe 70
Matthews, Francis 154
Maugham, William Somerset 166
May, John 20
McCowen, Alec 34, 113, 150, 174, 182

McCulloch, Joseph 89, 90, 134
McDiarmid, Ian 110
McGarrigle, Anthony 134
McKellen, Ian 65, 66, 104, 107, 109, 110, 111, 117, 133, 156, 157, 182, 187
McKern, Leon 99
McWhinnie, Donald 63, 159
Meaby, Phyllis 9, 10, 14
Measure for Measure 25, 26, 28, 41, 42, 59-60, 62, 63
Melia, Joe 105, 146
Melville, Alan 96
Mercer, Johnny 100
Merchant, Ismail 187
Merchant of Venice, The 84, 88, 92, 93
Merchant, Vivien 132
Merry Wives of Windsor, The 19, 34, 74, 83
Messel, Oliver 56
Michell, Keith 18
Middleton, Thomas 78
Mikado, The 56
Millar, Gavin 187
Miller, Gary 178
Mills, John 101, 102, 126
Mills, Mary 102, 126
Minnelli, Liza 73
Miser, The 46
Mitchenson, Joe 37, 53, 71, 84, 85, 177, 184
Mitford, Nancy 159
Moffat, Jean 5, 18, 20, 91
Moffat, John 5, 18, 20
Moffatt, John 54, 55, 159, 182
Molière 70
Molloy, Dearbhla 120, 123
Molnar, Ferenc 99
Montague, Lee and Ruth 182
Moore, Stephen 142
Morahan, Christopher 153
Morley, Christopher 75, 119
Morley, Robert 19
Mother Courage and her Children 140, 141-2, 175
Mount, Peggy 19
Moxon, John 154
Mr and Mrs Edgehill 187
Much Ado About Nothing 18, 37, 44, 105-106, 116, 122
Mulhare, Edward 31
Mulligan, Gerry 31
Murcell, George 40

Murray, Braham 100, 101
My Fair Lady 31

Napier, John 113, 142
Neighbours 154
Nelligan, Kate 17, 168
Neville, John 24, 25, 27, 28, 32, 47, 48, 50, 59, 60, 61, 62, 64, 145, 146
Newman, Paul 144
Newton, Robert 7
Nicholls, Anthony 25
Nights of Cabiria 71
Nkrumah, President 50, 82
Nott-Bower, Jill 180
Nunn, Trevor 44, 65, 66, 68, 74, 75, 76, 77, 78, 79, 80, 81, 84, 86, 87, 106, 107, 108, 109, 110, 111, 112, 113, 114, 115, 120, 121, 123, 124, 125, 126, 128, 155, 156, 157, 172, 174, 175, 180, 182

Obeyme, Mr 47
O'Casey, Sean 22, 120, 121, 122
O'Conor, Joseph 54
Old Possum's Book of Practical Cats 124
Olivier, Laurence 17
On Approval 154
On Giant's Shoulders 158, 160
Osborne, John 24
Othello 94, 107
Other Places 129

Pacino, Al 143
Pack of Lies 132, 136-140, 159, 165, 174
Page, Elaine 127
Page-Jackson, Richard 18
Palmer, Lilli 18
Parade's End 55, 152
Pasco, Richard 40, 76, 78, 94, 177, 180, 182, 183
Paterson, Bill 162
Peacock, Trevor 142
Pearman, Philip 25
Peck, Bob 110, 114, 119
Penhaligon, Susan 163, 164
Pennell, Nicholas 57
Pennington, Michael 117, 118
Percy, Esmé 23
Pericles, Prince of Tyre 74, 75
Pertwee, Roland 150
Peter, John 118

Phelan, Brian 146
Phillips, Sian 103
Pilbrow, Richard 68, 73, 100, 101
Pillars of the Community 116, 117
Pinero, Arthur Wing 102, 103
Pink String and Sealing Wax 150, 151
Pinter, Harold 8, 24, 120, 129, 131, 132, 155
Pirandello, Luigi 64, 65
Platts, David 134
Plays for Pleasure 157
Plenty 168
Plimsoll, Samuel 117
Poe, Edgar Allan 87
Porter, Cole 69
Power and the Glory, The 19
Preston, Duncan 110
Preview 127
Previn, André 100, 101
Priestley, J.B. 18, 100, 101
Prince, Harold 'Hal' 67, 68, 70, 73
Pringle, Annie 182
Pringle, Bryan 158, 159, 182
Private Lives 60, 63, 185, 187
Promise, The 65, 66, 67, 85, 99
Prowse, Juliet 71
Pursuit of Love, The 159
Purvis, Canon J.S. 4

Quilley, Denis 187

Rattigan, Terence 187
Raven, Simon 159
Redgrave, Michael 16, 19
Redgrave, Vanessa 17, 21, 143, 169, 177, 178
Redington, Michael 136
Rees, Roger 80, 110, 113, 114, 118, 119, 166, 177, 180, 182, 184
Relapse, The 74
Rennie, Malcolm 101
Representative, The 66, 85
Reynolds, Oliver 21, 22
Rhodes, Joan 57
Richard II 14, 61, 150
Richardson, Ian 42, 43, 44
Richardson, Natasha 187
Richardson, Ralph 19
Richardson, Tony 149
Rider, Penny 137
Rigg, Diana 43, 113, 178
Rintoul, David 162

Robertson, Annette 152
Robertson, Bryan 123
Robertson, Patrick 60, 62
Robertson, Toby 62
Robson, David 13
Robson, Flora 42
Robson, Michael 158
Rodgers, Anton 126
Rodgers, Richard and Hart, Lorenz 69, 113
Rodway, Norman 120, 146, 181
Rogan, John 121
Rogers, Paul 19, 30, 32, 34, 129, 131, 132
Rollason, John 65
Romeo and Jeannette 53, 57
Romeo and Juliet 36, 37, 38, 39, 54, 85, 107
Rose, Clifford 43
Rosmer, Milton 116
Rossiter, Leonard 64, 65
Roud, Richard 146
Rules of the Game, The 64, 65
Russell Taylor, John 148
Rutherford, Margaret 178
Rymer, David 10

Sacks, Oliver 131
Saigon — Year of the Cat 145, 165-167, 169, 182
Sailor Beware 19
Sallis, Peter 52, 53, 73
Saluz, Rex 149
Sandler, Bernard 136
Sands, Myra 127
Schlesinger, John 168
Scofield, Paul 19
Seal, Elizabeth 73
Seale, Douglas 34, 35
Search, Gay 136
Sekers, Miki 56
Selby, Nicholas 76
Sellars, Elizabeth 54, 55
Sellers, Peter 52
Shakespeare, William 60, 63, 70, 74, 78, 79, 86, 105, 107, 109, 111, 113, 115, 116, 119, 148, 149, 155, 158, 167, 177, 179
Shanks, Roasalind 103
Shaw, George Bernard 41, 47, 62, 87, 104, 138, 152, 157, 158
Shaw, Sebastian 148
Shawcross, Alan 187
Shelley, Frank 54, 57

She Stoops to Conquer 35, 36
Simmons, Jean 166
Simmons, Tony 55, 146, 158, 168
Simpson, Michael 187
Sinatra, Frank 28, 179
Sinden, Donald 79, 80, 87, 91, 105, 106, 114, 116
Sleep, Wayne 125
Smiley's People 126
Smith, Maggie 34, 154, 178, 187
Sondheim, Stephen 70
Spall, Tim 162
Spanier, Muggsy 31
Speaight, Robert 37
Spencer, Robert 180
Spriggs, Elizabeth 78, 88, 92
Spurling, Hilary 77
Standing, John 54
St Denis, Michel 38, 39, 40, 41, 85, 107, 161
Steedman, Tony 43
Steele, Tommy 35, 36
Stephens, Robert 154
Stewart, James 143
Stewart, Job 61, 63, 157
St Joan 61-62
Stockwood, Mervyn 184
Stride, John 36, 125
Suzman, Janet 113
Sweet Charity 71
Swift, Clive 42, 43
Swift, David 57
Szwarc, Jeannot 126

Tafler, Sidney 96
Tagg, Alan 103
Talking to a Stranger 33, 64, 152, 153, 154
Taming of the Shrew, The 64, 65, 66
Tanner, Tony 57
Taylerson, Marilyn 114
Teachers, The 154
Tebaldi, Renata 21
Tempest, The 23
Terry, Ellen 106, 176, 177, 178
Theocharis, John 62
Third Secret, The 145, 147
Thomas, Charles 84
Thomas, Miss 10
Thompson, Jimmy 59, 60
Thorndike, Daniel 30
Thorndike, Sybil 106
Three Sisters, The 46, 53, 54
Thurburn, Gwynneth 17

Time and the Conways 18
Time Remembered 18, 19
Tinker, Jack 114
Toad of Toad Hall 94
To Be or Not To Be 83
Tobias and the Angel 14
Tobin, John 87
Too True to be Good 104-105
Tosca 21
Toye, Wendy 34, 182
Traherne, Thomas 90
Travers, Bill 43
Treves, Frederick 162
Trewin, J.C. 43, 118
Troilus and Cressida 86
Trojan Women, The 123
Tubbs, Michael 79
Turner, Clifford 21, 22
Turner, John 54, 55, 57
Tushingham, Rita 144
Tutin, Dorothy 19, 29, 40, 67, 132, 174, 177, 178
Twelfth Hour, The 53, 55, 65
Twelfth Night 26, 27, 30, 31, 32, 47, 49, 51, 74, 79-81, 82, 83, 84, 85, 86, 88, 90, 94, 174
Two Gentlemen of Verona, The 19 23, 28, 69
Tynan, Kenneth 37

Ure, Mary 18

Van Druten, John 67
Vaughan, Sarah 28
Vernon, Richard 137
Victoria Station 129
Villiers, James 63
Virgo, Rosemary 62
Volonakis, Minos 57
Voytek (Woiciech Roman Szendzikowski) 15

Waiting for Godot 24
Walker, Hetty and George 5
Wallace, Marjorie 158
Waller, David 186
Walls, Tom 45
Walsh, Dr 11
Walter, Harriet 162
Wanamaker, Sam 19
Wanamaker, Zoe 129, 142
Ward, Simon 54, 57
Wardle, Irving 70, 77, 95, 101, 109
Warner, David 21, 84

Warren, Roger 105, 118
Warwick, Richard 163, 164
Waste 142, 186
Waterhouse, Keith 85
Watson, Cliff 5
Watson, Moray 154
Waugh, Auberon 157
Way of the World, The 116, 117-118
Wayne, John 29
Wayne, Naunton 29
Webb, Marti 101
Webster, John 93
Webster, Margaret 'Peggy' 26
Weigel, Helene 140
Weill, Kurt 70
Wells, H.G. 154
Wesker, Arnold 24
Wetherby 21, 169, 176
Whitehead, Sylvia 9
Whitemore, Hugh 136
Whiting, John 45
Whyte, Jerome 52
Wilde, Oscar 128, 129, 130
Wiles, Hazel 158
Wiles, John 149
Wiles, Len 158
Wiles, Terry 158, 159
William, David 150
Williams, Clifford 92, 93, 104, 113, 137, 138
Williams, Elizabeth 97, 98
Williams, Emlyn 85
Williams, Ewan 59, 61
Williams, Joe 31
Williams, Leonard 97, 98
Williams, Michael 43, 66, 72, 84, 85, 86, 87, 88, 89, 90, 91, 92, 93, 94, 95, 96, 97, 98, 99, 101, 102, 113, 114, 116, 119, 120, 126, 127, 128, 129, 133, 134, 135, 136, 137, 138, 139, 140, 149, 156, 159, 163, 164, 165, 166, 170, 172, 174, 177, 180, 181, 182, 183, 184, 185, 186, 187
Williams, Paul 98, 139
Williams, Tara 'Finty' 95, 96, 98, 126, 129, 149, 156, 159, 181, 182, 185, 186, 187
Williams, Tennessee 70
Wilton, Penelope 21
Winter's Tale, The 74-78, 83, 84, 86, 88
Wisdom, Norman 160, 161
Wolf, The 99
Wolfit, Donald 149
Women Beware Women 78, 84, 92
Woodthorpe, Peter 150
Woodvine, John 34, 110, 111, 114, 115, 118, 187
Woodward, Edward 59, 60, 61, 99, 151
Woolfenden, Guy 113, 114
Wycherley, William 63
Wymark, Patrick 40

Yeats, W.B. 45
York Mystery Plays 3, 14, 25
Young, B.A. 109, 123

Z-Cars 33, 64, 125, 150
Zeffirelli, Franco 36-38, 54
Zinneman, Fred 111